Integrity, Personal, and Political

Integrity, Personal, and Political

SHMUEL NILI

OXFORD
UNIVERSITY PRESS

OXFORD
UNIVERSITY PRESS

Great Clarendon Street, Oxford, OX2 6DP,
United Kingdom

Oxford University Press is a department of the University of Oxford.
It furthers the University's objective of excellence in research, scholarship,
and education by publishing worldwide. Oxford is a registered trade mark of
Oxford University Press in the UK and in certain other countries

Published in the United States of America by Oxford University Press
198 Madison Avenue, New York, NY 10016, United States of America

British Library Cataloguing in Publication Data
Data available

Library of Congress Control Number: 2020933981

ISBN 978-0-19-885963-5

Printed and bound in Great Britain by
Clays Ltd, Elcograf S.p.A.

To Jamie Dunn, who was right all along:

it is, indeed, "just like the gaffer said . . . "

Preface

Integrity, ironically, leads a divided life. The concept is almost omnipresent in everyday moral discourse. Yet it does not have anything like the same impact within professional moral philosophy, where appeals to moral integrity are often seen as lacking adequate foundations. Elsewhere within the ivory tower, among those who study various aspects of politics, invocations of moral integrity are similarly met with suspicion, though for different reasons. Scholars of politics worry less about integrity's philosophical foundations, and more about its supposed irrelevance to messy, real-world public life, with the numerous moral compromises it inevitably forces upon those who seek or hold power.

This book tackles both sets of concerns. I argue that moral integrity can be given solid analytical foundations, but also that, properly understood, integrity is highly relevant to individual as well as collective choices in real-world politics. This dual ambition means that different chapters will likely be of interest to different sorts of readers, depending on whether their interests are more applied or "purely" philosophical.

The first two chapters of the book, devoted to extensive normative foundations, should be of most interest to readers who study the more theoretical reaches of moral and political philosophy. "Realist" political theorists and scholars of international relations may be especially interested in Chapter 3, where I try (among other things) to show integrity's relevance to foreign policy and national security issues. Alongside realists, Chapter 4, offering a detailed discussion of "media demagogues" and the multiple threats they pose to the value of integrity, will be most useful for scholars of political communication. Chapter 5, applying integrity ideas to the awarding and withdrawal of political honors, should be of use not only to political theorists, but also to the various disciplines—from English and art through law to social and intellectual history—that have reflected on these honors. Notwithstanding their different starting points, I obviously hope that at least some readers will benefit from seeing how the book's theoretical and practical contributions stand together.

I should also say something here about the parallel, driving the book, between individual and collective integrity, and its relationship to previous essays. Much of the book is devoted to showing why the sovereign people in a liberal democracy, understood as a collective agent, can have its own morally important collective integrity. This is an idea I have already presented in other work, including *The People's Duty* (Cambridge University Press, 2019). However, my focus in that book was on combining claims regarding the people's integrity with other collectivist claims (regarding the people's property). And so I could not do full justice to integrity's import and complexity.

This book aims to do better, by offering a treatment of integrity that is broader—touching new policy areas—but that is also deeper, in at least two ways. First, in this work I give much more systematic attention to skeptics who think that invocations of moral integrity are entirely parasitic upon morality's overall verdicts: countering such skeptics is the core challenge of the book's opening part. Second, my work up to this point has said fairly little about the analytical relationship between the people's integrity and the integrity of ordinary citizens, and even less about how the people's collective integrity relates to the integrity of individual politicians. I try to fix these gaps here. In turn, these significant additions lead me to believe that the book will be of use even to readers who might be familiar with some of the collective integrity ideas discussed in Chapter 2 (such as that of the "global integrity test").

Even with these additions, however, I believe that much more can and should be said about integrity in public life, not least with regard to professional integrity. In future work, I intend, for instance, to examine how ideas regarding journalists' professional integrity might inform our thinking about the mass media's critical role in preserving liberal democracy. I could not discuss such topics here. But I will be satisfied if this work will convince readers that topics of this sort are both practically and philosophically worthwhile.

Acknowledgments

Integrity is a demanding ideal, but many individuals and institutions have made the challenge of thinking about it less demanding and more enjoyable. I am quite sure that I will not be able to recall everyone who ought to be acknowledged. So what follows is bound to be an incomplete list.

I presented on the themes of this book at the University of Adelaide, the Australian National University, Duke University, the European University Institute in Florence, Griffith University, the Hebrew University, Nuffield College Oxford, the University of Otago, the University of Ottawa, Stanford University, the University of Victoria, and Yale University. I am grateful to the organizers and participants in all of these events, especially Richard Bellamy, Luis Cabrera, Emilee Chapman, Ramon Das, Lisa Ellis, Cecile Fabre, Philip Gerrans, Simon Keller, Alex Kirshner, Patti Lenard, Mingh Ly, Alison McQueen, David Miller, Andrea Sangiovanni, Shlomi Segall, Rob Sparling, Jeff Spinner-Halev, and Patrick Tomlin.

A few paragraphs in Chapters 1 and 2 reuse material from my "Integrity, Personal, and Political," *The Journal of Politics* 80 (2018): 428–41 (though the shortcut-seeking reader should be warned that the most important arguments of the opening two chapters are nowhere to be found in that article-length essay, notwithstanding its title). The latter sections of Chapter 5 draw upon "From Charlottesville to the Nobel: Political Leaders and the Morality of Political Honors," *Ethics* 130 (April 2020). I am grateful to the editors and publishers of these journals for permission to reprint parts of those essays here.

The roots of my fascination with integrity skepticism can be traced to numerous conversations with Shelly Kagan, who remains the most intense skeptic I have yet to encounter; I deeply appreciate the sheer amount of time he spent trying to prove to me the error of my non-consequentialist ways (with often-amusing determination). Less skeptical, but no less supportive, were my other (formal and informal) graduate school teachers, including Seyla Benhabib, Helene Landemore, Daniel Markovits, Thomas Pogge, and Ian Shapiro. Thanks to all of them for convincing me that I had something worth writing about integrity. The list of fellow graduate students who contributed to my ideas is extremely long, but I should single out Paul Linden-Retek, who kindly taught me a great deal about Havel's legacy and ongoing Czech politics, thus inspiring the book's introduction.

Immediately following my PhD, I started spending various periods as a research fellow at the Australian National University's School of Philosophy. Over many conversations and meals in the land of kangaroos, several wise ANU colleagues convinced me that what I should write about integrity is ultimately a book, and allowed me to see much better what this book should and should not say. Christian Barry, Renee Bolinger, Geoff Brennan, Jesse Hambly, Josef Holden, Seth Lazar, Shang Long Yeo, Philip Pettit, Nic Southwood, and Lachlan Umbers all deserve thanks. Visiting Canberra, Tom Parr was gracious enough to offer to read the book's first complete draft. Making good on this offer, Tom provided extraordinarily detailed written comments, almost all of which I have taken on board.

My colleagues at Northwestern have been equally helpful in thinking through many issues related to the book. Thanks in particular to Mary Dietz, Jim Farr, Andy Koppelman, Dan Krcmaric, Christina Lafont, Sara Monoson, and Andrew Roberts. Thanks also to Northwestern's Kaplan Institute for the Humanities, whose research fellowship facilitated the manuscript's timely completion. I have further benefited from discussing individual and collective integrity with many of my students at Northwestern, including Agneska Bloch, who provided superb research assistance.

Working on the book with Oxford University Press has been a delight. From the very beginning, Dominic Byatt has been a prompt and enthusiastic editorial backer of the project. The readers for the Press, in turn, offered many perceptive comments throughout the review process. My thanks to them all, including to Matthew Kramer and Richard Bellamy, who chose (at different stages) to shed their anonymity.

My penultimate acknowledgments go to Elizabeth Anderson, Eric Beerbohm, Paul Bou-Habib, Garrett Cullity, David Enoch, Lior Erez, Jeff Green, Clarissa Gross, Burke Hendrix, Jeff Howard, Tom Hurka, Lizzie Krontiris, Kate Moore, Jiewuh Song, Annie Stilz, Matt Vermaire, Leif Wenar, Jim Wilson, and Alex Zakaras. All of these individuals were extremely generous with their time on multiple occasions; all of them provided me with deep insights on integrity, without having the slightest obligation to do so.

Last but very far from least, I owe a profound debt to my dear friend James Dunn. Jamie simultaneously accelerated my work on this book and improved its quality by showing me that the best version of its sixth chapter is the non-existent one. In addition to this marvelous feat, Jamie has long imprinted in my mind, through his inimitable imitation of Steven Gerrard, that plain and yet meaningful wisdom: "keep pluggin' away, and you'll get your rewards." I don't know anyone who plugs away at their academic work with more devotion, healthy intellectual ambition, and scholarly integrity than Jamie.

Contents

Introduction

"Living in the Truth"

"Václav Havel has become the symbol of our modern Czech state."
—President Václav Klaus, 2011[1]

Two questions, corresponding to two morally fraught situations, provide a useful entry point into the themes of this book. The first situation was described by "the symbol of the modern Czech state," Václav Havel, in his celebrated 1978 essay *The Power of the Powerless*.[2] In this essay, Havel depicts an anonymous grocer in Czechoslovakia behind the Iron Curtain. Like everyone else around him, the grocer's daily conduct meets the expectations of the dictatorship to which he is subject. This means that Havel's grocer leads a false life: he routinely displays outward conformity to a regime in which he does not believe. The grocer obediently participates in trade union meetings as the regime expects; he takes part in multiple regime-sponsored competitions; he participates in elections widely known to be a charade. The grocer, moreover, pronounces his loyalty to the regime in a distinctly public manner, by placing at his shop window the familiar slogan, "Workers of the world, unite!" Havel rhetorically asks, "why does he do it?" and answers:

> I think it can safely be assumed that the overwhelming majority of shopkeepers never think about the slogans they put in their windows, nor do they use them to express their real opinions ... The slogan is really a sign, and as such it contains a subliminal but very definite message. Verbally, it might be expressed this way: "I, the greengrocer XY, live here and I know what I must do. I behave in the manner expected of me. I can be depended upon and am beyond reproach. I am obedient and therefore I have the right to be left in peace."[3]

---

[1] "Statement by the President of the Czech Republic Reflecting on the Death of Former Czech President Václav Havel," December 18, 2011, at http://www.klaus.cz/clanky/3002.

[2] Václav Havel, "The Power of the Powerless," in Havel and Paul Wilson, *Open Letters: Selected Prose 1965–1990* (New York: Random House, 1991). Also available at https://www.nonviolent-conflict. org/wp-content/uploads/1979/01/the-power-of-the-powerless.pdf—all page references are to this online source. I am very grateful to Jim McAdams for introducing me to Havel's essay, many moons ago.

[3] Havel, "The Power of the Powerless," 6.

Integrity, Personal, and Political. Shmuel Nili, Oxford University Press (2020). © Shmuel Nili.
DOI: 10.1093/oso/9780198859635.001.0001

At a later point in the essay, however, Havel asks his readers to envision a day in which "something in our greengrocer snaps and he stops putting up the slogans merely to ingratiate himself":

> He stops voting in elections he knows are a farce. He begins to say what he really thinks at political meetings. And he even finds the strength in himself to express solidarity with those whom his conscience commands him to support. In this revolt the greengrocer steps out of living within the lie. He rejects the ritual and breaks the rules of the game. He discovers once more his suppressed identity and dignity. He gives his freedom a concrete significance. His revolt is an attempt to live within the truth.[4]

Now, at least in some parts of the essay, Havel clearly maintains the hope that if a sufficient number of individuals similarly attempt to "live within the truth," their courage will be contagious, encouraging others to follow their lead, and ultimately generating seismic political change.[5] But it is not hard to imagine circumstances where a dissident living under a dictatorship is deprived of hope of any such positive consequences. Thus, for example, it may be that others have clearly succumbed to the regime's propaganda. Or it may be that the regime presents extremely compelling evidence showing that one is virtually alone in dissenting— a predicament that Havel himself experienced during his first prison spell.[6] Considering such a dire situation from the moral point of view, it is far from obvious that one's familiar moral duties toward others point in any way toward dissent.[7] But then, how are we to explain the moral unease generated by the thought of our would-be dissident remaining entangled with the regime?

Bearing this question in mind, consider the second morally fraught situation. This situation pertains not to any particular Czech individual, but rather to the policy that the Czech people, as a collective agent acting through its government, is currently pursuing with regard to foreign dictatorships in general, and the Chinese dictatorship in particular. The most recent Czech governments have

---

[4] Havel, "The Power of the Powerless," 18.

[5] At least one influential social scientist has argued that it was precisely such a snowball effect that led to the remarkably quick collapse of Eastern European dictatorships. See Timur Kuran, "Now Out of Never: The Element of Surprise in the East European Revolution of 1989," *World Politics* 44 (1991): 7–48.

[6] That he let himself be convinced by the regime's evidence was a source of long-lasting torment for Havel, even though his resulting promises to the dictatorship, to refrain from future dissidence in exchange for an early release from prison, were widely agreed to have caused no harm to other people. Michael Zantovsky, *Vaclav Havel: A Life* (Grove Press: New York, 2014), 187, 191.

[7] In fact, if one is, for example, a parent to young children, and these children will predictably be harmed by the regime in case one opposes the regime, then it may seem as if one's other-regarding duties (at least when considered as a whole) point quite firmly *against* dissent.

pursued "normal" diplomatic and commercial ties with the Chinese regime.[8] On the one hand, this pursuit has added to the dictatorship's international standing, and has further enhanced its material power-base. On the other hand, given the nature of international politics, any China-related commercial opportunities that the Czech ignore are bound to be taken up by less scrupulous nations, who are unlikely to even try to use any influence they may acquire over the Chinese regime to push it to reform its repressive ways.

All this suggests that our observation about the individual Czech grocer also seems to apply to the foreign policy of the Czech people as a collective agent. Here, too, it is not clear that our compunction about this agent's entanglement in (foreign) dictatorship can be grounded in any simple consequentialist arithmetic. Nor, for that matter, can this compunction be grounded in a familiar appeal to the rights of the dictatorship's victims. After all, there is no obvious reason to think that the victims of the Chinese dictatorship would prefer that the Czech avoid cooperating with the dictatorship.[9] So it is not implausible to think that, given the opportunity, the dictatorship's victims would actually consent to—and thus waive any rights they may have against—Czech involvement with the Chinese dictatorship, however repressive this dictatorship may be at present. Therefore, in the collective as in the individual case, we should at the very least entertain the possibility that other-regarding moral considerations cannot ground our instinctive compunction regarding entanglement in political repression. And so here too the question naturally arises: how can this compunction be explained?

The first key aim of this book is to defend a specific answer, which applies both to the sovereign people in a liberal democracy, as a collective agent, and to individual agents.[10] According to this answer, an agent's own moral integrity can provide an *independent* moral reason to engage in (and refrain from) certain actions and practices. This moral reason is defeasible. But it is genuine. In particular, this self-regarding moral reason is not simply reducible to what the agent owes to others. This is true, for example, in the case of our individual Czech

---

[8] See, e.g., Bethany Allen-Ebrahimian and Emily Tamkin, "Prague Opened the Door to Chinese Influence. Now It May Need to Change Course," *Foreign Policy*, March 16, 2018, at https://foreignpolicy.com/2018/03/16/prague-to-czech-chinese-influence-cefc-energy-communist-party.

[9] Just as there is no obvious reason to think that the victims of other dictatorships would prefer outsiders to take distance from the regime oppressing them, if such distance would only lead the regime to respond by "digging in its heels." See for example Ben Hubbard, "Saudi Arabia Escalates Feud with Canada Over Rights Criticism," *New York Times*, August 8, 2018.

[10] Throughout the book, I take liberalism and democracy to revolve around a shared egalitarian core (as I go on to elaborate). I therefore allow myself (for example) to use "liberal societies" and "democratic societies" interchangeably. Like many other theorists, I consider it a key task of contemporary political philosophy to show how liberal and democratic values can be reconciled despite apparent conflicts (see, e.g., Ronald Dworkin, *Sovereign Virtue* [Cambridge, MA: Harvard University Press, 2000]; Joshua Cohen, "A More Democratic Liberalism," *Michigan Law Review* 92 [1994]: 1503–46; Jürgen Habermas, "Constitutional Democracy: A Paradoxical Union of Contradictory Principles?" *Political Theory* 29 [2001]: 766–81). One of the ambitions underlying my account of collective integrity is to contribute to this task.

grocer: this grocer has an integrity-based moral reason to disentangle himself from the dictatorship he loathes, which is not simply reducible to his moral duties toward anyone else. But the same is also true for the Czech people as a collective agent: this people's own moral integrity gives it an independent moral reason not to be entangled (for instance) in the wrongs perpetrated by the Chinese dictatorship—a reason that is *not* simply reducible to the moral reasons that pertain to the rights and interests of this dictatorship's victims.

This parallel is surprising, insofar as we do not commonly think of "the people" or "the polity"[11] as a candidate for having its own moral integrity.[12] I argue, however, that we can and should think about a liberal polity in this way. More specifically—to anticipate some of my main contentions—I argue that we should view a liberal polity as an agent with its own fundamental moral commitments, revolving around certain collective institutions. These institutional commitments parallel the fundamental moral commitments that we hope to find in the case of individual persons. And these institutional commitments, I contend, can form the core of a morally important collective integrity, in much the same way that an individual's fundamental moral commitments can form the core of a morally important personal integrity.

Now, prior to philosophical reflection, one might very well expect it to be the case that "the people's" moral integrity, if it can be given content at all, would turn out to be (at best) a fairly pale version of individual integrity. In the pages that follow, however, I seek to prove otherwise. My second key aim is to show that, notwithstanding appearances to the contrary, the moral force of integrity considerations is actually *easier to defend* when reflecting on a liberal people as a collective agent, in comparison to individual agents.

The book's ultimate ambition builds on both of the aims I just outlined. Relying on the idea that a liberal people as a collective agent can have its own morally important integrity, my ultimate goal is to illuminate multiple aspects of the complex relationship between this collective integrity, and the integrity of individual persons. In Chapters 1 and 2, as well as in the early stages of Chapter 3, I advance this goal by examining the relationship between a liberal polity's collective integrity and the integrity of ordinary individuals. In the latter part of Chapter 3, as well as in Chapters 4 and 5, I focus on the intricate relationship between a liberal polity's collective integrity and the integrity of individual

---

[11] I will use these two terms interchangeably, though I am aware that this involves a certain awkwardness.

[12] Even if some theorists have argued that "systems of governance" can have their own integrity. See for example Matthew Kramer's *Capital Punishment* (Oxford: Oxford University Press, 2011) and *Liberalism with Excellence* (Oxford: Oxford University Press, 2017), which place far less weight than I do on the idea of the sovereign people in a liberal democracy as a collective agent. Kramer (as an absolute deontologist) is also far more suspicious than I will be here of attempts to forge common ground with consequentialists regarding integrity. Other philosophical and practical differences between our views will become clear as I proceed.

political actors. More generally, throughout the book, I seek to show that integrity inquiries yield both broad philosophical dividends and important practical judgments, concerning individual as well as collective conduct.

The remainder of this Introduction sketches the book's core claims in a bit more detail. I start with the basic concept of moral integrity, and with the defense of its moral significance that I will offer in the first two chapters, both of which are devoted to philosophical foundations. I then briefly summarize the content of Chapters 3, 4, and 5, which move from foundations to concrete political problems. Following this summary, I distinguish between two different contributions that integrity ideas can make to our moral thinking, both of which run throughout the book. Finally, I further motivate the book's structure by explaining why it gives such sustained attention to critics of "integrity talk."

I.1 "My Moral Truth," "Our Moral Truth," and the Moral Truth

On my usage, an agent's "integrity" consists in fidelity to those commitments which are central to the agent's self-conception.[13] My interest in this book is specifically in *moral* integrity, which I take to consist in fidelity to those *moral* commitments that are central to the agent's self-conception (or, as I shall also call them, "fundamental" commitments). An agent whose actions and most fundamental moral commitments conflict is bound (especially in those cases where the conflict extends over time) to experience a kind of *self-betrayal*. This, I assume, is the experience that lies at the heart of our grocer's predicament, for example. A key part of my effort here will be to defend the thought that such self-betrayal— when connected to certain moral principles—has its own moral significance.

Now, why is such a defense necessary? Why isn't the significance of moral integrity simply self-evident? Perhaps the most obvious reason is the following. Moral integrity—being true to one's deepest moral convictions—may seem like a noble aspiration on first blush, but it becomes far less noble in cases where one's deepest moral convictions happen to be deeply flawed.[14] A person who truly believes in the morality of Stalinism, for example, including the most extreme elements of Stalinist repression, may very well experience self-betrayal akin to that of the grocer if forced—for instance, by social or economic pressures—to pretend that he is delighted to live in a society that firmly distances itself from Stalin's

---

[13] This conception of integrity has traditionally played a key role in the philosophical literature on the concept—a role that continues in recent scholarship. See, e.g., Greg Scherkoske, "Whither Integrity I: Recent Faces of Integrity," *Philosophy Compass* 8 (2013): 28–39.

[14] As Stuart Hampshire put it: "If a person has lived a blameless life 'according to his lights'...the question always arises—were his lights good enough, or could they have been better?" Stuart Hampshire, *Morality and Conflict* (Oxford: Blackwell, 1983), 159.

legacy. Should we therefore say that this person's predicament is on a par, morally speaking, with that of Havel's grocer? Does the deeply committed Stalinist have a genuine *moral* reason to make public, for example, his contempt for all of those "soft liberals" who fail to see the "virtues" of (say) Stalin's gulags?[15]

I do not think that we should endorse such a view. At the very least, I do not think that the idea of moral integrity would be of much interest—philosophically or practically—if we were to treat it in this way, as *purely* subjective. However, if we refuse to do this—if we assume, as I will here, that there must be some objective constraints on the kinds of fundamental moral commitments that agents may adopt—then we must also deal with a further challenge. Once we incorporate objective morality into our thinking about moral integrity—once we bear in mind that integrity talk about "commitment to my moral truth" must be constrained by some objective judgment as to what is *the* moral truth—why not go further? Why not say that the only "fundamental commitment" that really matters morally is simply the commitment to do what morality, all-things-considered, objectively requires?[16]

Some theorists have suggested that this is obviously the right way in which to proceed. Thomas Nagel, for instance, complained long ago that even "the notion that one might sacrifice one's moral integrity justifiably, in the service of a sufficiently worthy end, is an incoherent notion. For if one were justified in making such a sacrifice (or even morally required to make it), then one would not be sacrificing one's moral integrity by adopting that course: one would be preserving it."[17] Martin Hollis, to take another example, made much the same point, illustrated through the evocative case of the distinctly unpopular Pontius Pilate:

> Despite the terrible press which he has had, it is not obvious to me that *integrity* required him to protect a just man at the cost of a riot. Integrity does not offer a separate lever. The question is what it was right for the Roman Governor of Judaea to do and, once that question is answered, integrity simply demands that the Governor go ahead and do it.[18]

[15] For examples in similar spirit, see Susan Mendus, *Politics and Morality* (London: Polity, 2009), chap. 1.

[16] Here and throughout, like most moral and political philosophers, I use the term "all-things-considered" as a shorthand for "taking all relevant moral considerations into account." Similarly, following standard philosophical terminology, when referring to "presumptive," "prima-facie," or "pro-tanto" moral considerations, I have in mind considerations that, in the relevant circumstances, are susceptible to being outweighed by countervailing moral factors.

[17] Thomas Nagel, "War and Massacre," *Philosophy & Public Affairs* 1 (1972): 123–44, at 132–3.

[18] Martin Hollis, "Dirty Hands," *British Journal of Political Science* 12 (1982): 385–98, at 394. Italics in the original.

If these claims are correct—if an agent's moral integrity is simply identical to action in accordance with morality's overall requirements—then integrity would once again turn out to be devoid of philosophical and practical interest. Integrity would be only a trivial *output* of morality's all-things-considered requirements in any given situation, rather than an input informing these requirements. Havel's grocer, for instance, would not have any independent reasons of moral integrity to dissent from the regime under which he lives. Rather, if it turns out that, all-things-considered, Havel's grocer ought *not* to engage in dissent (say, because of his moral duties to care for his children, who would be imperiled if he made himself "an enemy of the state"), then the grocer ought to see conformity to the regime as aligning, rather than conflicting, with his moral integrity. Similarly, according to the "integrity skeptic," if the Czech people as a collective agent has compelling, all-things-considered moral reasons to foster ties with the Chinese dictatorship, presumably because of the benefits that such ties might yield for this dictatorship's victims (at least in the long run), then *that* is what Czech collective integrity requires. To invoke "Czech collective integrity" as an independent moral reason—whether for or against any action— is therefore confused.

The principal effort of Chapters 1 and 2 is to vindicate integrity's independent moral significance, in the face of this skepticism. More specifically, I argue that it is *easier* to defeat this skepticism when reflecting on a liberal people's collective integrity, as compared to the integrity of an individual person. This comparative ease, in turn, is central to my claim that integrity's moral significance is easier to defend in the collective as compared to the individual realm.

Although I shall leave the specific elements of my defense to the relevant chapters, it might be helpful to give already here an example of the kind of defense I shall offer. This defense starts with the temporal nature of the very notion of a "commitment," which I briefly left undefined. On one definition, which I find quite attractive and which I shall assume throughout this book, a "commitment" is "a normative determination made in the past to govern the future."[19] Once we adopt this understanding of "commitment," talk about agents' fidelity to their fundamental moral commitments acquires a historical dimension. At least in some circumstances, this talk is sensitive to the particular moral commitments that agents have adopted in their past, to govern their future conduct. This point, in turn, allows us to capture a simple and powerful, but also elusive, moral intuition—namely, that an agent's particular moral history can

---

[19] I borrow this definition from Jed Rubenfeld, *Freedom and Time* (New Haven, CT: Yale University Press, 2001), at 92. See also Cheshire Calhoun, "What Good Is Commitment?" *Ethics* 119 (2009): 613–41. I should note that virtually any plausible understanding of the term "commitment" can align with most if not all of the claims I want to make in this book.

bear on its moral situation, including in the kinds of entanglement cases introduced above.

To make this thought more concrete, and show why it matters, we can go
back to the case of the Czech relationship with China. Some of us, I assume,
hesitate when confronted with the skeptic's claim that the Czech people should
see the demands of moral integrity with regard to the Chinese dictatorship as
entirely parasitic upon the overall moral judgment as to how to deal with this
dictatorship. In turn, I believe that at least part of this hesitation is due to Czech
moral history and its formative influence on Czech foreign policy. Directly
continuing the dissident legacy of the "Prague Spring" and the "Velvet
Revolution," Czech foreign policy following the Cold War firmly emphasized
opposition to dictatorship, as well as support for peaceful protesters against
repression. Moreover, this stance, so central not only to Havel's presidency but
also to much of Czech civil society, has been perhaps most evident in traditional
Czech support of Tibet's peaceful struggle to liberate itself from Chinese rule, as
well as in general criticism of China's human rights record.[20] And this particular
Czech history, I believe, matters morally. It matters, furthermore, not just for
morality in general, but for the moral integrity of the Czech polity in particular.
This history means that for the Czech Republic to effectively turn its back on
Tibet and its dissidents, for example, arguably amounts not just to a betrayal of
the Tibetan struggle, but also to a form of collective *self*-betrayal, given the Czech
Republic's own history. And this (historical) self-betrayal means that, contrary to
the integrity skeptic, the Czech Republic has especially stringent and weighty
integrity reasons *not* to cooperate, legitimate, and reap benefits from the Chinese
dictatorship.[21]

Now, there are several grounds for why I think such "historical" arguments are
more powerful when bearing on the integrity of a liberal polity, as compared to the
integrity of an individual person. These grounds—as well as skeptical responses,
my rejoinders, and so on—will have to wait for Chapters 1 and (especially) 2. The
aim of the last pair of paragraphs was merely to provide more of a glimpse of the
kinds of arguments that these chapters will develop.

[20] This support, in turn, was manifest not only when Havel as President extended official recognition to the Dalai Lama, for example, but also when hundreds of Czech towns simultaneously raised
flags commemorating past Tibetan protests violently crushed by the Chinese regime. See, e.g.,
"Hundreds of Czech Towns Hoist Flags in Support of Tibet," *Prague Daily Monitor*, March 11, 2016,
at http://praguemonitor.com/2016/03/11/hundreds-czech-towns-hoist-flags-support-tibet.
[21] To be clear: it is not my claim that liberal democracies that lack the relevant moral history do not
have such integrity reasons. As Chapters 1 and 2 will explain, I simply believe that these reasons are
especially evident, and important, where the relevant history does obtain. I also believe that once we see
integrity reasons to be operative in historically laden cases, it is easier to be convinced of their broader
independent existence.

I.2 Integrity on the Ground

Having argued in the opening part of the book that both personal and political integrity can function as an independent moral factor, I turn in its latter, more applied part to discuss multiple resulting questions.

In Chapter 3, I take up the concerns of those who worry that, even if integrity is an independent moral factor, putting integrity at the center of our moral outlook is objectionably self-absorbed. I seek to undermine the appeal of this charge, and, in the process, establish further ways in which integrity can contribute to our practical reflections, on both personal and political morality.

The self-absorption concern on which I focus has a distinctly practical form. It holds that integrity talk dangerously pushes us to prioritize our own clean hands at the expense of others' needs—even quite vulnerable others. After explaining why this particular form of the self-absorption complaint should be our focus, I develop multiple responses to this complaint. For one thing, I contend that even when integrity's dictates push in the opposite direction from the rights and preferences of vulnerable others, there are still important cases where acting on these dictates will *improve* the position of the vulnerable. Moreover—and more centrally—I challenge the familiar equation of "integrity" with "clean hands," arguing that there are important cases where integrity might be compatible with "dirty hands," and may even actively push agents to dirty their hands. Integrity's relationship to "clean hands," I suggest, is causally contingent: agents ought to engage in a serious assessment of the causal pathways bearing on their conduct options, in order for their moral integrity to align with "dirty deeds."

Such assessment, in turn, exposes further weaknesses in the self-absorption charge. This charge, I contend, ignores the effort that ought to precede a binary choice between our own integrity and others' needs—namely, the effort to validate the causal premises on which such a binary choice rests. Moreover, I argue that since integrity demands of us to engage in this effort as a necessary condition for "dirtying hands," integrity's pressures, rather than leading us to neglect vulnerable others, typically *protect* vulnerable others—especially the likely victims of our potential dirty deeds. I illustrate this claim using the key example of ethically fraught decisions by corporate executives, and then turn to the political realm, where I discuss for the first time the integrity of individual politicians. Appearances to the contrary notwithstanding, I suggest that the self-absorption charge is particularly inappropriate when it comes to political decision making. Not only does it ignore the process of verifying that the only relevant policy choices really are between "our own purity" and others' practical needs; the self-absorption charge also ignores the significant political question of who is it that sets the policy-making agenda in these binary terms. In the context of international affairs, at least, I suggest that the answer once again points to self-seeking corporations, who cannot be relied upon to provide anything like the rigorous causal analysis that integrity requires. Given the familiar thought that integrity talk is particularly out of place in international politics, this is an important finding. And this finding, I further argue, turns out to be especially applicable to national security issues, which often demand dirty deeds.

Like the book's opening chapters, Chapter 3 largely highlights cases where individual and collective integrity point in the same direction—not only sharing an analytical structure, but also aligning in their practical verdicts. In contrast, the last two chapters of the book highlight issues on which individual and collective integrity seem to provide conflicting practical guidance. More specifically, the last two chapters examine important circumstances where the integrity of individual *political actors* seems to conflict with the polity's integrity. I therefore try to show how the resulting "integrity indeterminacy" can be resolved in a systematic fashion.

In Chapter 4, I focus on the apparent indeterminacy brought about by elected leaders whom I label "media demagogues." Media demagogues are distinguished by their combination of dangerous populism, systematic lies and manipulation, and an overwhelming reliance on media activity as a substitute for substantive government work. Using Donald Trump, Silvio Berlusconi, and Benjamin Netanyahu as my running examples,[22] I explore the integrity stakes involved in the decisions of those who are considering whether to serve or ally with media demagogues. These decisions fundamentally concern "dirty hands"—lying and manipulating for the demagogue, and more generally becoming complicit in his wrongdoing.

Initially, it may seem that such dirty deeds can align with integrity's dictates. In particular, it may seem as if one can advance one's fundamental public policy commitments by working with a media demagogue who is in power, and that one's personal integrity points toward such work. I argue, however, that the predictable threat which media demagogues pose to the integrity of liberal democracy has moral primacy. This threat provides extremely weighty reasons against collaborating with media demagogues. I end the chapter by explaining why ignoring these threats to collective integrity, and collaborating with media demagogues out of a blind devotion to extremely narrow policies that one wishes to advance, is a mark not of moral integrity, but rather of morally dangerous fanaticism.

This discussion of the relationship between dirty hands and integrity connects Chapter 4's inquiries to the more familiar concerns taken up in Chapter 3.[23] But

---

[22] My choice of these three examples is not meant in any way to suggest that media demagogues are to be found only on the political right. Rather, this choice is driven by the thought that right-wing populism, led by such demagogues, is especially salient to the current political climate.
[23] I am aware that there may seem to be a tension between the two chapters, since Chapter 3 shows how integrity can be compatible with dirty hands, whereas Chapter 4 shows that integrity prohibits

I should stress already here that my discussion of media demagogues' (actual and potential) allies and servants is also meant to expand upon these familiar concerns, by going beyond political theory's classic "dirty hands" debates. Parting with these debates' virtually exclusive focus on leaders at the apex of political power,[24] I aim to show the philosophical and practical value of reflection on those standing under, and next to, such leaders.[25] In the process, I hope to update the scholarly discussions of dirty hands problems. Whereas these discussions still reflect a structure going back to the Renaissance, it is important to adjust this structure in a way that is attuned to the tremendous political impact of contemporary mass media.

If the claims of Chapter 4 will be cogent, then they will help to further dispel the familiar suspicion to which much of Chapter 3 is also dedicated: that integrity talk is fundamentally ill suited to the dirty realities of politics, and specifically to the fact that real-world politics is dominated by actors whose integrity is often questionable at best. This theme is also central to the book's final chapter, in which I examine one more aspect of the complex relationship between collective integrity and the integrity of individual political actors: the way in which integrity considerations should guide collective decisions about symbolic political honors in general, and symbolic honors centered on individual politicians in particular.

The topic of political honors has been generating extensive public attention around the world, from the United States (consider heated controversies surrounding monuments to confederate leaders[26]), through the United Kingdom (consider the "Rhodes must fall" protests[27]) to the former Soviet Union (where debates persist about the proper commemoration of communist-era leadership[28]).

---

getting our hands dirty in certain ways. But this apparent tension dissolves once we obtain a clear understanding of the specific conditions under which dirty hands are morally justified: showing that these conditions cannot be met in the case of media demagogues will be a key part of Chapter 4's task.

[24] For still-too-rare exceptions, see Dennis Thompson, "Responsibility for Failures of Government: The Problem of Many Hands," *The American Review of Public Administration* 44 (2014): 259–73; Matthew Kramer, *The Ethics of Capital Punishment* (Oxford: Oxford University Press, 2011), chap. 6.

[25] Admittedly, the renewed philosophical interest in political parties, evident in recent years, may lead to more attention to those standing "next to" leaders. But I take this recent scholarly trend to be largely concerned with more abstract questions than the ones on which I focus here. See, e.g., Nancy Rosenblum, *On the Side of the Angels: An Appreciation of Parties and Partisanship* (Princeton, NJ: Princeton University Press, 2008); Russell Muirhead, *The Promise of Party in a Polarized Age* (Cambridge, MA: Harvard University Press, 2014); Jonathan White and Lea Ypi, *The Meaning of Partisanship* (Oxford: Oxford University Press, 2016).

[26] See, e.g., Tegan Wendland, "With Lee Statue's Removal, Another Battle of New Orleans Comes to a Close," *NPR*, May 20, 2017, at http://www.npr.org/2017/05/20/529232823/with-lee-statues-removal-another-battle-of-new-orleans-comes-to-a-close.

[27] Yussef Robinson, "Oxford's Cecil Rhodes Statue Must Fall—It Stands in the Way of Inclusivity," *The Guardian*, June 19, 2016, at https://www.theguardian.com/commentisfree/2016/jan/19/rhodes-fall-oxford-university-inclusivity-black-students.

[28] See, e.g., Sarah Rainsford, "Russian Communists Look to Reinstate 'Iron Felix' Statue," *BBC News*, July 19, 2015, at http://www.bbc.com/news/av/world-europe-33549850/russian-communists-look-to-reinstate-iron-felix-statue.

Yet normative political philosophy has had remarkably little to say about this topic. Seeking to fix this gap, I consider what an integrity-based perspective might have to say about political honors.

Initially, it may seem as if an integrity-centered perspective would lead us to focus political honors on individual leaders who, on the spectrum of moral admiration, stand on the opposite end from media demagogues. The aforementioned Havel (honored by renaming Prague's international airport after him[29]) is only one case in point. Emblematic public monuments honoring Mandela, Gandhi, and Lincoln could be offered along similar lines. But I argue that, despite its initial appeal, there are serious problems with the idea of hinging political honors on the honorees' individual integrity, no matter how admirable these honorees may have been in many ways. Several of these problems, moreover, follow quite directly from collective integrity concerns, not least because of the collective manipulation that inevitably accompanies any attempt to cast flesh-and-blood political leaders as modern-day saints. Building on this and other problems, I defend a conception of political honors that reconceives their moral function. Political honors should not aim to honor individual integrity—nor, for that matter, should such honors aim to honor individual desert, contrary to the conventional wisdom. Rather, decisions about both the awarding and the withdrawal of political honors should aim to mark and reinforce morally appropriate collective commitments.

Political honors, I contend, can typically fulfill their central collectivist functions even when they involve no individual honorees—when revolving instead around "anonymous heroes," around substantive laws or policies, or even around non-human animals. I show how this collectivist approach can account for important cases where there is a particularly firm intuition that individual leaders should be at the center of political honors, and argue that this intuition is compatible even with honoring leaders whose personal integrity could well be questioned. I similarly argue that the collectivist outlook can provide compelling guidance with regard to the withdrawal of honors given to political leaders, without falling back on either individual integrity or individual desert claims.

I.3 Integrity's Multiple Roles

The preceding paragraphs were meant to provide not only an overview of each chapter of the book, but also an initial sense of its structure—starting with abstract philosophical questions about integrity, and gradually moving toward concrete

---

[29] "Prague Airport Renamed After Czech Ex-Leader Vaclav Havel," *BBC News*, December 5, 2012, at https://www.bbc.com/news/world-europe-19854293.

political questions on which integrity, both personal and political, can be usefully brought to bear.

Even with this basic narrative arc in view, however, it will be helpful to note here a few other important features of the relationship among the different chapters. One such feature, which may have already occurred to the reader, is that the invocation of integrity plays a somewhat different philosophical role in different chapters. This difference is intentional, since I believe that we can and should expect the idea of moral integrity to play more than one role in our moral thinking.

One essential philosophical role of moral integrity was already made explicit above—that is, the role of an independent moral consideration. If my arguments in the opening part of the book will be convincing, they will establish that moral integrity can be an independent moral factor, to be weighed alongside familiar moral factors such as rights and interests, when trying to identify what we ought to do. However, alongside this philosophical role, I shall also try to show that the idea of integrity advances our moral thinking by increasing the *unity* of our moral outlook. The idea of moral integrity can play a unifying role in our moral thinking, by fruitfully bringing together a variety of moral concerns that typically seem quite removed from one another.

Consider, for instance, a liberal democracy's commemoration of its most emblematic moral failures and successes (a theme that will be prominent in Chapters 2 and especially 5). The language of collective integrity may not be unique in capturing the moral significance of such collective commemoration. But the idea of collective integrity nonetheless makes a contribution to our reflection on commemorative practices, by allowing us to see often-overlooked connections between them and other morally important phenomena. To go back to my earlier, Czech examples: we may not need the language of collective integrity in order to agree that there is moral value in the Czech Republic remembering the Czech dissidents who undertook the most severe risks to bring democracy to the country. But it is partly because the language of integrity provides an especially ready way to capture the moral significance of this collective memory—of making this memory essential to "who we are as a people"—that it is also able to illuminate how this collective identity might bear on moral problems that might initially seem quite distinct, such as the aforementioned problem of Czech engagement with dictatorships.

Furthermore, I believe that the idea of integrity can play a fruitful unifying role in our moral thinking by bringing together a variety of moral concepts that are commonly understood to lie in its vicinity, showing how these concepts can be combined to form a whole greater than its parts. Steadfastness and self-respect, for example, are often thought to be allies of integrity, whereas self-seeking rationalizations and self-deception are commonly understood to be antithetical to integrity.[30] To be sure, all of these concepts can be invoked and discussed without reference to the core notion of integrity—that is, without referring to any "fidelity to fundamental commitments." But while keeping this core notion firmly in mind, we can also think about integrity as a *broader moral framework*—one featuring multiple moral concepts that orbit around the core notion.

This broader framework is powerful—I shall argue—insofar as the concepts it brings together carry extra dividends once combined. These dividends will be apparent, for example, in Chapter 1's discussion of how attention to self-respect undermines the appeal of integrity skepticism. These dividends will also be apparent in Chapter 3's discussion of how self-seeking rationalizations generate false binary choices between compromising our most fundamental commitments and dirtying our hands. And these dividends will similarly be manifest in Chapter 4's discussion of how media demagogues' self-deception directly contributes to the threats they pose to the integrity of liberal democracy.

I should stress that while this unifying moral framework is ambitious in some respects, it is also modest in others. In particular, this framework is modest insofar as it does not necessarily involve a uniqueness claim. I certainly do *not* mean to say that every single moral problem that I discuss in this book can be grasped *only* by referring to integrity—either in the narrow sense, of fidelity to fundamental commitments, or in the broader sense, encompassing the additional concepts I just mentioned. But I do think that the idea of integrity allows us to see, in a very immediate way, crucial connections among several moral problems—including problems that existing philosophical frameworks have virtually ignored.[31]

I should also note that in different stages of the book, I will develop my arguments by highlighting different elements of—or different "orbiting concepts" within—the integrity framework. In particular, the book's earlier chapters will focus on how the orbiting concepts of self-respect, self-deception, and self-seeking rationalizations relate to the central notion of fidelity to fundamental commitments. The book's later chapters will add to these concepts other moral ideas that

---

[30] There are difficult philosophical questions as to whether self-deception is, upon examination, actually possible. I am inclined to think that self-deception is indeed possible, and that it is best understood, following Donald Davison, in terms of a "partitioned mind." See Davidson's "Who Is Fooled," in his *Problems of Rationality* (Oxford: Oxford University Press, 2004), 213–30, at 220, as well as (in the same volume) "Deception and Division."

[31] Chapter 4's inquiries into the menace of media demagogues and their collaborators provide an especially sharp example of this point. I do not mean to suggest that without the language of individual and collective integrity, we have no way to condemn either the personal failings of media demagogues, or the grave damage they inflict on core institutions of liberal democracy. But, for one thing, thinking about distinctive dangers posed by media demagogues—and even by their collaborators—is something that analytical political theory has yet to do. Moreover, the prism of integrity allows us to draw immediate links among multiple dynamics—both individual and collective—that (together) render these dangers particularly acute.

are naturally associated with integrity—such as wholeness, honesty, and reflection on one's commitments.

My attempt to bring all of these ideas under the umbrella of integrity should not be seen as a way of making "integrity" a moving target. Rather, this attempt simply reflects the concept's inherent complexity. Integrity, as some philosophers have already noted, is best thought of as a "cluster concept,"[32] which, like other "plural ideals,"[33] weaves together multiple notions.[34] If the specific weaving I shall propose here will be successful, it will allow us to regiment this concept—and to keep its core meaning firmly in sight—without rendering it artificially narrow.

I.4 Integrity and Its Critics

Before turning to the book's substantive arguments, I want to offer a last set of remarks about its setup. Specifically, I want to explain why I think it is essential to devote so much space, in the opening chapters of the book, to integrity skeptics. I am aware that this strategy may seem to give the early stages of my argument an overly negative structure. But I think that there are at least three reasons to opt for this structure nonetheless.

First, even the brief sketch of integrity skepticism provided earlier should show its considerable intuitive appeal. Moreover, this appeal—as I go on to stress in Chapter 1—is arguably so obvious to so many philosophers that they take the force of integrity skepticism to be self-evident. But if that is true, then no discussion of integrity's independent practical import, in either private conduct or public life, can really get off the ground unless and until we have at least tentative reasons to oppose integrity skepticism. That is partly why I wish to present the reader with such reasons very early on.

Second, as should become clear in what follows, my presentation of integrity's positive contributions, and my "defensive" effort to undermine integrity skepticism, will turn out to represent two sides of the same coin. Even when I will be advancing "negative" arguments, countering those dismissive of integrity's moral significance, my arguments will have a clear constructive edge. I hope that this edge will be evident from the very start.

---

[32] See, e.g., Damian Cox, Marguerite La Caze, and Michael Levine, *Integrity and the Fragile Self* (Aldershot: Ashgate, 2003).

[33] I borrow this phrase from James Wilson's characterization of social equality throughout his *Democratic Equality* (Princeton, NJ: Princeton University Press, 2019).

[34] Different philosophers can obviously disagree on which are the relevant notions here. Cheshire Calhoun, for example, concludes that integrity is a "master virtue" which "presses into service" a wide range of "other virtues," including "self-knowledge, strength of will, courage, honesty, loyalty, humility, civility, respect, and self-respect." See Cheshire Calhoun, "Standing for Something," *Journal of Philosophy* XCII (1995): 235–60, at 260. My own list, as we will see in due course, partly overlaps with Calhoun's.

Finally, I believe that integrity skepticism lies at the root of the key discrepancy I noted in the Preface, between everyday moral discourse on the one hand, and professional moral philosophy on the other. Integrity talk—even talk that focuses specifically on the sense of moral integrity I am deploying here, of fidelity to one's deepest moral convictions—is ubiquitous in everyday discussions of morality. But such talk is not nearly as influential, at least not in present times, within professional moral and political philosophy. I believe that this divide speaks against professional philosophy, and should be closed by bringing philosophy closer to everyday moral discourse. Closing this divide—partly by confronting integrity skepticism—will be a key part of my task.

1

Organizing Integrity

This opening chapter has three aims. The first is to spell out the key concepts I will be deploying throughout this book. The second is to argue, against integrity skeptics of various types, that personal integrity can actually have independent moral significance. The third aim is to lay the ground for parallel arguments that I will make in Chapter 2, where I will try to show that a polity too can have its own morally significant integrity.

I pursue these aims as follows. In 1.1 I present my understanding of personal integrity as revolving around fundamental commitments. Here I motivate my interest in fundamental *moral* commitments, and indicate how I intend to deal with the problem of repugnant commitments that agents may adopt. In 1.2, I briefly outline three ideas—steadfastness, self-seeking rationalizations, and self-deception—that will play an important role throughout my inquiry.

In 1.3 and 1.4, I present, and then begin to respond to, a central source of skepticism about integrity's moral significance—namely, the thought that a person's integrity can only be a trivial output of morality's overall requirements, rather than an independent factor feeding into these requirements, meaning that integrity is merely a fifth wheel in moral deliberation.

The claims I develop in order to undermine this "fifth-wheel skepticism" lead me to a related source of skepticism about integrity's moral significance—the thought that integrity's concerns are ultimately psychological rather than moral. In 1.5 and 1.6, I confront this complaint by linking unconditional commitments underlying an agent's moral integrity to several notions related to the "self"—especially self-distrust, self-respect, and duties to self. In 1.7, I offer a further defense of integrity's moral significance, by considering how the force of moral commitments that we expect all agents to incorporate into their identity can be amplified by fundamental commitments associated with an agent's particular moral history. Many of these arguments—not only regarding agents' particular histories, but also regarding unconditional commitments, self-distrust, and duties to self—will turn out to have powerful parallels when we consider political integrity in Chapter 2.

1.1 Setting the Stage

As I said in the Introduction, for the purposes of this book, an agent's integrity consists in fidelity to the commitments that the agent considers fundamental to its

Integrity, Personal, and Political. Shmuel Nili, Oxford University Press (2020). © Shmuel Nili.
DOI: 10.1093/oso/9780198859635.001.0001

self-conception.[1] The term "commitment"—to repeat the other definition mentioned in the Introduction—refers to "a normative determination made in the past to govern the future."[2] I shall use "fundamental commitments" and "identity-grounding commitments" interchangeably. I shall also—especially in Chapter 2—use "commitments" and "projects" interchangeably.[3]

Alienation provides the most basic reason why fidelity to one's fundamental commitments can have moral value. Experiencing recurrent conflict between her conduct and convictions, a person may become alienated from herself - unable to explain to herself how the actions she takes in the world cohere with the commitments constitutive of who she is. Any plausible normative theory, I assume, should see such "psychological fragmentation"[4] as at least potentially alarming.[5] In what follows, however, I will pay attention only to fundamental commitments or projects that fall within a certain range. One reason for this limitation is that agents can clearly adopt commitments that are abhorrent from an objective perspective, and it would be disturbing, I think, to ascribe even presumptive moral value to such commitments. Therefore, it is essential for my purposes to show that even if one grants external constraints on the kinds of commitments that agents may pursue, at least some of the commitments that lie within that permissible range can still have their own moral significance.

Proceeding down this path means thinking about substantive moral commitments that agents may adopt in a manner that is similar to the morality of promises. While promises can have their own moral significance, this is true only for promises that fall within the boundaries delineated by independent

---

[1] The classic formulation of integrity in these terms remains Bernard Williams' "A Critique of Utilitarianism," in Williams and J.J.C Smart, *Utilitarianism—For and Against* (Cambridge: Cambridge University Press, 1973). For a tiny portion out of the huge literature engaging Williams' views, see Barbara Herman, "Integrity and Impartiality," *Monist* 66 (1983): 233–50; Mark Halfon, *Integrity: A Philosophical Inquiry* (Philadelphia, PA: Temple University Press, 1989); Christine Korsgaard, "The Reasons We Can Share: An Attack on the Distinction between Agent-Relative and Agent-Neutral Values," *Social Philosophy & Policy* 10 (1993): 24–51; Edward Lawry, "In Praise of Moral Saints," *Southwest Philosophy Review* 18 (2002): 1–11. Though my own debts to Williams will be apparent throughout, I should stress already here that my position is independent: I take inspiration from Williams without claiming to offer an interpretation. For one thing, whereas Williams saw integrity as conflicting with the traditional "morality system," I see integrity as always constrained by, and often being in the service of, this system (hence my explicit interest in *moral* integrity, which sets me firmly apart from Williams). Furthermore, there is very little in Williams' political writing to suggest that he would have been sympathetic to any talk of "a liberal people" as a bearer of its own morally important integrity. See, e.g., Williams' *In the Beginning Was the Deed* (Princeton, NJ: Princeton University Press, 2005).

[2] Jed Rubenfeld, *Freedom and Time* (New Haven, CT: Yale University Press, 2001), 92.

[3] I prefer to put more emphasis on the language of moral "projects" in the context of the polity's integrity, since I think this term connotes more immediately the thought that a liberal polity ought to actively pursue certain collective moral undertakings, rather than treat morality solely as a constraint on its amoral projects. I say more about the difference between "active" and "passive" commitments below.

[4] Elizabeth Ashford, "Utilitarianism, Integrity, and Partiality," *The Journal of Philosophy* 97 (2000): 421–39, at 422.

[5] Later on, I shall try to diffuse some possible doubts about this assumption.

moral constraints. Most if not all of us would agree that if one man promises another to help him rape a woman, for instance, this promise is morally irrelevant—it has no moral force at all. Here I will try to show that it is sensible to view fundamental commitments in parallel fashion—seeing *some* such commitments as exerting their own moral force, even while ruling out *ab initio* the moral force of clearly repugnant commitments.[6]

There is a sense in which this claim is unsurprising. After all, there are many commitments that are morally permissible for agents to adopt, and that, once adopted, can exert their own independent force. Thus, for example, the fact that a musician may have a fundamental commitment to certain artistic pursuits, or a businessman to certain professional goals, will often have rational force—making it rational for them to pursue certain actions and to avoid others. My interest here, however, is not in the rational functions of such amoral commitments. Rather, I wish to shed light on the distinctly moral functions of fundamental commitments that center on moral principles. I want to explore how the *moral* integrity of characters such as the pacifist should affect their *moral* deliberation, without making any judgments about how the musician's artistic integrity, for example, should affect her rational deliberation.[7]

1.2 Steadfastness, Self-Seeking Rationalizations, Self-Deception

The core notion of moral integrity—the appeal to fundamental moral commitments as an independent factor in moral deliberation—will be at the heart of my argument in what follows. But while trying to vindicate integrity as a moral factor, I will also be deploying multiple moral ideas that lie in integrity's vicinity.

Several such accompanying ideas will play recurring roles in different chapters. In this chapter, however, three of these accompanying ideas will be especially useful, and I therefore want to say something about each of them here. The first idea is that of steadfastness. A person who is steadfast in her adherence to her moral convictions—who not only tries to act in accordance with certain moral convictions, but is also clearly willing to incur non-trivial costs for the sake of

---

[6] For a powerful rebuttal of heterodox attempts to assign normative force to repugnant promises, see Gary Watson's defense of promising as a "constrained normative power," in his "Promises, Reasons, and Normative Powers," in David Sobel and Stephen Wall (eds.), *Reasons for Action* (New York: Oxford University Press, 2009), 155–77.

[7] In saying this, I do not mean to deny that, in some contexts at least, there will be parallels between moral and amoral commitments, and consequently between the respective invocations of integrity that each grounds. Thus, for instance, just as one person may intelligibly invoke his pacifist commitments to explain why joining the military will betray his integrity, so can another person intelligibly invoke his artistic commitments to explain why sacrificing his artistic ideals will be a betrayal of his integrity. But the former integrity revolves around a principle that is undoubtedly moral in character. This is not true in the case of artistic integrity.

these convictions—is far more likely to strike us as a person of integrity.[8] Conversely, we will hesitate to ascribe moral integrity to a person who only acts upon the moral principles he professes in fair weather—only when doing so costs him little. In fact, we might go so far as to suggest that a person's integrity can *only* be ascertained in circumstances where fidelity to his commitments involves (at least modest) sacrifices.[9]

The second idea concerns hostility to self-seeking rationalizations. An agent who claims to be committed to certain moral principles, but who repeatedly tries to exempt himself from the hold of these principles whenever following them requires real sacrifices, is not very distinct from the person who adheres to his professed principles only in fair weather. Insofar as there is a distinction between the two, it is simply that the person who engages in self-seeking rationalizations does not merely hope for fair weather, but tries to create one himself whenever his hopes are disappointed. Morally speaking, this seems to be a distinction without a difference.

The third idea is that of self-deception. While we often try to explain to others why it is that our apparent deviation from our stated principles is morally warranted, or perhaps not even a deviation at all, just as often, *we ourselves* are the addressees of our self-seeking rationalizations. And when this is the case, we frequently engage in a particular practice that I take to be especially alien to integrity—namely, self-deceit.

What exactly is the relationship I envision between integrity as a moral factor and these three ideas? The answer is complex. On the one hand, I do not mean to claim that the three ideas I just sketched are *only* available to someone who endorses integrity as an independent factor in moral deliberation. Integrity skeptics too can believe that steadfastness is morally valuable, that self-seeking rationalizations are morally objectionable, and that the same is true for self-deception. On the other hand, I hope to show here that for someone who wishes to defend integrity as an independent factor in moral deliberation, these three ideas represent natural allies.

This alliance, in turn, might be best understood as a form of reflective equilibrium. I will argue that concerns about steadfastness, self-seeking rationalizations, and self-deception reinforce the appeal of seeing a person's moral integrity as an independent factor in her moral deliberation. Yet the same is true in the other direction. Once we view a person's moral integrity as an independent factor in her moral deliberation, it is easier to explain why we should care greatly about steadfastness, self-seeking rationalizations, and self-deception. Through this

---

[8] I borrow this emphasis on "steadfastness" from Stephen Carter's *Integrity* (New York: Harper, 1996), although my aims, especially at the political level, are quite distinct from Carter's.

[9] This is not to say that a person who never had to pay any price at all for her convictions is thereby deprived of integrity. It is only to say that others (and perhaps even the person herself) cannot really tell whether she is a person of integrity.

mutual reinforcement, the core notion of integrity as an independent moral factor joins adjacent concepts to form a powerful, unifying framework, clarifying and organizing our moral outlook.[10] Or so, at least, I will try to show.

1.3 Is Integrity a Moral Fifth Wheel?

Why is defending integrity's moral significance a challenging task? One key reason has to do with what I am going to call "fifth-wheel skepticism" concerning moral arguments that appeal to integrity. According to this view, if an individual is going to have any fundamental *moral* commitment at all, then this commitment should simply be to "do the right thing." But if this is so, then a person's fundamental moral commitment will merely track the balance of impersonal moral considerations. Therefore, it is profoundly wrongheaded to ever treat moral integrity as an independent factor that can help one understand how one ought to act. To proceed in this manner is to try to answer a question with the help of a concept that can only have content once that very question is settled.

One way to appreciate the significance of fifth-wheel skepticism is to note its centrality to moral philosophy's most well-known debate on integrity, between Bernard Williams and his utilitarian critics. Williams famously argued that utilitarianism (or, at least, act utilitarianism) "cannot hope to make sense, at any serious level, of integrity," not least because it demands that agents regard their fundamental commitments as entirely dispensable in the pursuit of overall utility.[11] In turn, the main act-utilitarian response to Williams' criticism has been to assert that agents who adopt the utilitarian goal of maximizing moral value in the world as their fundamental commitment would never have to experience a loss of integrity when advancing utilitarian aims.[12]

---

[10] To be clear: in proposing that we think of this unifying framework as "a form of reflective equilibrium," I am not pointing at any sort of family resemblance. The thought here is not "We should care about integrity because we care about some other concept X or Y that lies in its vicinity." Rather, by invoking reflective equilibrium, I simply wish to invoke the Rawlsian thought about moral justification being "a matter of the mutual support of many considerations, of everything fitting together into one coherent view." See John Rawls, *A Theory of Justice* (Cambridge, MA: Harvard University Press, revised edition, 1999, hereafter *TJ*), 19. In similar spirit, my suggestion is that there is an ensemble of concepts, which are commonly understood to have important affinities to one another, and which can be brought together in such a way to allow us to do more with them, in combination, than we can do with any of them individually. I am grateful to an anonymous reviewer for pushing me to clarify this point.

[11] Williams, "A Critique of Utilitarianism," 114–15.

[12] Moreover, at least some utilitarians hold that agents *ought* to adopt the utilitarian project as fundamental, and that if we do not insist on agents viewing the utilitarian project in this way, we run the risk of allowing agents to adopt any project whatsoever, no matter how disturbing. See, e.g., Spencer Carr, "The Integrity of a Utilitarian," *Ethics* 86 (1976): 241–6; Gregory Trianosky, "Moral Integrity and Moral Psychology: A Refutation of Two Accounts of the Conflict between Utilitarianism and Integrity," *The Journal of Value Inquiry* 20 (1986): 279–88.

It must be emphasized, however, that one does not have to be a utilitarian in order to endorse some form of fifth-wheel skepticism about moral integrity. One does not have to be a utilitarian to argue, as Shelly Kagan, for instance, does, that real moral integrity requires that an agent be able to "defend his moral outlook against the challenge of critical self-examination,"[13] and that only agents who adopt the correct all-things-considered moral outlook possess this ability. In fact, even avowed opponents of utilitarianism can endorse fifth-wheel skepticism concerning moral integrity.[14] One may believe that utilitarianism is an implausible moral doctrine, while also believing that the force of agents' moral integrity is entirely parasitic upon familiar factors of impartial morality. Hence fifth-wheel skepticism regarding integrity is not only simple, but also, at least on the face of it, attractively ecumenical.

Now, many philosophers, I believe, take it for granted that invocations of moral integrity that are independent of morality's overall requirements are simply "confused."[15] In fact, I suspect that fifth-wheel skepticism strikes many as so obviously fatal to integrity arguments that it may not even seem necessary to actually *defend* it.[16] If this is the case, the impact of fifth-wheel skepticism might very well exceed its published appearances. And this makes undermining such skepticism especially important for my purposes.

1.4 Integrity as a Moral Factor: The Commitments of Decency

Equipped with these remarks, let us now turn to see why—*pace* fifth-wheel skeptics—an agent's integrity can be an independent factor in moral deliberation. We can start by examining particular commitments that might underlie an agent's moral integrity.

The commitments I have in mind here are those associated with basic moral constraints. We do not only demand of individuals to abide by basic moral constraints in their dealings with others (for instance, to refrain from murder, from assault, or from rape). Alongside the requirement that individuals refrain from committing paradigmatic wrongs, there is moral value in individuals seeing paradigmatic wrongs—or even support for such wrongs—as fundamentally alien to who they are. And that is partly why we have the moral expectation that individuals incorporate a rejection of such wrongs into their self-conception. At

---

[13] Shelly Kagan, *Ethics and the Limits of Morality* (New York: Oxford University Press, 1991), 391.
[14] Recall, for instance, Nagel's remarks cited in the Introduction.
[15] See, e.g., Gerald Gaus, "Dirty Hands," in *A Companion to Applied Ethics*, ed. R.G. Frey and Christopher H. Wellman (Oxford: Blackwell, 2003), 167–78, at 178.
[16] As Brian Barry has pointed out in another context, many people can be expected to hold certain objections without actually airing them, if they take these objections to be so obvious that they do not bother to confront their targets. See Barry's *Culture and Equality: An Egalitarian Critique of Multiculturalism* (Cambridge, MA: Harvard University Press, 2001), 6.

the very least, we have the moral expectation that social and political institutions will cultivate this kind of commitment, as will those agents who have special responsibilities to nurture others' moral personality (parents, teachers, and so on). It is this expectation that is present, I think, when we say that parents and teachers, as well as social and political institutions, ought to cultivate the decency of children, pupils, and citizens. I shall accordingly term the kinds of fundamental commitments we associate with basic moral constraints the *commitments of decency*.

I believe that the commitments of decency can function as an independent factor in an agent's moral deliberation. But in order to develop this claim, I first want to note two points that make this independent role easy to overlook. One point is that such commitments are typically *passive*—existing only in the distant background of the agent's self-understanding. Under (morally) normal circumstances, if you were asked what your most fundamental commitments are, it is unlikely that your first answer would be "I am committed to the rejection of murder." This is true even if you very much have this commitment. It is simply the case that your rejection of murder does not consciously inform your everyday life, pursuits, and projects. Only extraordinary circumstances will "activate" this commitment—will move it to the foreground of your self-conception (that, presumably, is what should happen if someone invites you to murder a third person).

The other point that makes the commitments of decency easy to overlook is that, from a moral perspective, it may seem tempting to skip these commitments and focus instead on their more fundamental grounds. It is tempting, in other words, to focus directly on familiar impartial justifications for why it is important that agents adopt the commitments of decency. Yet we should resist this temptation. Even if the moral weight of the commitments of decency can ultimately be traced to some deeper source, it is not the case that references to these commitments are superfluous from a moral point of view.

While this claim may initially seem odd, the idea I am invoking here about the moral significance of non-foundational concepts is in fact familiar. To give just one example, this idea is central to certain interest-based conceptions of rights. On these conceptions, rights ultimately derive their moral significance from important interests they protect. Yet proponents of these conceptions rarely if ever argue that rights are merely a place-holder for morally important interests, and that we should therefore focus exclusively on "morally protected interests," doing away with "rights talk" altogether. Even if the moral weight of rights, on this view, can ultimately be traced to interests they safeguard, rights can still have their own moral significance: X's right can still yield morally important constraints on Y's actions, for instance, even if X's interests that underlie this right will not be best advanced or protected by Y upholding the constraints. Hence we might say that rights have their own independent moral force.

My suggestion is that we think in analogous terms about the relationship between individuals' fundamental moral commitments and basic moral constraints. Even when the moral significance of individuals' fundamental moral commitments can ultimately be traced to impartial moral constraints, these commitments too can have their own moral force. We might capture this force by saying that *a person's having a moral commitment can provide her with an independent moral reason for action, which is not reducible to the reasons that justify adopting this commitment.*

In order to make this thought concrete, it will be helpful to examine a case where the two come apart: where reference to personal moral commitments captures crucial moral intuitions, which cannot be explained through direct appeal to an impersonal (consequentialist or deontic) justification of why it is important to have these commitments. Consider, then, the following, real-life example.[17] It is June 1940; a person appalled by Nazism is sitting in a German café, witnessing his compatriots celebrating wildly as the radio announces France's surrender to the Nazis. Virtually everyone in the crowd spontaneously raises their arm in the regulation Hitler salute. The person knows that refusing to give the salute would expose him to the risk of serious harms (at the hands of the crowd and perhaps at the hands of the regime). Yet many (if not all of us) are nonetheless bound to think that this person still has *some* reason not to salute. Even if it may be outweighed by opposing considerations—most straightforwardly, by his legitimate interest in self-preservation—it is a genuine reason. But what is this reason?

An appeal to consequences may initially seem like a natural answer. One may suggest that there is a chance that many of the other individuals in the crowd in fact share our protagonist's disdain of the Nazi regime, and are only pretending to support the Nazi cause for fear of the repercussions that might follow if they displayed their true convictions. So if our protagonist conspicuously refused to give the salute, he might thereby embolden others in the crowd to similarly refuse. Such collective refusal, in turn, may influence the attitudes and actions of many who are present—maybe pushing them to re-consider their support of the regime, making them more hesitant to contribute to the regime's practical aims, and, going forward, more willing to sabotage these aims to the degree that they can. All of these would be consequences of non-trivial moral value.

This consequentialist rationale is elegantly simple. But it nonetheless falls short if we add further—eminently plausible—assumptions into our description of the case. Given the terrifying effectiveness of the Nazis' propaganda and

---

[17] This case has some obvious parallels to the Czech grocer case with which I began, though it may seem more challenging for my view—one reason to take it up here. My thinking about this case is indebted to Robert Adams' treatment of it in his *Finite and Infinite Goods: A Framework for Ethics* (New York: Oxford University Press, 1999), chap. 9 (although, unlike my inquiry, Adams' discussion ultimately has theistic aims). I am grateful to Paul Bou-Habib and Shelly Kagan for drawing my attention to Adams' argument.

brainwashing, our protagonist has very strong grounds for believing that him refusing to give the Hitler salute would have no positive impact on the crowd's attitudes or behavior. To drive the point home, we can further suppose that our protagonist has known the vast majority of the crowd members over an extended period—they have all been frequenting this local café for many years—and he has witnessed how they have gradually become genuine supports of Nazism. Even under these assumptions, it seems sensible to think that our protagonist still has *some* moral reason—whether or not it is decisive—to refrain from saluting. Yet this thought cannot be explained through any positive impact that his refusal to salute would have on the crowd.[18]

Might a deontic perspective do better here? The most natural deontic explanation would focus on complicity in the wrongs that the Nazis have been perpetrating against their victims. If our protagonist were to give the Hitler salute in honor of the Nazi defeat of France, he would thereby be complicit in the wrongs that the Nazis have done to the French—and maybe more generally in the wrongs that the Nazis have done (and will go on to do) to their many other victims.

This appeal to complicity comes closer to the mark. But, at least so long as it is focused on the victims, this appeal ultimately fails as well. For one thing, complicity in wrongdoing is typically thought to involve some *causal* contribution to wrongdoing.[19] But there is no obvious sense in which our protagonist makes a causal contribution to the Nazis' crimes simply through the symbolic act of giving the salute. Furthermore, it is not obvious why any of the Nazis' victims would prefer our protagonist to refuse to give the salute, if we assume that such refusal would only expose him to severe harms without producing any benefits for the victims. We can certainly imagine, for instance, French friends of this man who

[18] Some may insist that a rule-consequentialist alternative can provide a stronger explanation. But it is worth noting that even the most sophisticated defenses of rule-consequentialism, which seek to show that it can avoid collapsing into act-consequentialism, build caveats into the consequentialist code to avoid deontic rigorism, and there is no reason why these caveats would not apply here. Thus, for instance, if we follow Brad Hooker's elaborate defense of rule-consequentialism, we are likely to think that a sensible rule-consequentialist position must incorporate a requirement to "avoid disaster" into its favoured code (see Hooker's *Ideal Code, Real World* [Oxford: Oxford University Press, 2000]). But then why would we also think that such a code generates *any* reason for our protagonist to risk bringing disaster upon himself by refraining from giving the salute? Furthermore, most (if not all) rule-consequentialist accounts—including Hooker's—presuppose that the code of rules they favor is adopted by an overwhelming majority of the relevant population. But this presupposition might very well render rule-consequentialist accounts silent in the face of moral complexity that arises precisely because the relevant code (such as "do not support evil ideologies") is manifestly violated by an overwhelming majority. Thanks to Christian Barry for discussion of this point.
[19] See, e.g., Eric Beerbohm, *In Our Name* (Princeton, NJ: Princeton University Press, 2012); Alex Zakaras, "Complicity and Coercion: Toward an Ethics of Political Participation," in David Sobel, Peter Vallentyne, and Steven Wall (eds.), *Oxford Studies in Political Philosophy* 4 (New York: Oxford University Press, 2018), chap. 8. There are admittedly some views of complicity that try to steer away from this causal emphasis—see for example Christopher Kutz, *Complicity: Ethics and Law for a Collective Age* (Cambridge: Cambridge University Press, 2000), although whether this is a viable move is questionable—as noted, for instance, in John Gardner's review of Kutz's book in *Ethics* 114 (2004): 827–30.

tell him in advance that if he were to find himself in such a situation, he should not risk himself unnecessarily.[20]

Finally, a complicity argument focused on the victims is unable to capture a crucial intuition concerning repeated iterations. Imagine that our protagonist had to consider symbolic identification with the Nazis not as a one-off act, but rather as a repeated practice, present in everything from his dress (should he always wear Nazi insignia in public?), through his everyday exchanges (should he feign support for the Nazis in every social or professional conversation?), to the events he regularly attends (should he be present in many Nazi celebrations and rallies?). The intuition seems strong that *repeated* display of identification with the Nazis would be *qualitatively* worse, at least in some sense, than a single such display. But it is not clear how a complicity argument focused on the Nazis' victims could account for this qualitative difference. This complicity argument, then, like the consequentialist argument, ultimately fails to give a satisfactory account of our intuitions in this case.

The idea of integrity, I wish to suggest, is a more promising alternative. A person who loathes the Nazis yet associates with them through his actions is, in an important sense, compromising his integrity. More specifically, to use the terminology introduced above, we may say that our protagonist's extreme circumstances mean that his rejection of the Nazis cannot be a merely passive component of his self-conception. This rejection may stem from basic standards of decency that we expect all individuals to have in passive mode, "in the back of their minds." But our protagonist's predicament means that his rejection of Nazism cannot be passive in this way. Rather, the circumstances render it an *active* fundamental commitment—moving this rejection to the front of his self-conception. That is why associating with the Nazis would be, for this person, a form of self-betrayal. And this self-betrayal is the best explanation for why he has a moral reason not to display identification with the Nazis.

The most immediate way to see the attraction of this integrity explanation is to contrast it with the complicity argument we have just considered. Unlike this argument, the integrity explanation does not depend on any kind of causal impact

---

[20] A similar point would apply, I believe, if one argued simply that the equal moral status of the Nazis' victims generates some kind of expressive requirement not to display support for the Nazis' crimes (whether this status is understood in terms of equal autonomy, equal dignity, or some related notion). For we can imagine the victims saying that it is precisely *because* of their equal moral autonomy and dignity that their voice should matter when they insist that they do not want well-meaning others to pursue risky symbolic gestures. As far as I can tell, the only way to resist such insistence is to hold that the victims have certain inalienable rights. But such rights apply far more easily to the conduct of perpetrators than to the conduct of third parties. Suppose, by way of comparison, that a given regime's victims believe that the regime is violating their inalienable rights, but are also afraid that foreign divestment from the regime will make them economically worse off. As a result, these victims publicly oppose foreign divestment. Would we really say that the victims are simply confused about the moral situation? Would we really say that they are trying to waive rights vis-à-vis foreign actors that are in fact inalienable? I say more about such political questions in Chapter 2.

that our protagonist's symbolic action will have on the Nazis' crimes. Nor does it depend on showing that the Nazis' victims prefer, or would have strong grounds for preferring, that our protagonist refrain from giving the salute. Last but not least, the integrity explanation, unlike the complicity argument, can capture the thought that there would be something qualitatively worse about our protagonist *repeatedly* displaying identification with the Nazis, as opposed to a single deviation from his real convictions. While he may be able to justify to himself a "one-off aberration"—say, a single salute—with the thought that "this does not really represent who I am," such a claim would ring hollow if he routinely displayed conformity to Nazism in every aspect of his life.[21]

To make this gap between the one-off aberration and the repeated practice especially vivid, we may imagine that there is no sheltered, private space in which the man can express his real convictions (say, because of the kind of pervasive regime surveillance that is one of the hallmarks of totalitarianism). Under such extreme circumstances, there would simply be no difference in any area of life between the outward behavior of this man and that of avowed, genuine Nazis—no way to tell him apart from them. Accordingly, such a man might very well lose the ability to recognize himself, experiencing especially acute alienation from his own actions. The idea of integrity, in turn, directly captures this alienation.[22]

Now, if all this is cogent, then it seems that the integrity account provides a powerful explanation of the intuitions associated with the case we have been considering.[23] But the implications of this conclusion extend beyond this particular case. For our conclusion suggests, more generally, that an agent's integrity can have its own independent moral force.

One immediate upshot of this finding is that an agent's integrity can be an independent factor affecting what, all-things-considered, the agent ought to do.

[21] It is worth adding that not just the complicity argument, but in fact any familiar deontic (or consequentialist) argument would arguably have trouble explaining this qualitative difference between one-off and repeated identification with the Nazis.

[22] Adams (*Finite and Infinite Goods*, 218) makes a similar point in his reflections on the case: "suppose that, under the pressure of persecution, and perhaps justifiably, you suppress all outward expression of your loyalties. After a while you yourself may begin to wonder how much reality there is in your opposition to Nazism. Are you actually opposed to it, or do you only wish you could be?"

[23] Some may suggest that it is equally powerful to simply invoke a deontic constraint against displays of support for evil ideologies. But, arguably, such a constraint can only be seen as *agent-directed*. As Thomas Nagel observes when reflecting on deontic constraints, "the evil at which we are constrained not to aim is *our victim's* evil, rather than just a particular bad thing, and each individual has considerable authority in defining what will count as harming him for the purpose of this restriction." (Nagel, *The View from Nowhere* [New York: Oxford University Press, 1986], at 182, italics in the original.) When that authority is operative (when the relevant individuals are not trying to waive inalienable rights) then, as Nagel says, the "particular evil" at which one aims is "swallowed up in the larger [good] aim for deontological purposes." Of course, one's reason not to display support for evil might be directed at oneself, rather than at the victims of evil. But to invoke this first-personal reason is not to present an alternative to the integrity explanation. Rather, it is to *restate* the integrity explanation. Notice, finally, that this point does not depend on whether one believes (as do I happen to believe) that *all* moral reasons are directed toward some agents (contra, e.g., Simon Cabula May, "Directed Duties," *Philosophy Compass* 10 [2015]: 523–32).

The precise effect that integrity will have will obviously depend on the configuration of other pertinent factors. But two such configurations are worth mentioning. First, when the balance of other factors is undecided, integrity might be a tie-breaker.[24] By way of illustration, suppose again that a morally decent person is considering whether to join a crowd celebrating a profoundly unjust war waged by a dictatorship. If this dictatorship has engaged in less brainwashing than the Nazis (or if its brainwashing techniques have been less effective), there is more of a chance that conspicuous refusal to identify with the dictatorship will have a meaningful impact on the crowd. We can at least imagine a case where the moral weight of this chance for positive developments is (roughly) equal to the moral weight of concerns about the risks involved in refusing to display identification with the regime. And in such a case, integrity might act as a tie-breaker, settling the all-things-considered moral judgment against public identification with the regime.

A second configuration features countervailing considerations that are simply not significant enough to overcome integrity's weight. For instance, imagine a case where a morally decent person has very strong grounds for believing that her symbolic refusal to identify with a brutal dictatorship will have no positive effect on anyone else, but also knows that the costs of such refusal will be relatively modest given her particular circumstances. This may be an affluent person, for instance, who knows that her family's social pedigree effectively protects her from the regime's worst methods, meaning that she will only incur some limited economic costs as a result of refusing to associate with the regime. This refusal may cost her certain business opportunities she would have enjoyed otherwise. And these opportunities would simply be taken up by her competitors, all of whom (she has good reason to believe) are genuine in their adoption of the regime's ideology, and unlikely to be moved by her actions. But we can still imagine circumstances where the economic costs to this person are sufficiently contained so as to be outweighed by the countervailing normative force of her integrity. And, in line with what was said above, this outweighing would be especially clear if the issue at hand involved not a one-off decision, but rather repeated, continuous association with the regime.

With these claims in mind, I want to temporarily put aside integrity skepticism, taking a brief detour to consider the question of just how far integrity considerations can go in shifting the moral status of our actions. This question arises in light of the following worry. It might be true that the presence of integrity considerations can turn an action that, in their absence, would be morally permissible into one that is morally required. But it is harder to see how integrity considerations can render otherwise-*prohibited* actions into ones that are morally

---

[24] I do not mean to suggest that the "moral math" will frequently (if ever) work out so neatly. But I think that the conceptual point here is important apart from its empirical regularity.

permissible, let alone required.[25] The main reason, in turn, is that it is hard to see how agents can plausibly cite their own integrity as a justification for imposing costs on *others*, in ways that would be prohibited were integrity not in play.

I believe that my account of integrity can accommodate this worry, to the extent that it merits accommodation. To see how the account can do this, recall 1.1, in which I conceded that a morally tenable account of integrity must incorporate external moral prohibitions on the kinds of commitments that agents may adopt. In that section, I highlighted commitments that are simply repugnant, such as those of the misogynist, the racist, and their ilk. Here, however, we can add that agents can espouse commitments that are plainly morally untenable not so much because their substantive focus is repugnant, but because they involve a plainly indefensible imposition of costs on others. When that is the case, the account I am offering denies *ab initio* that the relevant agents can claim the mantle of integrity as providing even a pro-tanto justification of their actions. A committed propon-ent of animal rights, for example, may plausibly claim the mantle of integrity when accepting certain personal costs that stem from his ethical convictions—for instance, the various costs associated with maintaining a purely vegan diet. But such a proponent cannot cite integrity, not even as a pro-tanto justification, for murdering 10,000 people in order to save a single non-human animal. In my view, a proponent of animal rights who is willing to impose such costs on others in order to advance the moral principles in which he believes is not a paragon of integrity, but rather a *fanatic* (a distinction on which I say more in Chapter 4).

In this way, my view of integrity partially accommodates the concern about imposing costs on others. But why only partially rather than fully? The answer is that there are *some* costs which one may be morally permitted, or even required, to impose on others in the name of one's own integrity, even if this imposition would

---

[25] Here and throughout, I am relying on what I take to be the standard understanding of the morally "required," "prohibited," and "permitted," which refers to whether under a certain set of circumstances, taking all relevant moral considerations into account, a given act (respectively) ought to be done, ought not be done, or is optional. Some deontologists who write on integrity favor a more complex terminology distinguishing between "strong" and "weak" moral permissibility, in order to support the thought that even in moral conflict situations where infringements upon deontic constraints are warranted, such infringements (being merely "weakly" permissible) are always wrongful in some sense, and therefore always give rise to remedial duties. For an elaborate argument emphasizing this reasoning, see Matthew Kramer, *Torture and Moral Integrity* (Oxford: Oxford University Press, 2014), e.g. at 2–10. I stick here to the simpler, more familiar terminology, for three related reasons. First, while I share the concern with moral remainders in the aftermath of moral conflict situations, I am not convinced that such remainders are always best explained through reference to infringed deontic constraints and to remedial duties associated with such constraints. Accordingly, I am more inclined to view my integrity account as an alternative to the deontological conception of moral conflicts and moral remainders. Second, whether infringements upon deontic constraints should always count as wrong and as generating remedial duties (as Kramer holds) is a substantive question; I do not think that we can make meaningful progress on this question (even in part) by making our terminology more complex. Finally, given these points, it seems to me that the gains involved in departing from the standard moral vocabulary are not significant enough to outweigh the loss of terminological simplicity.

be prohibited were one's integrity not in play. Consider, for instance, the afore-mentioned scion of an affluent family who abhors the dictatorship ruling her country. Taking a symbolic stand against the dictatorship may involve costs not just for her, but also for others. Thus, for example, by conspicuously refusing to identify with the regime, she may (directly and indirectly) set back the educational and socio-economic prospects of her children, who would be cast out of elite circles dominated by the regime and its lackeys. In my view, there could very well be circumstances where the moral weight of her integrity would be sufficient to make the imposition of these costs permissible, possibly even required, even though such an imposition would be prohibited were we to take her integrity out of the moral picture. This example suggests that we cannot offer a precise rule indicating how integrity may or may not affect the moral status of our actions. The answer will have to be given on a case-by-case basis, and it will hinge, as I said earlier, on the overall configuration of moral factors pertinent to the case at hand.

Now, the reason why I designated my discussion of shifts in moral status as a "detour" is that this discussion presupposes that we have already defeated fifth-wheel skepticism about integrity: we can only discuss integrity's relative weight in comparison to other moral factors if we assume, *contra* fifth-wheel skepticism, that integrity itself *is* a moral factor. And, of course, I do hope that the claims I have been making will help to quell the doubts of many drawn to such skepticism.

I also recognize, however, that at least some skeptics are likely to remain unpersuaded. The reason, I believe, has to do with another influential source of skepticism about integrity's moral force, which has to do with the distinction between psychology and morality. The thought here is that if an agent does what morality, all-things-considered, requires in a morally fraught situation, then any regret that the agent may experience should be dismissed as a psychological pitfall that the agent ought to overcome as much as possible. Certainly, one may "feel compromised"[26] when acting in ways that conflict with one's fundamental com-mitments. But such a feeling will have no more moral weight than other kinds of psychological phenomena whose moral significance we readily dismiss (think about greed, domination, and "weakness of the will").[27]

I think this "mere psychology" complaint is misguided. But it is also intuitive. I therefore want to respond to this complaint too in some detail, first by offering two general observations. The opening observation is that there is nothing

[26] See Chiara Lepora and Robert Goodin's discussion of the "phenomenology of compromise" in their *On Complicity and Compromise* (Oxford: Oxford University Press, 2013), chap. 2.
[27] This point finds traction even with some who are otherwise sympathetic to integrity arguments. See, e.g., Daniel Markovits, "Integrity and the Architecture of Ambition," in Daniel Callcut (ed.), *Reading Bernard Williams* (London: Routledge, 2009), 110–38, passim. Markovits responds to this point by trying to distance integrity's significance from psychology, instead connecting integrity's import to human beings' bounded rationality. My strategy is different, if nothing else because, as I stressed above, I am interested precisely in the moral rather than simply rational force of integrity.

unfamiliar about the claim that theories aiming to guide human action should be sensitive to facts about human nature that are not easily alterable.[28] But if we treat this venerable claim as at least somewhat credible, then the idea of incorporating recurring features of human psychology into our moral outlook should not seem so immediately implausible.

The other general observation I wish to make is that the psychological tendencies we are most inclined to ignore for moral purposes all seem to represent a practical indifference to the moral claims of others. Consider, for instance, a person who says, "I understand that vulnerable others have a compelling moral claim to my assistance, but my will to respond to this claim is simply too weak." Or a person who says, "I understand that it would be unfair to exploit a certain group that I have the opportunity to exploit, but I am just too greedy to avoid it." We are likely to think that such individuals do not really take others' moral claims to provide reasons of significant practical force. This is why we are so ready to deny that such individuals can cite their psychological traits as morally salient facts. But there is no reason to think that *all* appeals to psychological constraints necessarily reflect such practical indifference to the moral claims of others. The anguish that our protagonist in the Nazi salute case, for example, feels about associating with the Nazis stems not from practical indifference to others' moral claims, but precisely from taking seriously the moral claims of the agents whose moral status the Nazis deny. Stated more abstractly, we can say that an agent who is anxious about actions that conflict with his fundamental moral commitments is anxious *because* he engages the universe of morality, rather than because he is detached from morality. This distinction gives us a principled basis for distinguishing the psychology associated with certain moral commitments from the psychological phenomena whose moral importance we readily dismiss.[29]

What I want to do in the next two sections (1.5 and 1.6) is to build upon these general observations. I do so by developing two more specific and sustained arguments. Both arguments are meant to further reduce the apparent distance between my conception of integrity and morality's traditional concerns. In due course, I will suggest that these arguments have surprising implications for our thinking about political integrity. But these arguments should prove useful already here, when discussing personal integrity.

[28] See Samuel Scheffler, *The Rejection of Consequentialism* (New York: Oxford University Press, 1982).

[29] To be sure, this form of engagement with morality may still be vulnerable to the complaint that it does not sufficiently engage others' practical needs. But that is a different complaint, which I discuss in Chapter 3.

1.5 Unconditional Commitments and Self-Distrust

The first specific argument I wish to examine in detail has to do with the relationship between integrity, unconditional commitments, and self-distrust.

This argument begins from the thought that integrity is closely linked to unconditional commitments. Lynn McFall provides an elegant description of this link:

> Unless corrupted by philosophy, we all have things we think we would never do, under any imaginable circumstances, whatever we may give to survival or pleasure, power and the approval of strangers; some part of ourselves beyond which we will not retreat, some weakness however prevalent in others that we will not tolerate in ourselves. And if we do that thing, betray that weakness, we are not the persons we thought; there is nothing left that we may even in spite refer to as I ... *it is in this sense that some commitments must be unconditional: they are conditions of continuing as ourselves ... There are things we could not do without self-betrayal and personal disintegration.*[30]

I do not wish to try to settle the question of whether having unconditional commitments is a necessary condition for having integrity. I am only going to make the more minimal assumption that when a person has such commitments, acting in ways that are diametrically opposed to them unequivocally threatens integrity.[31]

This assumption makes it easier to challenge a firm division between morality's familiar concerns and the (ostensibly) "merely psychological" concerns I have been stressing. In compressed form, this challenge can be stated as follows. Morality *itself* pressures agents to incorporate various unconditional commitments into their identity, and to treat them as an independent factor in moral deliberation. Therefore, it is unfair to admonish agents who actually treat these commitments in this way. Since morality itself encourages agents to view certain actions as profoundly alien to who they are, and to make this view central to their moral deliberation, it is unreasonable to also tell agents that whenever the overall balance of moral reasons favors the very same actions, they should regard any alienation associated with these actions as a mere psychological pitfall that is to be resisted.

We can begin to unpack this argument by asking exactly how and why morality pushes agents to incorporate unconditional moral commitments into their

---

[30] Lynn McFall, "Integrity," *Ethics* 98 (1987): 5–20, at 12–13. Throughout the book, all italics are mine unless noted otherwise.

[31] This is especially so when the relevant actions occur repeatedly (think again of the example of repeated displays of Nazi allegiance).

self-conception. The commitments of decency discussed above provide some helpful clues. I noted earlier our moral expectation that teachers and parents cultivate the commitments of decency in those under their tutelage. And the normal way in which teachers and parents (as well as broader social and political institutions) try to cultivate these commitments is in unconditional form. We are inculcated, from our earliest years, with the conviction that there are some things—such as the most extreme forms of violence and disrespect—that a decent person *necessarily* and *always* avoids. Parents and teachers typically focus on such unconditional moral commitments because they have obvious reasons not to trust that their children and (at least very young) pupils possess the capacities needed to master and apply more complicated moral guidelines. But adults too have an important reason to adopt an unconditional perspective with regard to commitments of decency. This reason again has to do with lack of trust, of a particular sort—*self-distrust*.

Let me elaborate. If we are aware of the all-too-human propensity to rationalize our way out of the hold of moral principles whenever these principles are burdensome, then we should have a healthy distrust of ourselves. We should be honest in recognizing that, just like so many other human beings, we too are overwhelmingly likely to seek exceptions from moral principles whenever they seem demanding. But if awareness of our propensity for self-seeking rationalizations leads us to distrust ourselves as moral umpires—as it should—then we have strong reasons, of a decidedly moral nature, to *pre-empt* our rationalizations.

To make this pre-emption vivid, imagine, for example, a couple whose income and investments would have been more than enough to take care of the entire family, if it weren't for the husband's weakness for gambling—a weakness that, time and again, blows out a substantial portion of the couple's savings, and puts the children's future in jeopardy. The husband recognizes in advance that given recurring, easy opportunities to gamble, it is overwhelmingly likely that he will— time and again—find a way of explaining to himself why "just this one bet" is warranted. But instead of meaningfully acting on this self-knowledge, the husband takes a job right next to a casino (convincing himself, implausibly, that it has real benefits over another job in a safer place that is clearly just as good), and even signs up to receive constant updates from an online sports website that "just happens" to also alert him to attractive-looking bets (telling himself that he signed up only because he likes to follow various sports teams). Predictably, he makes more bets, and loses more money.

Now suppose that the gambler's wife unequivocally expresses her moral outrage. If her husband were to defend himself by arguing that he really thought prior to making his latest bet that it was a good one, we would want to say—as his wife surely would—that he is missing the point entirely. The pivotal point is that he ought not to have let himself get into a situation where he even *begins* to engage in calculations about whether or not to bet. He should have known that once he commences this process, his mind will inevitably find a way to rationalize yet another gamble. Therefore, if nothing else because of his duties toward his children, he had very strong moral reasons to commit unconditionally to steer clear not only of bad gambles, but even of situations where the temptation to *calculate* whether to gamble will present itself.[32]

My suggestion is that, when it comes to many important moral principles we hold, there is a sense in which we are all in the gambler's predicament. There are numerous contexts where our ubiquitous tendency to engage in motivated reasoning will predictably lead us to engage in morally dangerous calculations that will, "surprisingly," turn out to rationalize deviations from our principles. Thus morality itself tells us what it tells the gambler: that healthy self-distrust should lead us to pre-empt our predictable rationalizations, by preventing ourselves from even entering into various morally fraught calculations.

In turn, one of the very best strategies for steering clear of these calculations, and thus a strategy that morality itself should cherish, is to adopt certain unconditional moral commitments, and to take these as essential to our self-conception—in other words, to treat these unconditional commitments as the core of our moral integrity. If we succeed—if we manage to incorporate unconditional moral commitments into our identity in this way—then action directly contradicting these moral commitments will seem entirely *alien* to us, and indeed, in the vast majority of circumstances, *unthinkable*. Williams captures the appeal of this idea as follows:

> An effective way for actions to be ruled out is that they never come into thought at all, and this is often the best way. One does not feel easy with the man who in the course of a discussion of how to deal with political or business rivals says, "of course, we could have them killed, but we should lay that aside right from the beginning." It should never have come into his hands to be laid aside...some concerns are best embodied in this way, in deliberative silence.[33]

One way to evince the moral value of this pre-emptive strategy is to consider how it allows us to overcome familiar obstacles facing standard consequentialist and deontic approaches. We can see these obstacles by considering morally fraught issues concerning the treatment of vulnerable others. There are many situations where one could try to rationalize what seems like questionable—and in some cases even seriously objectionable—treatment of the vulnerable, either

---

[32] This is a subtly different point than the more familiar idea of self-binding. The thought here is not simply that we should bind ourselves at an early point in time so as to resist the temptations we know will come our way later on, in the manner of Ulysses tying himself to the mast to resist the sirens he knows he will encounter later in his journey (an image that is familiar from constitutional theory). The thought is rather that unconditional commitments should prevent us from ever embarking on certain journeys. For other variants of self-binding and their complex relationship to integrity see Korsgaard, *Self-Constitution: Agency, Identity, and Integrity* (New York: Oxford University Press, 2009), chap. 9.
[33] Bernard Williams, *Ethics and the Limits of Philosophy* (London: Routledge, 1985), 206.

through consequentialist calculations or the removal of deontic constraints. Consider, for instance, the head of a major company, who convinces himself that if he does not bribe foreign officials in a developing country to win contracts for the supply of essential services to the population, his less scrupulous competitors will win and only provide worse services, to the overall detriment of the country's most vulnerable. Or consider an affluent tourist traveling in a poor country, convincing himself that enjoying sexual favors from young women in clearly dire straits satisfies basic moral constraints because these women consent to sexual relations.

Self-seeking rationalizations similarly loom large when reflecting on the vulnerable who are much closer to us, spatially and emotionally. Think about care for one's elderly family members, for example, and in particular care for family members who have suffered severe cognitive decline. In such circumstances, there will inevitably be moments where one may ask whether one's attention and energy makes "any real difference," and whether it would therefore be appropriate to use this time and energy differently. Reasoning in this way, one may also cling either to the expressed consent of the vulnerable (think of an elderly mother who tells her middle-age son that since she can rarely recognize him, she wants him to stop "wasting time" visiting her, using it to work instead). Or one may invoke assumptions about what the vulnerable would consent to if they had the chance (thus the children of demented parents might tell themselves that their parents, had they been capable of giving informed consent, would consent to them working instead of visiting).

I do not mean to suggest that these examples are all identical in terms of the moral severity of self-seeking rationalizations. But I do take these examples to illustrate the moral value in individuals pre-empting the distinct probability of self-seeking rationalizations, by incorporating into their self-conception unconditional commitments to do or avoid certain actions. The affluent tourist who sees it as essential to his self-conception to never engage in exploitation of women in dire straits, for example, will not enter into consequentialist arithmetic or even consider appealing to any kind of consent from the women as an excuse for accepting their "offers," because his own integrity will pre-empt, *ab initio*, any deliberation on whether or not he should actually accept. Similarly, the businessman who has a fundamental moral commitment never to engage in bribery will not even embark on the calculation—that is bound to be self-serving—of the outcomes that would follow from his refraining. And the children who have a fundamental commitment to care for their parents, even when (and perhaps especially when) their parents suffer from severe cognitive problems, will not even contemplate consent considerations, or concerns about effective use of their time, as potentially licensing abandonment of their parents, because such abandonment, being fundamentally alien to who they are, will be simply unthinkable for them.

Of course, even if we pursue the pre-emptive strategy I have just described, such that certain actions (or omissions) are unthinkable for us, specific circumstances might arise in which "the unthinkable" *has* to become, for the lack of a better word, thinkable. Take again the Nazi salute example. Presumably, our protagonist in this example never thought before the Nazis' rise to power that even symbolic identification with a monstrous ideology would be a live conduct option for him. But now circumstances have developed in such a way that it *is* a live option—and perhaps even the morally dominant option, all-things-considered. How can the account I have been outlining make sense of this shift?

Three answers come to mind, in ascending order of significance. First, to recognize that certain specific situations render thinkable what was previously unthinkable is also to recognize, in a very immediate and powerful way, a core feature of these situations—namely, their profoundly *tragic* character (a point to which I return below).

Second, I have suggested above that healthy self-distrust gives one a reason, as an adult, to sustain the same unconditional moral commitments with which one was imbibed as a child: one has a reason to tell one's parents and teachers, as Rousseau's Emile tells his tutor, "I have chosen to become what you have made of me."[34] But everything I have said up to now is fully compatible with recognizing that our capacities as adults nonetheless alter our moral responsibilities. In particular, as adults we have the responsibility of recognizing that in tragic circumstances, we must acknowledge the presence of other salient moral considerations apart from those given by our fundamental moral commitments—including considerations that may force us to act against these commitments.

However, third, none of this means that morality can reasonably demand of us to simply *ignore* our fundamental moral commitments in tragic circumstances—to throw them out of our moral deliberation as a mere psychological distraction. For one thing, such a sharp boundary between the moral and the psychological would also require of us to ignore morality's own pressures to anticipate our rationalizations in response to moral principles—rationalizations which are, after all, psychological phenomena. Furthermore, morality itself should recognize that part of what makes the work of cultivating our fundamental moral commitments so hard is precisely the fact that these commitments can only reliably help us anticipate our rationalizations if they are, to a significant extent, *resistant* to change. If our commitments were too flexible, and we treated them as entirely dependent upon changing circumstances, then these commitments could not do

---

[34] Given the political purposes of our inquiry, it is worth noting that this Rousseauian process had political parallels. According to Patrick Riley, for example, Rousseau hoped that "political society would finally, at the end of its political education, be in a position to say what Emile says at the end of his domestic education." See Riley's *Will and Political Legitimacy: A Critical Exposition of Social Contract Theory in Hobbes, Locke, Rousseau, Kant, and Hegel* (Cambridge, MA: Harvard University Press, 1982), 118.

the job that morality itself should want them to do—and, in fact, they may not really be *commitments* at all.

Before moving on, it may be helpful to remark on the relationship between the claims I have been making so far and two of the dominant camps of contemporary moral philosophy—deontologists on the one hand, and utilitarians on the other. Consider deontology first, and specifically absolute deontology. The foregoing should already make clear that my emphasis on unconditional moral commitments is not simply equivalent to absolute deontology. To reiterate, I am *not* suggesting that certain moral constraints always ought to be upheld, regardless of circumstances.[35]

What makes the commitments in which I am interested "unconditional" nonetheless is the thought that it is virtually impossible to "cleanly" break them. In line with McFall's aforementioned remarks, we can say that *whenever* we break our unconditional moral commitments (or at the very least, whenever we do so in a manner that extends beyond a one-off aberration), we seriously jeopardize our most basic sense of our identity.[36] Indeed, it is precisely because this jeopardizing

[35] I am referring to the standard understanding of absolute deontology. I also mentioned above Kramer's less common variant of absolute deontology, which holds that we sometimes ought to infringe upon deontic constraints, but that such infringements are (nonetheless) always wrong, and thus always generate remedial duties. Here is the place to say something about why I think this is an unstable position. The instability that worries me can be illustrated via apologies, which I take to be at play whenever we seek to convey recognition of the wrongful status of our actions. A view that classifies every infringement of a deontic constraint as wrong (arguably) implies that every such infringement—even one that we ought to have committed—necessitates an apology. Genuine apologies, however, reflect admission that we ought *not* to have acted the way we did. If I apologize to you for breaking my promise to have lunch, for example, my apology can only be genuine if I really believe that I ought to have kept the promise. But suppose I skipped our lunch because that was my only way to save someone else's life. In that case, it would still be true that I owe you an *explanation*. But I do not owe you an apology (and if I say, "I'm sorry about skipping our lunch," I am best construed as conveying regret over the fact that the *world* turned out the way it did, not over the fact *I* acted the way I did). Indeed, if I provide the needed explanation, adhering to the social convention of framing it as an apology, then surely what you should say is "you don't need to apologize—I would have done exactly the same thing if I were you." And in any case where that is the appropriate reaction to the infringement of a deontic constraint, it is at the very least an open question whether the relevant infringement was actually wrongful. These thoughts place serious pressure on the idea that *all* infringements upon deontic constraints are "wrong always and everywhere" (*pace* Kramer, *Torture and Moral Integrity*, e.g. at 21). I hasten to concede, though, that the morality of apologies is a large topic, and it is obviously possible to endorse a different conception of apologies than the one on which I am relying here. For discussion, see, e.g., Nick Smith, *I Was Wrong* (Cambridge: Cambridge University Press, 2008); Adrienne Martin, "Owning Up and Lowering Down: The Power of Apology," *The Journal of Philosophy* 107 (2010): 534–53; Marc Cohen, "Apology as Self-Repair," *Ethical Theory and Moral Practice* 21 (2018): 585–98.

[36] Some might worry that understanding "unconditional" commitments in this way involves a problematic circularity: if these commitments turn out to be defined simply as those commitments that, once incorporated into our self-conception, cannot be infringed without compromising our integrity, then we have not really advanced our cause vis-à-vis the integrity skeptic. This worry, however, misconstrues the role that unconditional commitments play in my argument. My claim is not that once we understand what unconditional commitments (in my sense) *are*, we will be convinced of integrity's moral significance. Rather, my claim is that the unfairness argument (in this section) and the self-respect argument (in 1.6), both of which revolve around unconditional moral commitments, should convince us of integrity's moral significance. Thanks to Garrett Cullity for pushing me to clarify this point.

is so often constitutive of tragedy that tragic circumstances make unconditional commitments—and one's betrayal of these commitments—loom especially large.[37]

What, then, about utilitarianism? One can imagine a utilitarian who agrees with much of what I have been saying here. According to this utilitarian, we should indeed treat unconditional moral commitments as an independent factor in our moral deliberation, simply because making our moral judgments this way increases the probability that we will get more of them right, on average. Thus, for example, even if the moral truth is that in a given instance it would have been better for the head of a major company to bribe foreign officials because of the positive consequences that would be associated with this act, there will be multiple other instances where his unconditional commitment not to bribe would have far better consequences than the consequences that would arise if he had no such commitment, meaning that the adoption of unconditional commitments would yield a net gain for morality overall.

There are at least two differences between this utilitarian position and my view. The first difference concerns the relationship between morality's evaluative and prescriptive functions. The utilitarian firmly separates these functions: morality in its prescriptive role may yield a decision procedure centered on unconditional commitments, even though morality in its evaluative role may assign agents a "negative score" in any given case when their adherence to these commitments yields outcomes that are suboptimal from a purely impartial perspective (for example, in a case where the CEO bribing the foreign official to win the contract really would have produced the most good possible). In contrast, I am highly skeptical of any attempt to distinguish between these two functions of morality, not least because I believe that *there is no* "evaluative morality" that exists apart from morality's prescriptions. In my view, a standard for evaluating the world that does not seek in any way to offer prescriptions to any agent in the world is not a *moral* standard, whatever else it may be.[38]

Second, I am inclined to think that utilitarianism is ultimately an implausible moral doctrine. Its implausibility, in turn, is evident partly in its misconception of the very nature of tragic choices associated with unconditional commitments.

---

[37] Tragedy, in other words, often arises precisely because our unconditional commitments are "identity-conferring" in a way that our merely defeasible commitments are not. See McFall, "Integrity," 12–13, following John Kekes, "Constancy and Purity," *Mind* 92 (1983): 499–518. See also Martha Nussbaum, "The Costs of Tragedy: Some Moral Limits of Cost-Benefit Analysis," *The Journal of Legal Studies* 29 (2000): 1005–36.

[38] I do not mean to say that we can engage in moral evaluation of agents only if we can guide their actions (it seems clear, after all, that we can morally evaluate the dead, for example). What I *do* want to say is that our moral evaluation of agents is parasitic upon morality's prescriptions. That is why, if morality itself prescribes the incorporation of certain unconditional commitments into agents' self-conception, as I have argued, then it makes little sense to also castigate agents who actually incorporate these commitments in these ways.

By way of illustration, consider the classic example of "Sophie's choice," from William Styron's novel of the same name.[39] Sophie, a Polish mother in a concentration camp, is forced by a Nazi to pick which one of her two children will live, otherwise he would have both children murdered. Much has been written on this quintessential example of tragedy, evident in Sophie's repeated claim that she is simply unable to choose between her children.[40] My own view is that predicaments such as Sophie's lie beyond the reach of moral philosophy,[41] precisely because it is hard to see how any morally sentient agent can experience this kind of predicament without experiencing the most acute self-betrayal. In fact, it seems to me presumptuous, possibly even offensive, for any philosopher to insist on there being a "morally correct answer" as to what Sophie ought to do.[42]

However, even if you do not share this view, you may still share my thought that utilitarianism fundamentally mischaracterizes the considerations bearing on Sophie's choice. For, at the end of the day, the utilitarian must insist not only that there is a morally correct answer as to which of her children Sophie ought to try to save (an answer that evaluative morality coldly records). The utilitarian must also insist that which of these children can make a greater positive impact on the world is a salient moral factor, one actually bearing on the content of that answer. But such insistence is surely bizarre: it is simply false to say that Sophie ought (in *any* sense of "ought") to try to save the child with the better utility-producing prospects. Moreover, this utilitarian position remains bizarre even if we try to add to it the idea that Sophie can be "excused" for her all-too-predictable failure to engage in such utilitarian calculations. After all, a necessary condition for talk of moral excuses to make sense is there being real grounds for thinking that agents have not reasoned or acted as they morally ought to have reasoned or acted. But Sophie's "failure" to consider which of her children would be a better utility-producer yields no such grounds.

Now, there is obviously a great deal more that could be said about this and similar examples. One could discuss whether such examples are really a *reductio* of utilitarianism, or rather (as some utilitarians would likely have it) a Q.E.D.; one could also discuss the extent to which these examples trade on familiar complaints regarding utilitarians' inability to make sense of particularistic obligations and attachments. But I will not pursue any of these large issues here, nor will I delve

---

[39] William Styron, *Sophie's Choice* (New York: Random House, 1979).

[40] See, e.g., Gaus, "Dirty Hands," responding to Michael Stocker, *Plural and Conflicting Values* (Oxford: Clarendon, 1990), 19.

[41] In *Moral Luck* (Cambridge: Cambridge University Press, 1981), 18, Williams expresses what I take to be a similar view, though on somewhat different grounds.

[42] The same point could be made with regard to other famous cases, such as Jean-Paul Sartre's example of the son who has to decide whether to stay at the side of his ailing mother or to join the French resistance to the Nazis. See Sartre's "Existentialism Is a Humanism," in Walter Kaufman (ed.), *Existentialism from Dostoyevsky to Sartre* (New York: Meridian Publishing Company, 1989).

further into the large and ongoing meta-ethical debates at which the last few paragraphs have gestured.[43]

Instead of all this, I will simply point out that my choice not to put my differences with utilitarianism center stage is a conscious one. To reiterate my introductory remarks, the purposes of this inquiry are ultimately constructive rather than destructive. Therefore, if the claims I have been developing can extend integrity's appeal, bringing on board even some utilitarians typically thought hostile to it, then that is all to the good.

1.6 Unconditional Commitments and Self-Respect

Having developed the unfairness argument in some detail, let me now turn to a second argument against those inclined to view integrity claims as "mere psychology" devoid of moral significance. This argument, like its predecessor, relies on the thought that morality pressures us to make unconditional moral commitments central to our self-conception. But instead of associating this pressure with unfairness, as the first argument does, this argument goes in a different direction. Here the thought is that once incorporated into a person's self-conception, unconditional moral commitments can give rise to important moral duties that a person owes to *herself*. This is because, when a person who sees unconditional moral commitments as constitutive of her integrity infringes upon these commitments, she is also bound to be compromising her self-respect.[44] And according to this argument, persons have a moral *duty* to sustain their self-respect.

This is once again a compressed statement of the argument, and so it will again be helpful to unpack it gradually. We can start with the basic notion that persons have duties to themselves. Many, from Hobbes onward, have been critical of this notion. The main idea often invoked by such critics is that a person to whom a duty is owed has the prerogative of releasing the duty-bound from the requirement that they act or refrain from acting in the relevant ways (you are no longer under a duty to pay me in accordance with a contract we signed, for example, if I release you from this duty). Thus it seems that in the case of duties to self, a person has the prerogative of releasing herself from any "duties" to herself. But

---

[43] I have in mind here in particular the meta-ethical debate about "objective" versus "subjective" permissibility. See, e.g., Michael Zimmerman, "Is Moral Obligation Objective or Subjective?" *Utilitas* 18 (2006): 329–61; Zimmerman, *Living with Uncertainty* (Cambridge: Cambridge University Press, 2008); Peter Graham, "In Defense of Objectivism About Moral Obligation," *Ethics* 121 (2010): 88–115; Bas van der Vossen, "Uncertain Rights Against Defense," *Social Philosophy and Policy* 32 (2016): 129–45.

[44] As Gabriele Taylor elegantly puts it, "to have self-respect," one "must have a degree of integrity; without some integrity there would be no self to respect." See Taylor's "Shame, Integrity and Self-Respect," in Robin Dillon (ed.), *Dignity, Character, and Self-Respect* (London: Routledge, 1995), 157–80, at 168.

then these duties are ultimately illusory, and any invocation of them can at most be only metaphorical.[45]

Although this familiar suspicion of duties to self is intuitive, it can be resisted, in at least two important ways. First, the classic challenge to the idea of duties to self only gets off the ground if we presuppose that an individual may release others from any moral duty they have toward her. But this presupposition is extremely controversial, at least if we follow the conventional view according to which duties correspond to rights. On this view, in order to release others from a duty they have toward her, an individual has to waive her right that others treat her (or avoid treating her) in certain ways. So in order to insist that a person can always release others from any duty they have toward her, we have to insist that a person can always waive any rights she has vis-à-vis others—we have to insist, in other words, that there are no inalienable rights. Once this point is recognized, the appeal of the classic challenge to duties to self should diminish considerably.[46] To be sure, some may be willing to bite this bullet and simply reject the notion of inalienable rights. But biting this particular bullet requires especially strong teeth.

Second—moving closer to our specific interest in self-respect—we can shore up the idea of duties to self in general, and duties to respect oneself in particular, by considering our reactive attitudes in cases where those close to us fail to demand of others the basic respect they are due simply qua persons. Suppose, for example, that your partner suffers daily, non-trivial mistreatment at work, and recognizes it as disrespectful, but never demands to be treated better. Suppose further that his silence stems not from pragmatic calculations (for instance, "I don't want to risk the job by speaking out"), but rather from a dismissal of his own moral claims. Although you know that he would immediately speak out for co-workers who suffered even lesser mistreatment, you witness every day how he accepts his own situation as fait accompli. When you press your partner about the issue, he responds, "I am not that important." Arguably, there is going to be some point where you will react to this situation not only with morally warranted anger at those who are mistreating your partner. Eventually, you will be angry at your partner as well, for failing to take seriously his own moral worth. His servility at work will be not only a lamentable fact or an unattractive form of behavior (though it may also be that), but a *moral* failure: a failure to respect himself as he ought to. In other words, failing to acknowledge fully one's own basic moral

[45] Thus Hobbes famously wrote: "For he is free, that can be free when he will: Nor is it possible for any person to be bound to himself; because he that can bind, can release; and therefore he that is bound to himself onely, is not bound." See Thomas Hobbes, *Leviathan*, Richard Tuck, ed. (Cambridge: Cambridge University Press, 1991), chapter 26, section 2. See also Marcus Singer, "On Duties to Oneself," *Ethics* 69 (1959) 202–5; Singer, "Duties and Duties to Oneself," *Ethics* 73 (1963): 133–42.

[46] As pointed out, for example, in Connie Rosati, "The Importance of Self-Promises," in Hanoch Sheinman (ed.), *Promises and Agreements: Philosophical Essays* (Oxford: Oxford University Press, 2011), at 129–34.

worth, simply qua human being, can be considered a violation of a duty to respect oneself.[47]

Once we recognize this point, we should consider whether there are other morally fraught ways in which agents can lack respect for themselves. It is at this stage that the notion of unconditional moral commitments once again comes to the fore. Ignoring unconditional moral commitments that one takes to be constitutive of one's self-conception can also be an important form of failing to respect oneself.

One context in which such a failure might occur is when a person has a significant role to play in the making of morally fraught collective decisions. By way of illustration, consider again the case of the company that bribes a poor country's foreign officials. Suppose now that the decision to bribe is made not by a single person, but by a small group of company directors. Suppose further that one of these directors is unconditionally committed to the rejection of bribery, but finds himself silent in the moment of truth: confronted with his fellow directors' uniform enthusiasm for bribery as a business strategy, he puts up no resistance whatsoever in the crucial board meeting setting the bribery policy in place. In my view, this silence on the director's part means that he, too, fails a moral duty of self-respect. Whereas the servile worker disrespects himself by failing to take seriously his moral rights against mistreatment, the director disrespects himself by failing to make his most deeply held convictions heard, as part of collective deliberation on how the company ought to behave.[48] This failure makes it *morally appropriate* for the director to castigate himself—at least after the fact—for betraying his unconditional moral commitments.[49]

Now, integrity skeptics are likely to challenge this reasoning. Integrity skeptics will likely say that in a situation where morality's overall requirements actually push one to part ways with one's unconditional commitments, there is no reason to think that doing so violates *any* moral duty of self-respect. No self-recrimination is morally appropriate under such circumstances.

---

[47] Here I follow the spirit of Thomas Hill's "Servility and Self-Respect," *The Monist* 57 (1973): 87–104. See also Robin Dillon, "How to Lose Your Self-Respect," *American Philosophical Quarterly* 29 (1992): 125–39.

[48] As Cheshire Calhoun puts it: "Persons of integrity treat their own endorsements as ones that matter, or ought to matter, to fellow deliberators... concealing [one's views], recanting them under pressure, selling them out for rewards or to avoid penalties, and pandering to what one regards as the bad views of others, all indicate a failure to regard one's own judgment as one that should matter to others." See Calhoun's "Standing for Something," *Journal of Philosophy* XCII (1995): 235–60, at 258.

[49] To be sure, people may fail to stand up for their moral views even when these views do not involve any unconditional commitments. But insofar as unconditional moral commitments are particularly significant components of one's self-conception, the failure to express them is particularly relevant for the present discussion. Moreover, I am inclined to think that the relationship between one's *motives* and one's failure to stand up for one's moral views is especially morally fraught in the case of unconditional commitments. I say more about this relationship in a moment.

The best way to respond to this challenge is to bear in mind that agents' self-evaluations typically—and properly—feature a concern not only for the conduct options they have chosen, but also for the motives underlying their choices. The bribery example can be used to illustrate this point as well. Suppose that our company director now routinely votes in favor of bribing foreign government officials in order to secure major contracts. Each time, he voices no opposition, as the same narrative is presented to the board: if the company wins the relevant set of contracts, this would redound to the benefit of the most vulnerable people living under the relevant foreign government, because these people will be worse off if other firms win the contracts instead. It seems safe to assume that the director is not only going to ask himself each time whether the given bribery decision is indeed morally warranted overall, in a way that justifies him in retaining his self-respect. For his self-respect will be bound up not only with his vote as to how the company should conduct itself, but also with his inspection of the motives underlying his vote. Is it really a concern with the most vulnerable people abroad that leads him to defer to the company narrative without a fight, and to vote as he does? Or is it a much more dubious motive—say, the lure of ever-increasing personal wealth as he cements his standing in the company and its contracts multiply—that explains his toeing the company line?

Once questions of this sort come to the fore, the idea of self-distrust reappears. Earlier, I argued that self-distrust is a key part of the reason why morality pressures us to adopt unconditional moral commitments—self-distrust comes first, and those who have a healthy distrust of themselves are more likely to make such commitments essential to their self-conception. But here we can see that self-distrust also plays an important role ex-post, *after* a person acts in a way that is contrary to his unconditional moral commitments—when he evaluates his motives for acting this way. The person who repeatedly betrays his political commitments by feigning identification with the Nazis may be able to retain at least a significant portion of his self-respect, if he manages to convince himself that he is driven to act as he does by his emotional attachment for, and moral duties toward, his family. But in his most self-critical moments, this person may very well suspect that his feigned identification with the Nazis is driven by far less lofty a motive—that the real explanation for his actions is (for instance) sheer cowardice. Such—eminently predictable—self-doubts explain why even a person who recognizes the objective moral case in favor of departing from his unconditional commitments may nonetheless injure his self-respect in the process—perhaps even fatally.[50] And these doubts also explain why a simple insistence on

---

[50] We may think about such self-doubts as a different rendition of Kagan's aforementioned claim that real integrity requires "critical self-examination." That said, I do not mean to suggest that integrity should be associated with an obsessive form of self-distrust. I say more about such excess in Chapter 2.

the fact this person's actions were ultimately morally justified cannot, by itself, salvage his self-respect.[51]

This response deals with the problem of false negatives concerning self-respect. But it does not yet address the problem of false positives. This problem has to do with agents who sustain their sense that they have been true to their fundamental moral commitments, and thus sustain their self-respect, simply through self-deception. We surely want to criticize agents who maintain their self-respect in this artificial way. But how can the tools presented so far ground such criticism?

When we consider this question, we can see why it is important to keep the overarching notion of integrity firmly in mind as we delve into concepts such as unconditional commitments, self-distrust, and self-respect. After all, as I stressed earlier, any plausible rendition of "integrity" will see it as antithetical to self-deception. And that is one important reason why we should not discuss the moral significance of self-respect without reference to integrity. The idea that (at least under certain circumstances) there is a moral danger in agents losing their self-respect by acting contrary to their fundamental commitments is intelligible even without the language of integrity, to be sure. Nonetheless, thinking about such a danger through the prism of integrity adds something that a more direct reference to self-respect alone cannot capture. Thus we can see the problem of false positives with regard to self-respect as one particular illustration of a more general point I made early in the Introduction: that in the process of trying to defend the core notion of integrity as an independent factor in moral deliberation, we will find ready support in multiple concepts that orbit around this core notion, and, once combined with it, yield a sum that is greater than its parts.

---

[51] Some may worry that the combination of such self-doubts with unconditional moral commitments and duties to self makes my conception of integrity far too saintly to be appropriate for mere mortals—and especially for mortals engaged in politics, our ultimate business in this book. As I noted in the Introduction, the book's later chapters deal with different variants of this worry at some length. At this stage, I only wish to flag one thought. The fact that my conception of integrity accords much weight to the notion of self-respect makes it at the very least compatible with, if not actually supportive of, at least one practice often seen as the diametric opposite of saintliness—*schadenfreude* (see, e.g., Julia Driver, *Schadenfreude* [unpublished manuscript]). Consider, for example, people who have been victims of brutal behavior on the part of others—for instance, a brutal past dictatorship or a lethal drug cartel. Such victims should not dismiss the violations they have suffered as insignificant. Their self-respect requires that they take the wrongs done to them seriously, and—within familiar moral and legal constraints—seek redress. But suppose that redress cannot be had—say, because the cartel is too powerful to be held accountable by the law, or because the former dictator's henchmen were too effective in eliminating the key witness for them to be convicted in court. In such circumstances, there is nothing in my account of integrity that opposes the victims deriving pleasure from learning that the perpetrators who have wronged them so profoundly have been suffering at least some non-trivial predicaments of their own. I recognize that this favorable view of "cosmic justice" is controversial, unlikely to be supported, for example, by those who reject the idea that there is any intrinsic moral value in wrongdoers suffering punishment (e.g., Victor Tadros, *The Ends of Harm: The Moral Foundations of Criminal Law* [Oxford: Oxford University Press, 2011], 261). My point here is only that this "unsaintly" view is perfectly compatible with my conception of integrity, and indeed can perfectly be endorsed by someone who is an exemplar of moral integrity as I understand it.

1.7 Historical Commitments and the Commitments
of Decency

So far, I have discussed one important moral function that integrity might have. Focusing on one type of fundamental commitment underlying an agent's integrity, I have sought to show, against intuitive skepticism, that integrity can function as an independent factor in moral deliberation. In this closing section, I want to turn to other types of fundamental commitments, and to examine how these types too might affect an agent's moral situation. More specifically, having so far examined those commitments of decency that we morally expect all agents to incorporate into their self-conception, I now want to examine commitments that are contingent on an agent's specific moral history. In particular, I have in mind here those moral commitments that we expect agents to adopt in the wake of grave wrongs they have perpetrated in the past. I wish to suggest that these commitments can *amplify* the force of commitments of decency that we expect all agents to incorporate into their self-conception.

Here is an example, in two steps. First, suppose that Alex is a morally decent person who lives in a town effectively ruled by the mafia. Using its customary violent tactics, the mafia takes over many of the businesses that structure much of Alex's professional and social life. In each business, the criminals place their own men behind the counter, forcing the real owners to stay home and only accept a portion of the revenue, with the rest going to the mob. Yet these owners urge Alex to continue frequenting their stores, arguing that if he boycotts their stores as a way of boycotting the mafia, this will only make them worse off.[52] If we follow the analysis presented above, then we should be led to think that quite apart from deontic or consequentialist considerations, Alex's integrity is an independent factor militating against repeated association with the mafia. Given that, as a morally decent person, Alex sees the mafia's crimes as fundamentally alien to his convictions, associating with the mafia on an ongoing basis would undermine his integrity. And this is an independent consideration that feeds into the moral judgment of what, all-things-considered, he ought to do in this situation.

However, second, integrity's weight in this overall moral balance can increase if Alex approaches this situation with the background of a pertinent personal history. Imagine that Alex himself has previously committed many serious crimes as a member of a mafia (perhaps this very mafia). Given a chance to start anew (whether by legal authorities or through sheer luck), Alex sees the rejection of the mafia and its ways as one of his most fundamental commitments—breaking free

---

[52] Those who may find the example somewhat contrived should bear in mind that it will serve as a useful template for thinking about concrete real-world problems surrounding commercial ties with odious regimes—an issue that was already flagged in the Introduction, and that I discuss in more detail in Chapter 2.

from mafia life is now for him a fundamental struggle. But re-associating with the mafia, especially in a deep and ongoing manner, would directly conflict with this struggle. Such association would take Alex back to the person that he had promised himself never again to be. And this kind of self-betrayal would pose an *especially* severe threat to his integrity. Hence Alex's particular moral history amplifies the weight of his integrity in the balance of reasons bearing on what he ultimately ought to do.

This amplifying argument is likely to trigger two objections. The first objection is that insofar as Alex's particular history alters his moral situation, this is simply because of his past victims, rather than because of his own integrity. Alex should be especially reluctant to (re-)associate with the mafia because of his special duties to the victims of his past mafia crimes: such reluctance is morally appropriate because it reflects continued awareness of the wrongs that he has done to his past victims, and continued appreciation of the severity of these wrongs.

Our earlier discussion already indicates the best response here. Ultimately, we may be able to trace the moral significance of Alex's rejection of the mafia to his duties toward his victims. Nonetheless, insofar as Alex does come to see his moral effort to dissociate from the mafia as an identity-grounding struggle, this effort accrues its own independent moral momentum, which is *not* simply reducible to what he owes his victims. We can make this point vivid by imagining circumstances where Alex's special compunction still seems morally appropriate, although his past victims approve of him re-engaging the mafia. Suppose, for instance, that Alex's former victims have accepted the compensation and apologies that he had previously offered them, and have even formed a friendship with him. Within this context, Alex's former victims offer their blessing for his engagement with the mafia under the circumstances, making clear that they will not see such engagement as offensive, and even actively pushing Alex to seek it. At least some of us, I assume, will think that even given these victim preferences, it would be morally appropriate for Alex to have special reservations about associating with the mafia—stronger reservations than those of someone who lacked his particular history. But the moral force of these reservations cannot be explained solely in terms of what Alex owes his past victims.[53]

The second objection is based on the thought that Alex ought to refine the lessons he adopts from his moral history. Specifically, Alex ought to adopt a more conditional rejection of the mafia and its ways: he ought to see association with the mafia as a threat to his fundamental projects only when such association is all-things-considered wrong. But if that is true, then Alex's specific history cannot

---

[53] Some may want to suggest that the issue here is actually about potential *future* victims—that if Alex re-associates with the mafia, he will be more likely to act wrongly going forward. But it is not clear why this worry sets Alex apart from anyone else who may associate with the mafia.

really set his moral situation apart from the situation of any other agent who lacks this history.

One problem with this objection is that it yields a highly counter-intuitive understanding of the way in which agents' moral struggles unfold over time. According to this objection, if it turns out that the overall balance of moral reasons favors Alex re-engaging even in the most morally fraught acts that he has committed as a mafia member, then he should not see any deep conflict between his past moral struggle and his present conduct. Thus, for example, suppose that the police, having finally decided to act against the mafia that rules Alex's town, try to persuade Alex to serve as an informant, which would require of him to once again participate in mafia crimes, including (let us say) in routine assaults on innocents, so as to re-acquire credibility with the mafia. The difference is that this time (let us assume), Alex's participation in mafia activities will be morally justified, all-things-considered. According to the objection that we are now examining, this difference should prevent Alex from seeing any conflict between his renewed entanglement with the mafia and his fundamental moral struggle to break free from his previous life. The fact that Alex is now imposing the same grave harms on innocents as he did in his previous life makes no difference. Nor does it matter that Alex wishes precisely to dissociate from his "previous self" that inflicted these very harms. The only thing that matters is that the infliction of these harms is currently justified overall, whereas previously it was unjustified. This fact alone means that there is no deep conflict between Alex's past moral struggle and his present mafia actions, no matter how violent. Yet many will think that there very much *is* a conflict here. While it may be true that wrongful acts of violence are not identical to all-things-considered justified acts of violence, it is surely also true that the two share much more than a passing resemblance.[54] And it is implausible to demand that Alex entirely ignore this fact if morality, all-things-considered, now favors him doing the very same deeds that he has so firmly sought to distance himself from.

Second, this concern again becomes especially pertinent when we consider cases featuring not "one-offs," but rather repeated departures from constitutive moral struggles. According to the objection that we are now entertaining, there cannot be a fundamental difference between Alex re-engaging in mafia violence once, and Alex doing so time and again, so long as each instance of violence is all-things-considered justified. Yet it would surely be reasonable for Alex to think that engaging in repeated violence is qualitatively worse for him, because it would pose a far deeper threat to the coherence of his fundamental moral struggle to break free from his previous life. The objection, however, has no way to account for this

---

[54] This is, of course, a recurring, and in some cases even career-making, theme for many crime and espionage novelists. John le Carré is only the most famous example, illustrated most recently in his *A Legacy of Spies* (New York: Viking, 2017).

complaint: if any single act of violence that Alex commits is morally justified, all-things-considered, then the objection will continue to claim that Alex ought to see his fundamental moral struggle as coherent rather than as irreparably ruptured. But this claim strains credulity.

These points suggest that a person's reluctance to act in a manner that conflicts with his fundamental moral struggles has moral force that cannot be explained solely through reference to what this person owes to others. "Moral persons," as Daniel Markovits writes, "seek commitments and plans that leave them reflectively satisfied not just with what they have done to others, but also with what they have made of themselves."[55] And this is especially true when persons consider what they have made of themselves *over time*, in relation to their morally fraught projects. When persons seeking to break free from a morally haunted past *repeatedly* act in ways that take them back to what they had firmly sought never again to be, only part of the moral story lies with others. Whether or not such persons have betrayed their duties to others, it also matters morally that they have betrayed their own integrity.

1.8 Conclusion

It may seem tempting to think that an agent's moral integrity must be derived from morality's overall requirements, and therefore cannot inform our understanding of these requirements. It may also seem tempting to dismiss any residual hold that moral integrity may have on us by casting integrity concerns as merely psychological rather than genuinely moral. But in this opening chapter I have sought to show that both of these temptations, notwithstanding their pervasive presence in moral philosophy, should be resisted.

In the process of developing this claim, I have also introduced several core ideas related to the "self" which I believe have intimate connections with integrity. But these ideas—including self-distrust, self-respect, and duties to self—not only support the claim that we should view individual integrity as a genuine factor in moral deliberation. They also have various important parallels in the political realm—parallels which suggest that a polity too, as a collective agent, can have its own morally important integrity. The challenge of Chapter 2 is to articulate and defend the moral significance of this collective integrity.

---

[55] Markovits, "Integrity and the Architecture of Ambition," 110–11.

2

Integrity: Political, Not (Only) Personal

Having focused Chapter 1 on personal integrity, I turn in this chapter to political integrity. More specifically, I present three main claims with regard to political integrity. First, I argue that it is possible to talk about a polity of a certain sort—a liberal democracy—as an agent that has its own integrity. Second, I contend that this political integrity too, like personal integrity, can be an independent factor in moral deliberation. Finally, I seek to show that the integrity skepticism I battled in Chapter 1 turns out to be *especially* weak when directed toward political integrity.

I develop these claims as follows. Following preliminary remarks (2.1), I introduce my understanding of a liberal polity as a collective agent with its own moral integrity (2.2), and present some initial attractions of conceiving of a liberal polity in this way (2.3). In 2.4, I further develop these attractions by highlighting various international cases where the idea of liberal integrity captures important but elusive moral intuitions. In 2.5 and 2.6, I add to these arguments by outlining several parallels between a liberal polity's unconditional commitments and the unconditional commitments of an individual person. These parallels help dispute skepticism about integrity's independent moral significance, and allow me to argue that such skepticism is easier to combat at the political as compared to the personal level. In 2.7, I develop two additional arguments reinforcing this conclusion. Finally, in 2.8, I consider the objection that the discussion of a liberal polity's integrity might be a distraction from a proper focus on personal integrity.

2.1 Setting the Stage

In order to speak meaningfully about a liberal democracy as a group agent with its own integrity, one must first endorse the more general claim that talk about group agents need not be purely metaphorical. I should therefore start by briefly indicating my assumptions on this score.

In the course of this book, I will assume that group agents supervene upon, but are not readily reducible into, the mere sum of individual agents. This is the influential view of group agency espoused by Christian List and Philip Pettit.[1] One

---

[1] Christian List and Philip Pettit, *Group Agency: The Possibility, Design, and Status of Corporate Agents* (Oxford: Oxford University Press, 2011). Although the List-Pettit view is especially congenial for my purposes, it may still be the case that other accounts of shared agency can also align with at least

Integrity, Personal, and Political. Shmuel Nili, Oxford University Press (2020). © Shmuel Nili.
DOI: 10.1093/oso/9780198859635.001.0001

idea underlying their supervenience conception is the famous "discursive dilemma," showing the vulnerability of any attempt to read individual members' judgments off a group agent's judgments.[2] Another idea is that any account of social life which makes no room for group agents is necessarily impoverished. "It is not just theoretical convenience," as Pettit notes, "...that we would lose, were we to ignore group agents and describe things individualistically; we would also be likely to overlook some important features of the world we occupy."[3]

The normative import of this loss is especially clear when reflecting on corporate responsibility.[4] Consider, for instance, the accusation that in areas of key public concern, major corporations have deceived the public, with massive societal repercussions. This deceit may revolve around corporate products' health effects (as in the case of the big tobacco companies). Or it may concern the riskiness of investments that the corporation is peddling to its customers (as in the case of major banks embroiled in the financial crisis of the late 2000s). In either case, insofar as the deceit is believed to have been a *systematic, corporate-wide* practice, it seems mistaken to examine responsibility for the corporation's failures from a purely individualist lens. To be sure, particular individuals (most obviously, the most senior corporate executives) may plausibly carry special responsibilities (including legal responsibilities) for the corporation's conduct. Nonetheless, a sufficiently comprehensive *moral* account of corporate responsibility must involve, at least in part, a direct reference to the corporation itself, as a morally culpable group agent.

I will have more to say about major corporations later in this book. For the most part, however, my focus will be largely with a different kind of group agent—the sovereign people in a liberal democracy, which I will also refer to as "the body

---

some of my moral and practical claims. Since my interest ultimately lies with these more concrete claims, I do not try to adjudicate (possible or actual) disagreements between the List-Pettit account and alternative views of shared agency. For two prominent examples of such alternatives, see Michael Bratman, *Shared Agency* (New York: Oxford University Press, 2014); Margaret Gilbert, *Joint Commitment* (Oxford: Oxford University Press, 2013).

[2] See, e.g., List and Pettit, "Group Agency and Supervenience," *Southern Journal of Philosophy* 44 (2005): 85–105. The danger on which the discursive dilemma pivots is that "perfectly consistent individuals may vote in such a pattern that the group gets to be committed to an inconsistent set of judgements," meaning that "the group can be individually responsive to the votes of its members. Or it can be collectively rational...[b]ut it cannot be both." Adopting the latter option therefore requires of a group agent's individual members to often "put aside their own individual attitudes, recognizing that corporate coherence may require them to support positions that they individually reject," and in doing so "construct a mind that has an identity of its own. This mind will characterize the group, and only the group...." Pettit, "Corporate Agency: The Lesson of the Discursive Dilemma," in Marija Jankovic and Kirk Ludwig (eds.), *Routledge Handbook of Collective Intentionality* (London: Routledge, 2018), 249–59, at 255, 257. See also List, "The Discursive Dilemma and Public Reason," *Ethics* 116 (2006): 362–402; List and Pettit, "On the Many as One: A Reply to Kornhauser and Sager," *Philosophy and Public Affairs* 33 (2005): 377–90.

[3] Pettit, "Group Agents Are Not Expressive, Pragmatic or Theoretical Fictions," *Erkenntnis* 79 (2014): 1641–62.

[4] See Pettit, "Responsibility Incorporated," *Ethics* 117 (2007): 171–201.

politic," or (especially in the international context) as "the polity." For the purposes of this book, all of the individuals who permanently reside within each of the world's stable territorial jurisdictions comprise—at least on first approximation—different sovereign peoples.[5] This definition of sovereign peoples is partly motivated by the thought that, over time, stable territorial borders accrue normative significance, irrespective of their amoral (or even immoral) origins. By delineating a stable group of individuals as the polity's citizens, stable borders demarcate a group that has to work together over time in pursuit of common affairs. And the thought is that this temporally extended collective pursuit (in turn) yields important civic ties binding together even citizens coming from disparate ethnic, religious, or linguistic backgrounds.

Now, it may be easiest for us to envision powerful "civic bonds"[6] uniting each such civic people, when we envision perfectly just societies. But in fact, these civic bonds are at least equally relevant when set against the background of manifestly unjust conditions. This is particularly the case when considering the collective sentiments that appropriately arise against this kind of background. Collective guilt associated with grave wrongs that the polity has perpetrated in the past, for example, can and often should give rise to a joint, collective struggle to distance the polity from these wrongs. Indeed, it is partly by considering such past-oriented collective sentiments, and the future-oriented collective efforts that such sentiments yield, that we can see why it is important to incorporate a conception of "the people" as a collective agent into our analysis of liberal democracy, instead of simply analyzing the acts and omissions of each individual citizen. Consider, for instance, the following remarks from Ronald Dworkin:

> Collective action is communal... when it cannot be reduced just to some statistical function of individual action, because it is collective in the deeper sense that requires individuals to assume the existence of the group as a separate entity or phenomenon. The familiar but very powerful example of collective guilt provides a good example. Many Germans (including those born after 1945) feel responsible for what *Germany* did, not just for what other Germans did; their sense of responsibility assumes that they are themselves connected to the Nazi terror in some way, that they belong to the *nation* that committed those crimes.[7]

Much of what I will say below about the sovereign people's collective integrity will have to do with such temporally extended sentiments and struggles, and with their

---

[5] In this I once again agree with Rubenfeld, who writes: "What makes persons a people is simply this: coexistence, over time, under the rule of a given legal and political order." Rubenfeld, *Freedom and Time*, at 153.

[6] *TJ*, 5.

[7] Dworkin, "Constitutionalism and Democracy," *European Journal of Philosophy* 3 (1995): 2–11, at 4. Italics in the original.

relation to core institutions of liberal democracy. But in order to see how these temporal ideas feature in the account, we first need to examine more closely why it is even sensible to think about the sovereign people in a liberal democracy in integrity terms, as an agent with its own identity-grounding commitments and projects.

2.2 The Integrity of a Liberal Democracy

If we assume that shared political activity is what constitutes the liberal people as a group agent, then this activity is the natural point of departure for our inquiry into the people's integrity. More precisely, the natural starting point for thinking about the people's integrity is the creation of its legal system. At least for the purposes of normative analysis, we are often inclined to view the law of a liberal democracy as the work of the sovereign body politic, a work that is itself foundational to the very existence of the body politic as a group agent. The body politic's law-making renders it *into* a collective agent.

The normative significance of this collective agency is manifest when we consider questions of responsibility for paradigmatic moral failures embodied in the law. Take, for instance, the moral responsibility of the American body politic for the legal institution of slavery in the antebellum United States. What I have said above with regard to corporations' responsibilities as a group agent seems to apply here as well. Thinking about responsibility for American slavery in purely libertarian terms—focusing exclusively on the behavior of each individual American toward each particular slave—is surely inadequate. It is far more normatively plausible to understand the institution of slavery as the responsibility of the American body politic—that is, the *group* agent that had imposed and retained the laws of slavery. Insofar as we accept this point, we accept a normative sense in which collectively sovereign citizens form a group agent when making law. Borrowing a term from Dworkin's account of "law as integrity," we accept the normative assumption that the legal order they enact turns collectively sovereign citizens into a "*community personified.*"[8]

In turn, if we endorse these claims (at least for the sake of discussion), then we can already begin to see how a liberal democracy can have identity-grounding projects much like an individual person. If the law of a liberal democracy makes it a single agent in some morally salient sense, then the projects that underlie this law can be described as the core of this agent's identity. Moreover, we are not

---

[8] Dworkin, *Law's Empire* (Cambridge, MA: Harvard University Press, 1986), 167, and passim. I should point out that Dworkin's account of the law's integrity represents an intervention in jurisprudential debates, and ultimately an argument against legal positivism, whereas my aims belong much more squarely in normative political theory.

entirely in the dark when it comes to identifying at least some projects that ought to underlie liberal law. We can safely say that, whatever other projects it may adopt, no legal system can be liberal unless it is committed to the realization of the equal rights of all citizens. One way to see this point is to observe that if some citizens are omitted from the law's egalitarian task-description—say, on account of their race, religion, or gender—then the legal system effectively endorses a quintessentially illiberal natural hierarchy among persons. Another way to see the same point is to note the profoundly illiberal character of a legal system revolving around any fundamentally collectivist project—for example, a system venerating "the nation" over and above the moral claims of any individuals. These observations suggest that, insofar as the commitments that underlie the law can be seen as the core of a liberal polity's identity, *any* liberal polity must understand the realization of its citizens' equal rights as an identity-grounding project.[9]

In order to see how these thoughts lead to a picture of a liberal polity's integrity, and how this integrity might be threatened, we need to take one more step. We should note that for a society to have a liberal identity, it must *formally and effectively* instantiate equal rights through its legal system. One can accordingly say that from a liberal society's identity-grounding commitment to equal rights follows a certain set of *identity-grounding institutions* that guarantee equal rights for all citizens. To be sure, any attempt to offer an exhaustive list of such institutions is likely to be contentious. But our purposes here do not require such a complete list. We can instead settle for a fairly modest set of institutions, including, for example, legal protections of bodily integrity, property, freedom of speech, equality before the law, and a ban on racial, religious, and gender discrimination.[10] Any tenable account of liberalism will include these institutions as necessary corollaries of a commitment to citizens' equal rights.[11]

Only somewhat more controversially, I am also going to presume that among the requisite identity-grounding institutions there must be protections of at least the most minimal standards of *universal* human equality. Just as a legal system could not plausibly claim to be liberal if it treats people of color as at best second-

---

[9] I do not mean to suggest that a liberal polity cannot permissibly have other projects. But I am inclined to think that these projects (e.g. the preservation of a certain language over time) will typically be amoral in character, and so while the polity might have *rational* grounds for pursuing them, it will not necessarily have moral grounds to do so.

[10] For why such a view is compatible with endorsing the liberal status of policies such as affirmative action, see, among others, Tommie Shelby, "Justice, Deviance, and the Dark Ghetto," *Philosophy & Public Affairs* 35 (2007): 126–60.

[11] By appealing to these minimal standards, I am (partly) trying to outline a set of "constitutional essentials" (to use Rawls' phrase), which constrain, rather than fully adjudicate, familiar philosophical and political disagreements about equality's practical implications. Even this constraining, moreover, is modest, insofar as I do not offer here any account of how to adjudicate meta-disagreements as to where precisely to locate the bounds of legitimate political disputes. I will only note parenthetically that issues often presented as evidence of the intractable nature of such meta-disagreements (such as abortion) seem to me too *sui generis* to allow for easy generalizations about the overall viability of liberal constraints on democratic disagreements.

rank citizens, or if it sees women as the property of their husbands, so we can confidently hold that a legal system cannot be liberal if it fails to recognize even the most minimal moral rights of outsiders—for instance, if it allows its own citizens, with complete impunity, to enslave outsiders (hence our instinctive sense that a polity could not coherently claim to be a liberal democracy if, for example, it perfectly realized its own citizens' equal rights through conquest and colonial exploitation[12]).

All of this matters here because if in order to have a liberal identity, a society must have specific effective legal institutions, then there is a fairly direct sense in which a society with a liberal self-conception would not truly be able to live up to its self-professed identity if these legal institutions did not exist, existed formally only and were ineffective, or were removed or distorted. Hence, just as a person's integrity is threatened when her actions fundamentally conflict with her identity-grounding commitments, we can say that the integrity of a polity with a liberal self-conception is threatened when the institutions that its law enacts clearly conflict with its own grounding commitment to equal rights.

2.3 Integrity's Attractions (I): The Claims of Collective History

Having rendered the idea of political integrity more intelligible, I now want to begin spelling out some of its attractions, by noting salient parallels between personal and political history.

We can start to see these parallels by reflecting on existing practices that play a significant role in the politics of at least some liberal democracies. Consider the numerous official ways in which many liberal democracies mark historical failures and achievements with regard to the realization of equal rights as constitutive of the national identity—of "who we are as a people." Core curricula in public education, emblematic public monuments, national holidays, and official ceremonies are all part of the way in which liberal democracies strive to incorporate their successes and failures in realizing rights into their collective identity.[13] Thinking about the realization of rights as an identity-grounding project allows us to capture the conviction that such official recognition is morally required. This conviction quickly comes to the fore if we reflect, for instance, on hypothetical cases: a decision by the U.S. Congress to abolish Martin Luther King Day, or to

---

[12] See in this spirit Lea Ypi, "What's Wrong with Colonialism?" *Philosophy and Public Affairs* 41 (2013): 158–91.

[13] These claims have obvious affinities with accounts of liberal nationalism. But the practical problems that are my focus in this book differ in both substance and kind from those commonly taken up by liberal nationalists. See for instance Yael Tamir, *Liberal Nationalism* (Princeton, NJ: Princeton University Press, 1993); Anna Stilz, *Liberal Loyalty* (Princeton, NJ: Princeton University Press, 2009).

remove the Lincoln Memorial, would clearly be morally objectionable; the same would be true if the Bundestag voted to remove Berlin's Holocaust Memorial; or if the British Parliament voted to remove Gandhi's statue from Parliament Square. I will have much more to say about such examples in Chapter 5. At this stage we can simply note the more general point that these specific examples make vivid: that a liberal polity *ought* to recognize, as constitutive of its identity, profound historical failures and achievements tied to the realization of egalitarian norms.

These points suggest that it may be not only plausible, but in fact morally essential, to view a liberal-democratic polity as the kind of agent that has its own normatively significant history. Accordingly, we can view identity-grounding moral struggles in which such a polity engages over time as paralleling the identity-grounding moral struggles in which an individual might engage. In particular, we may think that a liberal-democratic polity can strive to distance itself from its "past self," much as in the individual-level examples discussed at the end of Chapter 1. A democratic society can mark this kind of self-transformation through diverse means, ranging from radical reform of core curricula in public education (consider educational reforms in post-soviet countries), through the removal of public monuments (consider Russia itself with the collapse of the Soviet Union), to the awarding of prominent political honors (think of the morally fraught history of the United States' Medal of Honor[14]). And, of course, all of these means can be pursued in tandem (consider Germany's "never again" ethos and its pervasive impact on the country's politics). There are thus numerous means through which a liberal democracy as a group agent may say of its past self "that is no longer who we are," in much the same way that an individual agent might say of her past self "this is no longer who I am."[15]

2.4 Integrity's Attractions (II): "The Global Integrity Test"

Bearing in mind these initial attractions of the idea of collective integrity, I now want to move from the domestic to the international realm. In this realm we should see especially clearly both collective integrity's philosophical benefits, and, more specifically, the appeal of seeing this integrity as an independent moral factor. Consider, then, the following international case. In 1986, the U.S. Congress enacted the Comprehensive Anti-Apartheid Act, "to prohibit loans to, other investments in, and certain other activities with respect to South Africa."[16] The

---

[14] See Scott Wilson, "Obama to Award Medal of Honor to Two Dozen Veterans, Including 19 Discrimination Victims," *Washington Post*, February 21, 2014. I say more about this case in Chapter 5.
[15] Here I again follow List and Pettit (*Group Agency*, 200).
[16] See PUBLIC LAW 99–440, at www.gpo.gov/fdsys/pkg/STATUTE-100/pdf/STATUTE-100-Pg1086.pdf. Note that a key part of what made the Act "Comprehensive" is that it prohibited *both* various forms of U.S. government ties with the apartheid regime *and* private firms based in the United

moral justification for this Act seems over-determined. But suppose that during the debates preceding the Act, the victims of South Africa's apartheid regime would have publicly opposed it, out of fear of its unknown economic consequences. We can easily imagine these victims saying that the regime ruling them is blatantly violating their rights, and that in an ideal world this would not happen. But given non-ideal realities, they nonetheless prefer that outsiders continue their customary commercial dealings with the regime, because the repercussions of an economic boycott of their country might very well be worse. Now, it seems safe to say that even in such a scenario, something like the Comprehensive Anti-Apartheid Act would still have moral appeal. But what explains this appeal? This question cannot be adequately addressed simply by invoking familiar liberal vocabulary. Suppose, for example, that one defended the Act by invoking the rights, autonomy, or dignity of apartheid's victims. It would seem perfectly sensible for the victims to respond that it is precisely *because* of their rights, autonomy, and dignity that outsiders should defer to their call not to pursue such an Act. And, along similar lines, if one appealed simply to the injustice of the apartheid regime, we could imagine its victims claiming that "constructive engagement" with the regime would be more effective in gradually mitigating its injustice.[17] In such a context, where the familiar liberal appeals to other-regarding duties seem to come up short, the claims of liberal integrity come into their own. If, even under the conditions I just described, there would indeed have been *some* moral reason in favor of American divestment from South Africa's apartheid, it is extremely intuitive to trace that reason to what the American polity as a collective agent owed to *itself*, as a matter of its own moral integrity.

This evocative case points toward a more general test concerning liberal democracies' foreign dealings, which we may label simply "the global integrity test." When considering partaking in any foreign practice, a liberal democracy ought first to determine whether it could implement such a practice within its own borders while retaining its identity-grounding egalitarian institutions. If the relevant practice could be institutionalized domestically without thereby threatening the polity's fundamental commitment to the equal rights of its citizens, then it passes the global integrity test. On the other hand, if enacting the relevant foreign practice at home would distort fundamental domestic institutions beyond

---

States from dealing with the regime. One way of understanding this combination is to say that the Act altered not only what the U.S. legal system officially called for (it not only prohibited official government cooperation with the apartheid regime). It also altered what the legal system merely *allowed* through its silence (since private actors' dealings with the apartheid regime that the U. S. legal system previously condoned were now prohibited). I say more below on the moral significance of the law's silence.

[17] This was, of course, the claim of the Reagan administration, on which more below.

recognition, then the liberal polity has reasons of integrity against legitimating, perpetuating, or reaping benefits from this practice through its own law.

One way to further unpack the implications of this test is to note its intricate relationship to the particular histories of specific liberal democracies. To the extent that the self-contradiction highlighted by the global integrity is especially evident in the case of U.S. ties with South Africa's apartheid regime, this is (arguably) because of the United States' fundamental struggle to break free from its own racist legacies. The conflict between this protracted historical struggle and continued American entanglement in apartheid explains why the force of integrity considerations is so readily apparent here. And this particular conflict, in turn, means that the United States had especially weighty and stringent reasons of integrity against entanglement in South Africa's apartheid. But if the general test I just presented is cogent, then *any* liberal polity, even one without its own racially charged history, would have had integrity reasons against such entanglement. The presence of a particular moral history, in other words, amplifies the moral salience of integrity reasons.[18] Yet the absence of such a history does not remove these reasons.

These points can be illustrated through another international case with a similar structure. Imagine a liberal democracy that is considering whether to engage in a massive sale of various technologies to a foreign military dictatorship. Though these technologies were originally developed for peaceful purposes, there is ample reason to suspect that they would be abused by the military regime, facilitating its efforts to violently crush peaceful opposition. At the same time, entering this business relationship will likely enable the liberal government to pressure the military regime to moderate its repression. And if the liberal government shies away from this relationship, other vendors will step in, sell the same technology, and not even try to monitor how the military regime uses it, or pressure it to moderate its conduct in any other way. So here too we can plausibly imagine the victims of foreign wrongdoing actively *encouraging* a liberal democracy to cooperate with the foreign regime that is violating their rights. Given this state of affairs, does the liberal democracy in question have any moral reason— *apart* from simple consequentialist uncertainty—to refrain from providing the relevant technologies to the dictatorship?

---

[18] An anonymous reviewer wonders whether what matters here is a polity's subjective conception of its own history, or some objective account of this history. My main answer is that *both* matter. In a first step, every polity ought to incorporate into its identity certain morally essential historical lessons, as identified from an objective standpoint. But second, *once* the polity incorporates the relevant historical lessons into its identity, then this history acquires the identity-effect I am highlighting (amplifying the weightiness and stringency of integrity reasons). We may be able to see this sequence more clearly by drawing an analogy to promises yet again: it is entirely coherent to say both (1) that there are some promises that we ought to make, whether or not we recognize this moral fact at present, *and* (2) that *once* made, the relevant promises will acquire a moral weight that is not reducible to the reasons why we ought to make them.

The global integrity test suggests that the answer is *yes*. Clearly, any liberal democracy would cease to *be* a democracy if it implemented the relevant repressive practices within its own borders. And so any liberal democracy would have integrity reasons against supplying the relevant dictatorship with technologies that are bound to be used for repressive purposes.[19] But now imagine that the experience of peaceful struggle against dictatorship has played a formative role in the identity of the particular liberal democracy in question—exercising a considerable influence over its constitution, education system, emblematic public monuments, and myriad other elements of the collective ethos. Such circumstances would amplify the sense that in selling the relevant technologies to the dictatorship, this liberal democracy is engaging in a form of collective self-betrayal. Such circumstances would therefore amplify the weight and stringency of this polity's integrity reasons against supplying the dictatorship.[20]

2.5 Political Integrity, Unconditional Commitments, and the Unfairness Argument

No man is allowed to be a judge in his own cause, because his interest would certainly bias his judgment, and, not improbably, corrupt his integrity. With equal, nay with greater reason, a body of men are unfit to be both judges and parties at the same time; yet what are many of the most important acts of legislation, but so many judicial determinations, not indeed concerning the rights of single persons, but concerning the rights of large bodies of citizens? And what are the different classes of legislators but advocates and parties to the causes which they determine?

(James Madison, *Federalist 10*[21])

Some integrity skeptics may be unmoved by the global integrity test I just presented. Specifically, such skeptics are likely to argue that, contrary to what the test suggests, a liberal democracy should not ask itself whether it would still be able to

[19] These integrity reasons, moreover, do not disappear whenever there is good reason to think that other nations will sell the relevant technologies instead. The appeal to collective integrity thus sidesteps standard collective action excuses. For a particularly clear example of such excuses, see Catie Edmondson and Edward Wong, "State Department Defends Saudi Arms Sales Before Hostile House Panel," *New York Times*, June 12, 2019.

[20] Some skeptics might be tempted to argue that these supposed integrity reasons are purely liberal reasons, with "integrity" doing no real work. But (first) even if "integrity" is not more fundamental than liberal values, it can still have an independent moral role (per my earlier remarks about the moral significance of non-fundamental concepts). Second, this skeptical response conflicts with the fact that (as we have just seen) there is no simple invocation of liberal values that could yield the duties we are discussing here.

[21] See, e.g., http://avalon.law.yale.edu/18th_century/fed10.asp.

"recognize itself" if a given foreign practice were institutionalized within its borders. This question bestows on specific institutions a level of moral significance that they do not actually have. The institutions of liberal democracy are valuable only in conditional form—only insofar as they help in the realization of morality's overall requirements. Therefore, given a clear picture of morality's overall requirements in a given situation, a liberal polity should see action in accordance with these requirements as aligning with its moral integrity, instead of identifying this integrity with fidelity to some fixed institutions.

This skeptical claim with regard to collective integrity closely parallels the skeptical claim that Chapter 1 examined in detail. And, as in Chapter 1, the link between unconditional commitments and healthy distrust will be my starting point for countering the skeptic. More specifically, having used this link to develop an unfairness complaint against the skeptic with regard to personal integrity, I want to develop a parallel complaint here, in defense of political integrity's independent moral significance.

It might be helpful to recall what that unfairness complaint consisted in. In Chapter 1, I argued that it is unfair to admonish agents who treat unconditional commitments as an independent factor in their moral deliberation. The unfairness is rooted in the fact that morality itself encourages agents to adopt certain unconditional commitments, and to treat them as an independent factor in their moral deliberation, as a way of pre-empting the all-too-human tendency to circumvent conditional moral principles. Since morality pushes agents to incorporate unconditional moral commitments into their self-conception and to treat these commitments as an independent factor in our moral reflection, it is unfair to castigate agents who refuse to dismiss such commitments as a mere psychological distraction, whenever they conflict with other weighty moral considerations.

I want to argue that a very similar unfairness applies when we move from the personal to the political level. Here, too, healthy distrust of all-too-human proclivities means that morality pushes agents—this time, liberal political communities as collective agents—to adopt unconditional moral commitments. And here as well, it is unfair to admonish agents who then go on to treat these commitments as an independent factor in their moral deliberation.

We can start to develop this claim by noting that morality pushes liberal societies to incorporate unconditional moral commitments into their identity-grounding legal institutions. The most obvious reason is the dangers that arise when core legal institutions of liberal democracy cast certain morally important legal commitments in a conditional form. In such circumstances, it is all-too-predictable that senior state officials will exploit every possible loophole created by the relevant conditionals, to maintain the façade of upholding the commitment even while violating it in practice.

Consider, for instance, how multiple U.S. administrations over the last decades have evaded a variety of legal constraints on their power. Their evasive tactics have often hinged on bad-faith interpretation of institutional definitions—as was the case, for example, during the Iran-Contra scandal, when the Reagan administration implausibly argued that the National Security Council was exempt from Congress' explicit prohibition on government support for the Contras in Nicaragua, since the Council was not explicitly included in Congress' Boland Amendment.[22] Just as often, the façade of presidential conformity to essential legal prohibitions has involved a systematic effort to produce "in-house" legal opinions that justify important exceptions to the standard legal rules, as was the case with the war-making decisions of the Bush and Obama administrations.[23] Even more drastic cases have featured presidents who managed to convince themselves that the very office they held gave them the authority to infringe upon weighty prohibitions. Richard Nixon's infamous pronouncement—"if the president does it, it's not against the law"—was only the most extreme example.[24]

One key reason why it is often essential, then, for a liberal people to incorporate unconditional moral commitments into its identity-grounding institutions is that such commitments are often necessary in order to pre-empt self-seeking rationalizations by the powerful. Yet the fact that morality itself commends such pre-emptive adoption of unconditional commitments makes it unfair to also admonish a liberal people, when it treats those unconditional commitments as an independent moral factor even in the face of countervailing considerations.

We can further bolster this point by connecting healthy distrust of political power—and the more general distrust of individuals' moral deliberation—to several themes discussed above. We can do so by considering again the liberal polity whose collective identity gives pride of place to its history of peaceful struggle against dictatorship. Suppose that this history began with a call by massively popular democratic leaders, who, about to be overthrown in a military coup, pleaded with the people to commit unconditionally to resist the incoming military dictatorship solely through peaceful means. Their pleas were heeded, and the population's consequent peaceful efforts, which eventually toppled the military dictatorship, have become a focal point of collective pride. These efforts have been incorporated into the polity's collective identity, enshrined not only in its current constitution, but also in its education system, public monuments and ceremonies, and so on.

Now, our integrity skeptic has to insist that it is simply confused to treat this collective identity as exerting an independent moral force of any sort. According

---

[22] See, e.g., Malcolm Byrne, *Iran-Contra: Reagan's Scandal and the Unchecked Abuse of Presidential Power* (Lawrence, KS: University Press of Kansas, 2014).

[23] See, e.g., Bruce Ackerman, "Legal Acrobatics, Illegal War," *New York Times*, June 20, 2011; Jeremy Waldron, "Torture, Suicide, and Determination," *The American Journal of Jurisprudence* 55 (2010): 1–30.

[24] Quoted, e.g., in Scott Shapiro, *Legality* (Cambridge, MA: Harvard University Press, 2011), 75. As Shapiro points out, "Nixon was forced to resign in disgrace for acting on such a view."

to the skeptic, it would be folly for the relevant society to view the unconditional commitments associated with its particular history as having any independent bearing on its moral deliberations. These deliberations are to be settled *exclusively* through reference to impartial moral considerations, which cannot involve any essential reference to "unconditional commitments" or "identity."

In my view, however, this kind of skeptical response is highly unfair, because morality itself would have ample reasons for encouraging the society in question to adopt the relevant unconditional commitments, and to see these commitments as an independent factor in its moral deliberation. Morality, it seems safe to assume, supported the unconditional commitment to peaceful resistance against the dictatorship, precisely because of healthy distrust. There would have been a good moral reason to fear biases in the reasoning of individual citizens who would treat the initiation of violence against the dictatorship as a live option, and an even better reason to suspect that the dictatorship would only see violent resistance as a further excuse to inflict far more violence of its own. Additionally, it is not hard to see why morality should welcome peaceful opposition to dictatorship becoming a focal point of collective identity, and an enduring source of collective pride. But if all this is true, then it clearly seems unfair to also criticize the relevant collective, if it treats its history of unconditional commitment to peaceful resolution of political disputes as an independent factor bearing on its moral deliberations.

Moreover, this sense of unfairness is further reinforced once we consider the counter-intuitive implications that follow from integrity skepticism. To see this point, we can add one more detail to our tale of the society that had overcome dictatorship through an unconditional commitment to peaceful struggle. Let us suppose that a key part of this peaceful struggle concerned opposition to the torture that the dictatorship systematically deployed. Now, however, the same liberal society that has overcome the dictatorship is forced to fight a predatory neighbor, and as part of this war must consider whether to torture some of its enemies. In my view, even if one holds (at least *arguendo*) that these predatory enemies forfeit their immunity from torture because of their aggression, there would still be reasons of integrity for the relevant liberal society not to torture them.[25] These integrity reasons, to be sure, would apply to any liberal democracy. But, in line with what I said earlier, these reasons are especially weighty and stringent for this particular liberal democracy, given its particular history.

The integrity skeptic whom we are now confronting has to deny all of this. For this skeptic, *any* liberal democracy, including one traumatized by the collective

---

[25] Kramer suggests that (1) predators of this sort may in fact deserve to be tortured, but that (2) the moral integrity of individual government officials nonetheless renders such torture morally wrong, given that it represents a "self-aggrandizing course of conduct...that is inconsistent with [one's] own elementary humility as a moral agent." (See Kramer's *Torture and Moral Integrity*, 187, 191–2.) Nothing in my argument hinges on accepting (1). Nor does my argument invoke any link between integrity and humility, though I would certainly grant humility's general moral importance.

memory of torture, should see its opposition to torture as always conditional on the relevant torture being wrong all-things-considered. When this is not the case, the skeptic argues, any liberal democracy that sees its fundamental opposition to torture as an independent moral consideration is simply committing a moral mistake.

As a general matter, I believe that this skeptical rejoinder strains credulity. But more specifically, this rejoinder ignores the fact that morality itself strongly encourages polities to *un*conditionally commit to oppose practices such as torture, and to reflect this unconditional opposition in fundamental institutions. The most obvious reason for this encouragement, once again, has to do with the healthy distrust of those who wield effective political power. The danger that such individuals will abuse conditional prohibitions on torture (for instance, by arguing that they or their country are somehow "exceptional"[26]) is too predictable, and too great, to license conditional institutional arrangements on such issues.[27] But if this is so, then it seems unfair to also criticize polities that go on to instantiate an unconditional commitment to oppose torture, that treat this commitment as essential to the collective identity, and that consequently insist on treating possible deviations from this commitment as a morally important threat to their self-conception.[28]

Now, as I stressed above, this unfairness argument has clear analytical parallels to the unfairness argument I made in Chapter 1, with regard to personal integrity. But I believe that the political version of the argument is especially compelling. This is because the political version of the argument is more immune than the personal version to concerns regarding excessive caution. More specifically, I have in mind here concerns about excessive caution inherent in the pre-emptive adoption of unconditional commitments—that is, the pre-emptive strategy on which the unfairness argument hinges.

The relevant concerns can take two main forms. First, some may think that the pre-emptive strategy is overly pessimistic in its assumptions about human beings' moral reasoning. It is only under special circumstances—such as those featuring serious, destructive addictions—that the pre-emptive adoption of unconditional commitments is really called for as a way of preventing self-seeking rationalizations from running rampant. In normal circumstances of everyday life, many individuals can have sufficient confidence in their capacity for moral reasoning to

---

[26] See, e.g., Dick Cheney and Liz Cheney, *Exceptional: Why the World Needs a Powerful America* (New York: Simon and Schuster, 2015).

[27] A point sharply made, for example, in Jeff McMahan, "Torture in Principle and in Practice," *Public Affairs Quarterly* 22 (2008): 111–28.

[28] Notice that this point is compatible with recognizing—as McMahan also does—that in the face of truly catastrophic costs, laws prohibiting torture are likely to be ignored. Even when that is the case, however, there is a genuine moral remainder arising in the aftermath of such drastic situations. I leave open here the question of whether this moral remainder should translate into legal sanctions against individual officials responsible for torture, or into other forms of collective reckoning—for instance, some form of truth commission forcing the public to come to terms with what was done, even if "it had to be done." I examine the latter option, as it applies to related policy contexts, in *The People's Duty*, chapter 3. For a discussion of the former option, see Kramer, *Torture and Moral Integrity*, chapter 5.

do without the pre-emptive adoption of unconditional commitments. So while it is true that a compulsive gambler, for example, has strong moral reasons to unconditionally commit to refrain from gambling (as I said in Chapter 1), it is *not* true that *all* of us should think of ourselves as facing the gambler's predicament.

As Chapter 1 made clear, I have general doubts about this optimistic line of thought. But even those who are attracted to such optimism as a general matter should concede that it faces serious problems when applied more specifically to the political realm. After all, a venerable tradition in political thought teaches us not only about the corrupting and addictive effects of political power, but also about the extent to which *none* of us is immune to these effects. Therefore, even if one grants—*arguendo*—that in everyday life not all of us are in the addict's predicament, this predicament should clearly loom larger the closer we get to the exercise of political power.

Now consider the second likely suspicion about the caution inherent in the pre-emptive strategy. Some philosophers, it is safe to assume, will hesitate to accept the pre-emptive strategy's concessions to what seem like deeply regrettable motivational limitations. Such philosophers will accordingly treat these concessions as a pale version of the first-best, "purer morality."

I have already sought to combat the appeal of this reasoning in Chapter 1, when discussing individual conduct. But once we move from individual conduct to collective affairs, there is less of a combat to wage *ab initio*. For even if one finds the notion of a "purer morality" for "perfectly motivated" individuals to be natural in the realm of individual ethics, it is clearly less natural in the realm of political philosophy. That political philosophy should take individual motivational limitations as one of its most basic building blocks is very much a mainstream view. Rousseau's insistence that political philosophy must take "men as they are" when reflecting on "the laws as they might be" is only one canonical instance of this view. Rawls' rejection of utilitarianism as incompatible with individuals' motivational limitations is another.[29] For these and many other political theorists, it is clear that the core business of political theory—the design of political institutions—must be sensitive, at least to some degree, to "the capacity of human nature."[30] And this is true even if one grants that theories of individual ethics can be less sensitive to this capacity.

This point, in turn, can be reinforced with a simple but, I believe, crucial observation. Political arrangements that pay no heed to human beings'

---

[29] *TJ*, sections 18, 29.

[30] *TJ*, 154. However, this mainstream view obviously has its critics. See, e.g., G.A. Cohen, *Rescuing Justice and Equality* (Cambridge, MA: Harvard University Press, 2008); David Estlund, "Human Nature, and the Limits (If Any) of Political Philosophy," *Philosophy and Public Affairs* 39 (2011): 207–37. See also Nicholas Southwood, "Does 'Ought' Imply 'Feasible'?" *Philosophy and Public Affairs* 44 (2016): 7–45.

motivational limitations are not simply naïve. Rather, such arrangements are—profoundly—*morally wrong*. This is true not only with regard to gory issues such as torture, but also with regard to more mundane issues. Consider, for instance, (entirely imaginary) designers of a tax code that pays no attention to human beings' motivational limitations, and so gives no thought to enforcement mechanisms, to possible loopholes, or to how such loopholes are likely to be exploited. Such designers would be not only professionally incompetent, but also seriously morally blameworthy. If these designers responded to criticism by saying, "yes, we designed our code for angels, but it's not our fault that everyone around refuses to be more angelic," surely the only plausible answer would be that they have—culpably and deeply—misunderstood the most basic features of their task.

2.6 The Divided Self and "Duties to Self": The Collective Version

Equipped with these points, let us now consider another set of reasons for why it is easier to defend the moral significance of political as compared to personal integrity. This set of reasons goes back to the connection I drew in Chapter 1 between distrust, unconditional commitments, and duties to self.

It might be helpful to recall the essence of that connection. In Chapter 1, I argued that a person who adopts unconditional moral commitments as the core of her integrity is bound to view her self-respect as hinging, at least partly, on fidelity to these commitments. This point is significant, I suggested, not only because morality itself encourages agents to adopt certain unconditional commitments, but also because one of the moral duties that persons have toward themselves is the duty to sustain their self-respect. Distrust, in turn, comes onto the scene because agents who deviate from their unconditional moral commitments may compromise their self-respect not only because of their actions, but also because of their distrust of their own motives underlying their actions: it matters to one's self-respect whether one is motivated to put aside one's unconditional moral commitments in a given case because of a genuine belief that this is what morality, all-things-considered, happens to require, or because of a far less salutary motive.

I wish to show that something like a parallel account can be used even more effectively to defend the significance of a liberal polity's unconditional moral commitments, as the core of its collective integrity.[31] One way to begin developing this argument is to note the following point. While there is some level of healthy

---

[31] I use the qualifier ("something like") advisedly: I do not mean in any way to suggest that the political analogy I will be constructing here will be perfect. But I do think the analogy is useful enough to warrant discussing these aspects of political and personal integrity side by side.

self-doubt that each person should have, an individual who *constantly* suspects the motives underlying his own actions is likely to strike us as behaving quite oddly— as someone who assumes an artificial distance from himself. Even if we sometimes have cause to be unsure as to what exact motivations drive certain actions we take, there are also numerous cases where we have sufficiently intimate knowledge of ourselves to be able to discern what motives underlie our choices. This is the familiar form of self-knowledge we express whenever we say that "deep down" we "just know" this or that fact about our own motives. Things are quite different, however, when we move from individual persons to political communities as collective agents. Here there is nothing odd at all about one part of the agent taking itself to be at a constant remove from the agent's decision making, and accordingly developing constant suspicions about the motives underlying this decision making.

A specific example will help to illustrate the remove I have in mind. Consider once again, then, the example of U.S. ties with South Africa's apartheid regime, but this time as viewed specifically from the perspective of the African-American minority in the United States. Throughout the 1980s, African-American civil rights activists repeatedly made clear their suspicion of "constructive engagement" with apartheid. This suspicion was based partly on the obvious fear that engagement was only entrenching the apartheid regime, rather than furthering reform. But another source of suspicion for African-Americans had to do with their perception of the motives underlying "constructive engagement"—especially the motives of the Reagan administration, which vehemently defended this policy.[32] Reagan's approach to civil rights concerns at home led African-American civil rights activists to suspect that the "constructive engagement" rhetoric was merely meant to feign a concern for South Africa's oppressed black majority.[33] It seemed clear to those activists that even if the apartheid regime never changed, the administration was happy to continue its cooperation with this regime, so long as this cooperation continued to yield the geopolitical benefits that were really the driving force behind the administration's decisions.[34]

[32] See, e.g., Donald Culverson, *Contesting Apartheid: U.S. Activism, 1960–1987* (Boulder, CO: Westview, 1999).

[33] Thus, for example, the Citizens Commission on Civil Rights, an organization formed in response to Reagan's attempt to undermine the official U.S. Commission on Civil Rights, argued that Reagan caused an "an across-the-board breakdown in the machinery constructed by six previous administrations to protect civil rights." Quoted in Joe Davidson, "Reagan: A Contrary View," *NBC*, June 7, 2004, at http://www.nbcnews.com/id/5158315/ns/us_news-life/t/reagan-contrary-view/#.WlTrH2inGUk.

[34] Even Reagan's own officials admitted that the President had little knowledge of or concern for the plight of apartheid's victims. Chester Crocker, a Reagan official who genuinely believed in constructive engagement and was one of its main proponents, noted with alarm: "all he [Reagan] knows about South Africa is that he is on the side of the whites." Quoted in Robert Massie, *Loosing the Bonds: The United States and South Africa in the Apartheid Years* (New York: Doubleday, 1997), 483. See also Crocker's *High Noon in Southern Africa: Making Peace in a Rough Neighborhood* (New York: Norton, 1992).

To be sure, African-Americans were not the only ones who were suspicious of the motives behind the Reagan administration's South Africa policy. Nor were African-Americans the only ones calling on the U.S. government to commit itself unconditionally to oppose institutionalized racism. But African-Americans were nonetheless in a distinctive position with regard to U.S. policy toward South Africa. From an African-American perspective, the fact that "constructive engagement" was driven by extremely dubious motives was not merely a general subject of moral concern. Insofar as the Reagan administration was in fact indifferent to egregious violations of racial equality, such as the those ongoing in South Africa, this indifference threatened African-Americans' standing as equally respected citizens of the American polity itself.[35]

This intimate link, between the struggle for racial equality within the United States and U.S. policy with regard to racial subordination in South Africa, ran through African-American efforts to shape the U.S. response to apartheid. This link was evident from the earliest stages of these efforts—when Martin Luther King, for example, started calling for a boycott of South Africa as a natural corollary of the struggle for civil rights at home.[36] But this link remained just as central all the way to the Comprehensive Anti-Apartheid Act itself. As Robert Massie writes:

> Despite the historical differences between the United States and South Africa, the racial struggles in the two countries had become ideologically fused ... opposition to apartheid [had] evolve[d] into an index of commitment to racial justice in the United States. The Comprehensive Anti-Apartheid Act had passed, complained Robert Dole, because it had "become a domestic civil rights issue."[37]

Reflecting on these historical details, we could well imagine an integrity skeptic responding along the following lines: "even if these historical facts track morally important facts, all they tell us is that policies such as 'constructive engagement' were wrong in broader ways than we may think. Such policies wronged not only the victims of racism abroad, but also its victims at home. But we do not need the notion of integrity—or any adjacent notion, such as 'duties to self'—in order to capture these broader wrongs."

This skeptical response is misleading. It is misleading to think of cases such as the African-American struggle for U.S. divestment from apartheid—or about the

---

[35] Such threats have generally mobilized African-Americans with regard to multiple African policy issues. See Alvin Tillery, *Between Homeland and Motherland: Africa, US Foreign Policy, and Black Leadership in America* (Ithaca, NY: Cornell University Press, 2011).

[36] Explicitly denying that he was calling on blacks "to fight on two fronts," King insisted that "the struggle for freedom forms one long front crossing oceans and mountains." See King's "Address to the South Africa Benefit of the American Committee on Africa," Hunter College, New York City, December 10, 1965, at http://africanactivist.msu.edu/document_metadata.php?objectid=32-130-1121.

[37] Massie, *Loosing the Bonds*, 620.

African-American demand that the U.S. government unconditionally commit to the rejection of racism more generally—simply as a matter of one segment of a liberal political community making particular demands upon those who wield effective political power. Rather, more deeply and more dramatically, it is plausible to argue that in cases of this sort what is ultimately at stake is the *very existence* of a liberal political community as a unified group agent. African-American activists who fought for divestment from South Africa were not only fighting for the enactment of an unconditional government commitment to the rejection of racism. They were also—crucially, if less obviously—fighting to sustain and deepen a unified American polity: a society in which all citizens, regardless of their race, could sensibly see themselves as members of *one* sovereign body acting as a unified collective agent, as opposed to a fundamentally divided society, in which skin color marks a separation between rulers and ruled.[38]

The African-American activists who were fighting against the Reagan administration's "constructive engagement" with South Africa were therefore partly fighting—quite literally—for the collective integrity of American liberal democracy.[39] Once we recognize this point, we can recognize that it is neither odd nor superfluous to say that the American people as a collective agent had a "duty to

---

[38] The sense that divestment from South Africa was intertwined with the struggle to overcome this separation was manifest in the striking appreciation by various African-American activists of the link between this foreign policy issue and the rare experience of actual political power at home. One African-American activist, for example, recalled years afterwards, almost with disbelief: "We had an impact. Reagan was accountable to me!", quoted in Ryan Irwin, *Gordian Knot* (New York: Oxford University Press, 2012), 186. As another scholar put it in the 1990s: "The increasing involvement of African-Americans in Southern Africa is part and parcel of the evolution of their community and politics inside the United States...it...represents a significant step into the long sought and yet unattained vision of African-American integration...by portraying their homeland's cause as an all-American concern, African-Americans were able to move one step forward toward their own domestic inclusion." See Yossi Shain, "Ethnic Diasporas and U.S. Foreign Policy," *Political Science Quarterly* 109 (1994–5): 811–41, at 835. For a sustained emphasis on the moral importance of such integration, as "an indispensable goal in a society characterized by categorical inequality," see Elizabeth Anderson, *The Imperative of Integration* (Princeton, NJ: Princeton University Press, 2010), at 180 and passim. See also Christopher Lebron, *The Color of Our Shame: Race and Justice in Our Time* (New York: Oxford University Press, 2013).

[39] One way to further drive this point home would be to imagine a stylized case, where the leaders of a politically dominant racial majority explicitly present their domestic concessions to a minority as a purely pragmatic necessity ("we are improving the position of this minority not because we view its members as our equals, but simply because we don't want them to riot en masse"). Such an explicit statement would surely undermine any suggestion that the relevant polity can be seen as a unified collective agent. In contemporary liberal democracies, however, such an explicit stance with regard to domestic affairs represents an exception rather than the rule. That is why foreign policy issues can be so significant. Members of long-discriminated-against racial minorities are unlikely to respond to foreign policy choices in ways that threaten basic domestic stability. Therefore, these choices seem to provide something of a litmus test. The more the dominant majority is indifferent to foreign racial equality issues, the more natural it is to think that any concessions it makes to the cause of racial equality at home would not be made in the absence of credible minority threats to disrupt basic social stability. But if that is really the case, then it is extremely hard to view the majority and the minority as meaningfully joining together to form one unified polity that can truly be said to function as a single collective agent. Instead, we have here, at most, a deeply antagonistic "modus vivendi" between multiple, highly distinct agents.

itself" to commit unconditionally to the rejection of racism, and to design its response to apartheid on the basis of this commitment.

2.7 Refuting (Collective) Integrity Skepticism: Two Additional Arguments

Up to this point, I have focused my defenses of political integrity on parallels with Chapter 1's central defenses of personal integrity. My aim in this section is to present two additional reasons for why it is actually easier to defend the moral significance of political as compared to personal integrity. The first reason concerns repeated iterations. The second concerns the weight of history. I discuss each of these themes in turn.

2.7.1 Repeated Iterations

In Chapter 1, I noted that integrity's moral significance is easier to defend in contexts featuring repeated conflict between the agent's fundamental moral commitments and its actions, as opposed to a "one-off." Whether or not a person can dismiss a single deviation from her fundamental commitments as "not really representative" of who she is, such dismissal is clearly less plausible when her actions *repeatedly* contradict her fundamental commitments. This observation bears on the comparison between political and personal integrity, because polities as collective agents encounter many more repeated iterations cases than do ordinary individuals.

One way to see this point is to consider the (in)famous trolley problem, which has vexed so many contemporary moral philosophers. The question of whether a person is justified in turning a speeding trolley toward some people in order to save the lives of a greater number of people has been understood by virtually all of the philosophers who have discussed it as a question about the force of deontological distinctions in the face of countervailing consequentialist considerations. The trolley problem has been taken to embody the clash between a third-personal perspective, which asks what would be the best state of affairs the protagonist can bring about, and a second-personal perspective, which emphasizes the protagonist's particular duties toward each potential victim of his actions. However, none of the leading philosophical treatments of the trolley problem has examined the problem from the first-personal, integrity standpoint. No attention has been paid to any conflict that may arise between the protagonist's own identity-grounding moral commitments and his actions, if he were to kill some in order to prevent others from dying.

Arguably, at least part of the reason for this neglect is that none of the problem's dominant permutations is ever conceived as featuring any repeated iterations. The protagonist who is deliberating whether to divert a trolley away from some innocents in order to save the lives of a greater number is typically understood to be considering this choice only once.[40] If this protagonist had to decide *every day* whether to throw a switch that would lead to the deaths of some in order to save the lives of others, the question of how such decisions affect his own integrity would clearly become more salient. Again: a person who has the one-off misfortune of being in a position to either kill some or watch others die may try to tell himself that whatever decision he makes in this isolated instance does not really represent who he is. But even if this is true, a person who has to confront such a situation on a *routine* basis clearly has no such luxury.

Why, then, does the huge trolley problem literature feature so little attention to repeated iterations? One reason might be precisely the dominance of integrity skepticism in contemporary moral philosophy (after all, if it is taken as virtually axiomatic that individual integrity cannot be an independent moral factor, then there is little point in discussing repeated iterations cases whose main function is to show otherwise). But another possible reason is the sensible assumption that it is the job of collective institutions to spare individuals from having to routinely confront such drastic moral choices. If it turns out that the tracks malfunction in such a way that every day, a fresh trolley hurtles toward a fresh group of innocents who can only be saved by killing a fresh group of other innocents, the main moral priority is surely not to figure out how individual bystanders ought to react. The main moral priority is clearly to get the responsible institutions to fix the tracks.[41]

However, when we turn from the moral conundrums surrounding individual action to the actions of political communities as group agents, we cannot develop parallel expectations with regard to overarching institutions. In many cases, there is little point in expecting that overarching institutions fix the structural conditions that *repeatedly* force polities into drastic—if not outright tragic—moral choices. This is especially true in the international context. A key reason why I have been using multiple international examples when defending liberal political integrity is that there is no overarching global institution (or set of global institutions) that can reliably alter the structural conditions triggering international threats to liberal integrity. When a liberal polity is considering, for instance, the moral status of various repeated interactions with corrupt, brutal, or racist regimes beyond its borders, there is no world government to which it may turn in order to simply "solve" manifestly non-ideal problems "once and for all." Enduring international anarchy, in other words, means that liberal democracies have to repeatedly confront drastic and sometimes tragic choices in their international dealings.

---

[40] As noted, for example, in Barbara Fried's trenchant critique of what she dubs "trolleyology." See Fried's "What Does Matter? The Case for Killing the Trolley Problem (or Letting It Die)," *The Philosophical Quarterly* 62 (2012): 505–29.

[41] I am grateful to Shelly Kagan for helpful conversations on these issues.

Under such circumstances, the independent moral force of their collective integrity is much easier to see and defend than is the case with individual integrity.

2.7.2 The Weight of History

We can now turn to the final set of reasons for why political integrity's moral significance is easier to defend in comparison to personal integrity. This set of reasons has to do with the weight of history. When discussing personal integrity in Chapter 1, I suggested briefly that an agent's particular moral history might amplify integrity's weight in the agent's moral deliberation. But in this chapter, I have been making much more extensive use of examples and intuitions related to a polity's particular moral history. This difference is intentional: I believe that the appeal to particular histories is more fruitful when defending the moral significance of political as compared to personal integrity. One reason why this is so takes us back to the integrity skeptic's trenchant call for agents to incorporate "all-things-considered" morality into their conception of their particular histories. Applied to political integrity, such a skeptical call would require of a liberal democracy as a collective agent to adopt conditional lessons from its moral history. A liberal democracy struggling to come to terms with its racist history, for example, should not commit itself unconditionally to the rejection of racism; rather, a liberal democracy should see itself as committed to the rejection of racism *unless* legitimating and cooperating with racists is what morality, all-things-considered, requires.

I have already argued against such a conditional understanding of agents' moral history, both in the personal context (at the end of Chapter 1) and in the political context (in 2.5). Yet here I want to offer one more reason for why this conditional understanding is especially vulnerable at the political level. There may not be any obvious cost when an individual manages to "take the broader view," and adopt all-things-considered lessons from his or her moral history (thus, to go back to Chapter 1's example, there may not be an obvious moral cost if an ex-Mafioso, for instance, only sees renewed association with the mafia as a threat to his integrity when such association is morally wrong overall). Yet when the relevant agent is a polity, there *are* such costs, due to intense collective disagreement about the overall requirements of political morality. In fact, the construction of a polity's historical self-understanding, even when morally driven, can often be interpreted as an attempt *to put aside* the overall requirements of political morality, precisely because these are so controversial.

When a polity, for example, officially commemorates particular past wrongs suffered by particular social groups, it is effectively saying, "we agree that remembering those victims ought to be essential to our identity, whatever other issues of public morality we disagree about." Similarly, when a polity celebrates the heritage of individuals who led anti-discrimination movements, it is effectively saying, "we agree that the particular moral aims for which these individuals fought are essential to our identity, even if there are many moral questions that we contest intensely." The construction of a polity's identity, *especially* when driven by moral projects, is an exercise in incompletely theorized agreement.[42] But this exercise cannot succeed if it is performed on the terms proposed by the integrity skeptic. So the intuition that there are no obvious costs to incorporating all-things-considered morality directly into the agent's historical self-conception seems particularly vulnerable when we move from individual agents to a polity as a collective agent.

Another "historical" reason why it is easier to defend the moral significance of political as compared to personal integrity is more straightforward. We can imagine individuals whose moral history is fairly uneventful. We can imagine an individual who has never committed any serious wrong in her personal conduct; who has never been the victim of seriously wrongful conduct by others; and who has no special relationship to any perpetrator or victim of serious wrongdoing. In this kind of case, it will be difficult to appeal to the agent's particular history to explain why her identity-grounding commitments have independent moral significance. Yet such cases are much harder (if not impossible) to find when reflecting on liberal polities as group agents: one would be hard pressed to identify any (let alone many) existing liberal democracies that lack a morally fraught past—or, for that matter, liberal democracies whose morally fraught past does not clearly affect their present.[43] After all, while individuals are always born innocent (at least for those not theologically inclined), political communities never are, insofar as their founding is virtually always intertwined with various forms of violence. This observation alone should suffice for us to think that in the political context, much more than in the personal one, we can reliably expect agents to have histories featuring concrete significant wrongs. And given that this is the case, we can much more reliably expect political communities—at least of a certain kind—to constitute key parts of their identity around particular moral struggles, which will in turn have independent force in the manner described above.

Finally, it is also worth noting that, unlike the history of individual persons, a polity's history is not necessarily finite. This fact is significant, since it means that, unlike individuals, a polity always has the possibility (and indeed, the moral duty) to *reclaim* its integrity, even after extremely long periods of wrongdoing. In contrast, individuals who have spent almost their entire lives committing certain wrongs cannot reclaim their integrity, even if at the very end they genuinely

---

[42] The term is due to Cass Sunstein's *One Case at a Time* (Cambridge, MA: Harvard University Press, 1999).

[43] See, in similar spirit, Jeff Spinner-Halev, *Enduring Injustice* (Cambridge: Cambridge University Press, 2012).

commit themselves precisely to those moral principles that they have long violated. A person who has to decide on his deathbed, for example, whether to confess various wrongs that he has kept secret for decades may have all sorts of complicated moral considerations to balance. But his integrity is not going to feature in that balance, simply because by this point he has lost his integrity *irretrievably.*[44] A polity, however, can never encounter such a situation. It always can—and ought—to try again.

2.8 Does the Real Action Lie with Personal Integrity?

With these claims in view, let us now consider a final, general objection to the arguments of this chapter. This objection holds that if the integrity of a liberal democracy is really going to have moral value, this will ultimately be because of the integrity of its individual citizens. But if that is the case, then a focus on political integrity is ultimately misdirected.

Two related thoughts hold the key to meeting this objection. The first has to do with the intimate links between individual and collective identity: that human beings are fundamentally social creatures, whose self-conception is bound up with their communal reference points, is arguably one of the least uncontroversial observations that one could make in political philosophy.[45] The second thought—that is arguably just as intuitive—is that there is moral value in citizens identifying with the constitutive moral achievements of their political community. There is moral value in citizens shaping their conception of social life in light of these moral achievements, and even in deriving pride from achievements that preceded their time. Moreover, as I stressed from the very beginning of this chapter, there is also a similar moral need for citizens to integrate into their personal identity, at least to *some* extent, their polity's constitutive moral failures, even when they carry no individual responsibility for these failures.[46]

Now, if individual identity often is, and *should* be, intertwined with collective identity, then there is no reason to view a focus on collective identity and integrity as a distraction from the truly significant individual level. To bring this point into sharper relief, consider Rawls' theory of justice. Nothing in Rawls' account requires of him to deny that individuals, and only individuals, represent the ultimate units of moral concern. Yet notwithstanding his ultimate interest in

---

[44] This is a variation on a case discussed in Carter, *Integrity*, 53–4, where Carter reaches different conclusions.

[45] Contrary to certain uncharitable accusations, this is true for liberal political philosophy as well. For a particularly explicit example, see Joseph Raz, *The Morality of Freedom* (Oxford: Oxford University Press, 1986), 209.

[46] For claims in similar spirit see David Miller, *National Responsibility and Global Justice* (Oxford: Oxford University Press, 2007), e.g. at 161.

individuals, Rawls consciously opted to focus his theory on collective institutions, not least because of the simple but crucial insight that these institutions exert "profound" effects on individual citizens, effects that are "present from the start."[47] Clearly, this "collectivist" Rawlsian choice does not represent a distraction from an individualist viewpoint. The exact same point applies to collective identity and integrity. If collective identity has and ought to have a profound impact on individual citizens, then even a perspective that is ultimately individualist through and through can and should take collective identity considerations seriously.

2.9 Conclusion

I have spent the first two chapters of this book arguing that we should see integrity—both personal and political—as an independent factor in moral deliberation. The key upshot of this argument is that, despite familiar philosophical suspicions, there is something to the recurrent invocations of "integrity" in everyday moral discourse. Contrary to the claims of "fifth-wheel skeptics," an ordinary individual is not simply confused if, for example, she sees her own integrity as an independent reason to dissociate from morally repellent people. But we are also not confused if we think that a liberal democracy has parallel integrity reasons to dissociate from repellent foreign regimes. Moreover, if my arguments have been cogent, then this independent role of political integrity is *easier* to defend in comparison to personal integrity.

However, showing that integrity has independent moral weight does not yet tell us how to deal with cases where integrity's demands seem to conflict with other weighty moral considerations. Once we examine this question, additional doubts about integrity are likely to arise. It is to these doubts that I now turn.

---

[47] *TJ*, 7.

3

Integrity, Self-Absorption, and Clean Hands

In Chapters 1 and 2, I have sought to show that both personal and political integrity can function as independent factors in moral deliberation. Yet even those who are convinced by this claim may still be critical of integrity talk, particularly when applied to politics. Such critics are likely to suspect that putting integrity at the heart of our political thinking amounts to an undue moralization of politics.

One key aim of the remainder of this book is to grapple with different forms that such undue moralization concerns might take, both in relation to individual political actors and in relation to collective policy decisions. But before I begin this task, I want to offer some very brief remarks about the one tradition in political thought that is most strongly associated with worries about undue moralization of politics—namely, political realism.

Virtually all theorists who identify as political realists share the claim that it is mistaken to directly apply the edicts of private, interpersonal morality to public or political life. But this claim has taken at least two different forms in realist writing. The bold form holds that the principles which should guide political conduct should not be seen as moral principles at all; instead, the political realm should be seen as a realm with its own, entirely distinct normativity.[1] Like much of mainstream analytical political philosophy, I find this bold claim very hard to pin down, and, when pinned down, highly counter-intuitive.[2]

There is also, however, a more modest variant, which is far more intuitive, and widely shared even among theorists who do not identify as "realists." According to this variant, consequentialist calculations have to be much more central to the morality of public policy than to private morality. The simple reason is that political realities routinely mean that familiar moral constraints—against lying, manipulating, coercing, and the like—cannot be upheld without serious consequences for millions of people.[3]

This claim has direct implications for integrity arguments. If taking consequences seriously means that familiar moral constraints must constantly be infringed in politics as a matter of course, even when such infringements directly

---

[1] See, e.g., Mark Philp, "What Is to Be Done? Political Theory and Political Realism," *European Journal of Political Theory* 9 (2010): 466–84.

[2] This mainstream view is neatly crystalized in Jonathan Leader Maynard and Alex Worsnip's "Is There a Distinctively Political Normativity?" *Ethics* 128 (2018): 756–87.

[3] As emphasized repeatedly, for example, in Robert Goodin's *Utilitarianism as Public Philosophy* (Cambridge: Cambridge University Press, 1995).

Integrity, Personal, and Political. Shmuel Nili, Oxford University Press (2020). © Shmuel Nili.
DOI: 10.1093/oso/9780198859635.001.0001

conflict with integrity considerations, then these considerations can ultimately provide very limited political guidance. In fact, any agent (individual or collective) who still assigns considerable weight to integrity talk about "duties to self," even in the face of countervailing consequentialist considerations bearing on so many others, is guilty of dangerous self-absorption.

This *self-absorption charge*, as I shall call it, has a great deal of pre-theoretical appeal. Indeed, it does not take either a realist or a utilitarian to attribute narcissism to polities and politicians who prioritize "duties to self" over their responsibilities toward numerous others.[4] The self-absorption charge, then, is worth examining in some detail. This chapter is accordingly devoted to such an examination.

As a first step, it is worth noting that self-absorption charge against integrity talk, although particularly vivid in the political realm, is actually not unique to this realm. At least in principle, a critic of integrity talk might argue that whenever agents' choices are likely to affect a large number of others—whether outside or within politics—agents ought to prioritize their duties to others, rather than any integrity judgment as to "what they owe to themselves."[5] But I shall argue that, both as a general matter and when applied to politics in particular, the self-absorption charge fails.

As in previous chapters, I will be offering a positive contribution alongside this negative thesis: in the process of trying to undermine the self-absorption charge, I will be trying to establish further ways in which integrity can contribute to our practical reflections, regarding both individual and collective conduct.

I pursue this dual effort as follows. In 3.1, I begin to narrow the scope of the self-absorption charge by distinguishing between two variants that it might take, and showing why only one of these should be of concern given the account of integrity developed so far in the book. This variant of the charge focuses on integrity's practical implications: it holds that integrity implausibly pushes agents to prioritize their own clean hands at the expense of others' practical needs—even quite vulnerable others.

Taking this claim as my focus, I start to contest its appeal in 3.2. Here I show that even when integrity's dictates push in the opposite direction from the rights and preferences of vulnerable others, there are still important cases where acting on these dictates will *improve* the position of the vulnerable. In 3.3, I challenge the familiar equation of "integrity" with "clean hands," arguing that there are

---

[4] Even while rejecting both utilitarianism and many realist tenants, Nagel, for example, can still pointedly ask about political leaders: "what gives one man a right to put the purity of his soul or the cleanness of his hands above the lives or welfare of large numbers of other people?" (*War and Massacre*, 132). See also Nagel's "Ruthlessness in Public Life," in Stuart Hampshire (ed.), *Public and Private Morality* (Cambridge: Cambridge University Press, 1978). I say more below about the ecumenical nature of the self-absorption charge.

[5] This is true even if the political realm generates conflicting role responsibilities more frequently than other realms, as is illustrated, for example, in Jeremy Waldron's "Dirtying One's Hands by Sharing a Polity with Others," *The Monist* 101 (2018): 216–23.

important cases where integrity might be compatible with "dirty hands," and may even actively push agents to dirty their hands.

Building on this argument, I suggest in 3.4 that integrity's relationship to "clean hands" is partly mediated through causal inquiries: agents must engage in a serious assessment of causal pathways relevant to their conduct options, in order for their moral integrity to align with "dirty deeds." I then show how attention to such inquiries exposes further weaknesses in the self-absorption charge. Specifically, I contend that by zooming in on binary choices pitting our own integrity against others' needs, the self-absorption charge ignores the effort that ought to come first, to validate the causal premises on which this binary choice rests.

In 3.5, I turn to the political realm, and with it to another misleading aspect of the self-absorption charge. In many cases, this charge not only ignores the process of verifying that the only relevant policy choices really are between "our own purity" and others' practical needs. The self-absorption charge also artificially ignores the significant political question of *who it is* that—self-servingly—sets the policy-making agenda in these binary terms.

In 3.6, I turn to discuss national security issues. This is an area that may initially seem like especially fertile ground for the self-absorption charge, given the dirty deeds often required in pursuit of national security. Yet I argue that moral integrity claims—both individual and collective—nonetheless have important implications for national security policies. Finally, in 3.7, I anticipate the concern that my arguments still leave open the possibility—in theory and in practice—of a conflict between our own integrity and the needs of vulnerable others. I try to show why we should not overestimate the force of this concern.

Before I delve into the actual argument, I should make an important framing remark, concerning the relationship between the core notion of integrity—fidelity to fundamental moral commitments—and what I have been calling the "orbiting concepts" surrounding this core notion. In the book's Introduction, I suggested that this relationship may be viewed as a form of reflective equilibrium, wherein the orbiting concepts help bolster the defense of the core notion's independent moral significance. In Chapter 1, I made extensive use of one orbiting concept in particular—hostility toward self-seeking rationalizations. Different variants of this concept will also play an important role in the argument of this chapter. In particular, I shall pay special attention to how knowledge and (self-induced) ignorance relate to self-seeking rationalizations. At various points in what follows, I will be assuming that both individual and collective agents ought to pursue certain forms of knowledge, and will show how failures to engage in such pursuits bear on the self-absorption charge against integrity arguments.

I see this assumption concerning knowledge and ignorance as also falling naturally within the "orbit" of integrity as a broad moral framework. More specifically, I assume that if Chapter 2's argument about liberal integrity was cogent—if we should indeed see the realization of equal rights as a liberal democracy's collective *project*—then we must also attribute to its individual citizens a set of moral responsibilities that hardly allows for massive political ignorance. The identity-grounding institutions constitutive of a liberal democracy's integrity do not appear like manna from heaven: they require continuous civic engagement and vigilance. Citizens who remain blissfully ignorant of the most basic facts bearing on essential public policies can hardly fulfill these requirements. The precise relationship between this integrity-infused rejection of ignorance and the other themes of this chapter should become clear as we proceed.

3.1 Sorting through Self-Absorption

Equipped with these preparatory remarks, we can begin our substantive inquiry into the self-absorption charge, by distinguishing between two variants it might take. The first has to do with the kinds of reasons that the language of integrity pushes us to consider. The second has to do, more straightforwardly, with the practical implications that follow from making our own integrity central to our moral deliberation. Although the former concern may seem more philosophically fundamental, it is actually the latter concern that we need to tackle in greater depth. In this opening section, I briefly explain why.

Consider, then, the complaint that integrity is self-absorbed, because it leads us to focus on ourselves as a key source of our reasons for moral action, instead of duly focusing on others. This may seem like a deep concern. Morality, after all, is commonly thought to be first and foremost about our relations to others, rather than to ourselves.[6] In my view, however, the idea of integrity—or at least the conception of integrity that I have been defending—withstands this sort of criticism quite easily. The reason is that few would deny that it is at least permissible for agents to weigh their own interests as one kind of factor among several bearing on their moral decisions. So integrity reasoning cannot be faulted simply because it directs agents' attention to their own interests. Rather, the self-absorption charge here has to be that integrity arguments direct agents' attention to the *wrong kind* of self-regarding interests. But it is not at all obvious why we should think this. Integrity considerations, as we have repeatedly seen in previous chapters, can clearly push agents to *sacrifice* precisely those self-regarding interests (for instance, economic interests) whose moral force often seems questionable.

---

[6] A point explicit, for example, in Sam Shpall's "Moral and Rational Commitment," *Philosophy & Phenomenological Research* 88 (2014): 146–72. This is perhaps why even Williams, notwithstanding his ardent defense of integrity's significance (and equally ardent criticism of traditional morality), considers it important to discuss integrity's apparent "self-indulgence." See Williams, *Moral Luck*, chap. 3.

The self-absorption charge that should concern us, then, is not about "the wrong kind of reasons." Rather, the more relevant charge is simply that a focus on integrity is self-absorbed in its practical implications. Such a focus pushes agents to be self-absorbed in their practical decision making—to avoid compromising their own purity, even if doing so may be of tremendous practical help to others.[7]

Not a few philosophers have found this self-absorption charge to be important. In a sense, this is understandable. The "dandy who prates on about his integrity while others are suffering needlessly,"[8] as Robert Goodin unflatteringly put it, is bound to strike many as morally suspicious. Moreover, while this suspicion may be especially natural for utilitarians (such as Goodin), it can be—and indeed has been—shared by their deontological opponents as well. "We must," Thomas Pogge, for instance, has argued, "attempt to be of practical worth to others, rather than be overly concerned with the moral worth of ourselves."[9] Thomas Hill, to take another deontological example, has similarly cautioned against an "obsessive and inflexible concern for maintaining a 'pure' and simple record, even at others' expense."[10] While other examples could be given, the basic point is clear: the *practical* self-absorption charge is intuitive enough, and ecumenical enough, to consider in some detail. This is what I shall do here.

3.2 Our Own Integrity, the Rights of Others, and Their Practical Needs

It might be helpful to start by considering a thought which arguably provides the self-absorption charge with much of its appeal: that an agent who lets integrity guide its treatment of vulnerable others, even when integrity pushes in the opposite direction from that of the vulnerable's rights and preferences, is bound to treat the vulnerable in ways that are detrimental to their position. The problem with this thought is that there are cases where the integrity's dictates do clearly push in the opposite direction from the vulnerable's rights and preferences, but where acting on these dictates will, equally clearly, improve the position of the vulnerable.

---

[7] One is reminded here of George Bernard Shaw, who had one of his protagonists admonish another: "Your pious English habit of regarding the world as a moral gymnasium built expressly to strengthen your character in, occasionally leads you to think about your own confounded principles when you should be thinking about other people's necessities." George Bernard Shaw, *Man and Superman*, e.g. at https://www.gutenberg.org/files/3328/3328-h/3328-h.htm.

[8] Goodin, *Utilitarianism as a Public Philosophy*, 69.

[9] Pogge, "The Kantian Interpretation of Justice as Fairness," *Zeitschrift für Philosophische Forschung* 35 (1981): 47–65, at 64.

[10] Thomas Hill, *Autonomy and Self-Respect* (Cambridge: Cambridge University Press, 1991), 84.

To illustrate this point, consider a political integrity case which occupied us at length in Chapter 2: U.S. ties with South Africa's apartheid regime. With apartheid's demise, the democratic South African government faced the question of how to handle the sovereign debt of the apartheid era. Concerned with South Africa's reputation in international credit markets, the new government decided to assume rather than repudiate this debt.[11]

Now, it seems clear that the new government had the moral right to make this decision as a representative of the South African people. One would therefore be hard pressed to explain why liberal democracies that held apartheid-era debt had a duty toward *the South African people* to contest this decision. But it seems less difficult to say that liberal democracies owed it to *themselves*, as a matter of their own integrity, to refuse to accept payments by the new South African government for apartheid-era debt.[12]

Of course, the principles laid out in Chapter 2 explain why liberal democracies had, *ab initio*, reasons of integrity against contributing to (and benefiting from) the accumulation of this debt. But these principles also explain why affluent liberal democracies in general—and especially those affluent liberal democracies with their own racially fraught history—ought to have rejected the Mandela government's offer to pay back apartheid-era debt. This is true even if Mandela's government clearly had the right to make this offer as the legitimate representative of the South African people, and even if the offer genuinely represented the people's informed preferences. This, then, is a case where reasons of liberal integrity pushed in the opposite direction to that of the rights and preferences of a deeply vulnerable people. But had affluent liberal democracies upheld the dictates of liberal integrity, the result would not have been detrimental to this people's position—on the contrary.[13]

---

[11] See Odette Lienau, *Rethinking Sovereign Debt* (Cambridge, MA: Harvard University Press, 2014), 191–2.

[12] Alongside its contribution to our subject in this chapter, I also take this example to illustrate a claim I made in chapter 1: that important ex-post responsibilities in the aftermath of moral conflict are not always best conceptualized via reference to deontic constraints. In chapter 5, I briefly discuss a further political example supporting the same point (concerning honors denied to Bomber Command pilots following the Second World War).

[13] Some might think that there is an alternative explanation for why liberal democracies ought to have rejected payment for apartheid-era debt—namely, the thought that it is simply wrong to enjoy ill-gotten gains, independently of any appeal to integrity. Even if such an alternative works in this case, it is not obvious that it helps the self-absorption charge (for it would still be the case that *integrity's* practical implications are not self-absorbed). But we can also doubt whether this alternative explanation really succeeds. In normal cases, we are supposed to be averse to keeping ill-gotten gains because of our duties to the victims of the process through which these gains were accumulated. But in a case where the relevant victims *actively wish* that we keep the gains that came at their expense, then it is surely more intuitive to trace compunction about retaining these gains to integrity reasons concerning our duties to *ourselves*, rather than to these victims (at least barring an appeal to victims' inalienable rights, which would seem irrelevant here).

3.3 The Complex Relationship between Integrity and "Clean Hands"

With these claims in mind, let me now turn to a further, deeper concern about the self-absorption charge. This concern pivots on the relationship between integrity and "clean hands." Many who are convinced by the self-absorption charge assume—whether implicitly or explicitly—that "integrity" and "clean hands" are pretty much interchangeable.[14] This assumption is supported by the etymological roots of the word "integrity."[15] Perhaps more importantly, it is also supported by the fact that the integrity cases that have been most prominent in contemporary moral philosophy (for instance, Williams' case of the pacifist chemist who is considering a job at a weapons factory, or his case of the innocent tourist asked to kill one person in order that the lives of multiple others be spared[16]) can clearly be seen as "clean hands" cases.[17] And yet, despite its appeal, the equation of moral integrity with clean hands is misguided. Even in cases where an agent's clean hands are clearly at stake, integrity will *not* necessarily push in the same direction as the "purity of one's hands." In fact, in some circumstances, integrity considerations may actively push agents to "dirty their hands."

The best way to develop this complexity is to circle back to Chapter 1's example, of the person appalled by Nazism who is considering whether to join the crowd in giving a Nazi salute, as a celebration of the French surrender to the Nazis. Suppose that our protagonist in this example gives the Nazi salute not simply in order to preserve himself but, much more specifically, in order to further pursue his fundamental project of bringing down the Nazi regime to which he is feigning allegiance. The moral analysis of the man's choice clearly has to be sensitive to his particular motivation for saluting. It clearly matters that he gives the Nazi salute in order to continue his effort to defeat the Nazi regime, as opposed to giving the

---

[14] In the more explicit variants, "integrity" and "clean hands" are lumped together in the same argument. See, e.g., Goodin, *Utilitarianism as Public Philosophy*, 69.

[15] John Beebe, for example, begins his analysis of integrity by pointing out that "Tag, its Sanskrit root, as the game we still call by this name implies, means to touch or handle. Out of this root come words like tact, taste, tax, and contaminate. Integ means not touched or handled." See John Beebe, *Integrity in Depth* (College Station, TX: Texas A&M University Press, 1992), 6. See also the discussion in the opening of David Bauman's "Integrity, Identity, and Why Moral Exemplars Do What Is Right," PhD Dissertation, Washington University in St. Louis, 2011, at https://openscholarship.wustl.edu/cgi/viewcontent.cgi?article=1033&context=etd.

[16] Williams, "A Critique of Utilitarianism," 97–9. Several interlocutors have wondered why these canonical cases do not feature more prominently in this book. The main answer is that I find the latter case at least—that of the innocent tourist—to be unhelpful as a way of defending integrity's significance. This is because the tourist who shoots some so that others may be spared is violating his victims' inalienable rights—meaning that their consent to be shot under the circumstances is neither here nor there. But if that is true, then "integrity talk" is entirely unnecessary to capture non-consequentialist intuitions about the case; familiar deontic reasoning will do just as well. That is why Chapters 1 and 2 put center stage cases with a different structure, where the victims' consent *does* remove standard deontic constraints. In such circumstances, I believe, it is much easier to see integrity's distinctive role.

[17] And, of course, the same might very well be said for the cases described so far in this book.

salute merely in order to protect himself. But this different motivation matters not just from morality's general perspective. It also matters from *integrity's* particular perspective. If a man whose fundamental project is to defeat the Nazis engages in an isolated act of symbolic identification with the Nazis with the clear and calculated aim of furthering that very project, then there is no automatic reason for why this isolated act should count as a betrayal of his integrity.

This point is brought out sharply by the real-life case that inspires this example. The protagonist in this case was Dietrich Bonhoeffer, one of the leaders of German resistance to Hitler. When sitting in that café in June 1940, and witnessing the crowd giving the Hitler salute, Bonhoeffer chose to give the salute as well. His friend and biographer, Eberhard Bethge, who was also present, described the event as follows:

> The people round about at the tables could hardly contain themselves; they jumped up, and some even climbed on the chairs. With outstretched arm they sang "Deutschland, Deutschland uber alles" and the Horst-Wessel song. We had stood up too. Bonhoeffer raised his arm in the regulation Hitler salute, while I stood there dazed. "Raise your arm! Are you crazy?" he whispered to me, and later: "We shall have to run risks for very different things now, but not for that salute!"[18]

The "very different things" for which Bonhoeffer wanted to run risks were specific: they revolved, first and foremost, around his core project of undermining the Nazi regime, a project he pursued clandestinely in the 1940s. And given that this was clearly the motivation behind Bonhoeffer's choice to give the Nazi salute on that occasion, there is no obvious reason why this choice should be seen as conflicting with Bonhoeffer's integrity, even if this choice did in some sense conflict with his maintaining clean hands.

But we might make an even bolder claim here: we might point to circumstances where integrity is not only compatible with dirtying one's hands, but may in fact *push* one to do so. To see this point, note that Bonhoeffer was eventually executed by the Nazis for his close ties to the group of conspirators that undertook the most famous assassination attempt against Hitler, in which a bomb planted in Hitler's East Prussia headquarters nearly succeeded in killing him (July 1944). Now, imagine that the reason why this attempt on Hitler's life had failed was not bad luck and logistical errors (as was actually the case), but rather last-minute "clean hands" reservations by the person who was supposed to place the bomb next to Hitler. Suppose that this person simply decided that, notwithstanding his fundamental commitment to defeating the Nazis, he is too reluctant to "dirty his hands"

---

[18] Bethge, *Dietrich Bonhoeffer*, 585, quoted in Adams, *Finite and Infinite Goods*, 215.

on his way to placing the bomb: he is too reluctant to harm any lower-level soldier that he may need to neutralize on the day to bring the bomb to its destination. In fact, he is even reluctant to dirty his hands in more limited ways—he is reluctant even to bribe some security personnel to get access to key points in Hitler's headquarters. It would have been an obvious mistake for this person to let this kind of "clean hands" reluctance have decisive weight in his practical deliberation. But this would not have been a mistake only from the perspective of morality's overall requirements. It would also have been a mistake from the more specific perspective of the man's own integrity. For if he was really serious about his fundamental project of defeating the Nazis, then he should have been willing to sully his hands in these ways for the sake of that project. That is one kind of risk that this person, to paraphrase Bonhoeffer's remarks, ought to have been willing to run. And he ought to have been willing to run it not in spite of, but partly *in pursuit of*, his integrity.

In saying all this, I do not mean to suggest that the connection between integrity and clean hands is simply spurious. Rather, my claim is that this connection is *more conditional* and less automatic than it is often taken to be. On the one hand, integrity and clean hands will come apart when agents have at their disposal a very clear causal picture of how the "dirty" deeds they are considering will reliably advance their fundamental moral projects. But, on the other hand, it is rare for agents to be in such a position. It is far more common for us to be deeply uncertain about the consequences of our actions.[19] And under these more common circumstances, integrity will tend to align with clean hands reasoning. This alignment, in turn, will especially likely in circumstances that trigger the repeated iterations concerns that I have been associating with the idea of integrity.

To make these points concrete, consider a variant of the mafia case elaborated in Chapter 1. If Alex the ex-mafia member had a clear, reliable, causal picture of how a single act of violence he might undertake could destroy the mafia for good, then it may very well be that his fundamental rejection of the mafia will align rather than conflict with this act. But suppose that Alex is instead considering whether to re-join the mafia and re-immerse himself in its most notorious activities over an extended period, only on the basis of the vague hope that an opportunity will eventually unfold to undermine the mafia from the inside. This kind of open-ended, speculative strategy repeatedly involves Alex in dirty deeds that, over time, make his behavior indistinguishable from that of the genuine criminals. And given such conditions, where Alex's everyday activities repeatedly take him back to the person that he had promised himself never again to be, his integrity should—at least at some point—push him to stop sullying his hands.

---

[19] A point forcefully brought out in James Lenman's "Consequentialism and Cluelessness," *Philosophy and Public Affairs* 29 (2000): 342–70.

3.4 Is There Really No Alternative? Integrity, Psychology, and Self-Absorption

Agents, I have just argued, must engage in a serious assessment of causal pathways in order for their moral integrity to align with them dirtying their hands. This point is worth reiterating, because once we bear this causal element in mind, we can see another important shortcoming of the self-absorption charge. This charge provides an overly narrow picture of ethical decision making, by zeroing in on circumstances where a binary choice has to be made: one must either "self-indulgently" remain true to one's convictions, or sacrifice these convictions in order to help vulnerable others. This binary setup, however, artificially ignores a morally crucial effort that has to come first: the effort to verify the causal premises on which this binary choice rests. More specifically, one ought to try to verify that departure from one's fundamental moral commitments really will be effective in helping vulnerable others (as we just saw when recalling the case of Alex the ex-mafioso). And one also ought to try to verify that equally effective alternatives to the dirty deed are not available.

To be sure, I do not mean to suggest that the only way to ground the moral weight of such causal inquiries is through the language of integrity. But integrity does lead to these inquiries quite naturally. This is because the efforts to verify that our dirty deeds will really help the vulnerable, and that we really have no good alternatives, are often costly. These efforts necessitate precisely the steadfastness that is so essential to integrity, and yet so often missing in us. That is why it is often tempting to avoid such efforts—to try to convince ourselves that striving to get the best possible measure of our situation is either unnecessary or futile. But if *that* is how we proceed, we cannot say in good faith that we "really had no choice" but to compromise our deepest moral convictions "for the sake of others."[20]

This observation, in and of itself, should already dampen the appeal of the self-absorption charge. But if we link this observation to the psychological aspects of the self-absorption charge, we can weaken this charge even further. Let me explain. A key part of the force of the self-absorption charge arguably derives from the thought that integrity talk elevates objectionable psychological impulses onto the level of important moral principles. Those who fear for their own untainted self-image, to such an extent that they see it as a serious contender when pitted against the practical needs of vulnerable others, are not moral exemplars. They should be castigated, not lauded. Or so, at least, the complaint goes.[21] This complaint, however, ignores the multiple ways in which integrity,

---

[20] If that is what we say nonetheless, then there is clearly ample room to question whether we really hold these convictions.

[21] Brian Barry provided one particularly explicit version of this complaint: "If I were the man who was fleeing death, I would not think much of ... somebody who was agonizing about whether to pollute his precious 'integrity' to save my life ... if we take God and the soul out of the picture, the emphasis on

precisely by calling for the kind of costly inquiries I just emphasized, *restrains* psychological impulses which so often lead to decisions that neglect the vulnerable.

It might be helpful to illustrate the impulses I have in mind with a further example. The example of decision-making by corporate executives, especially as it concerns their firms' operations abroad, is particularly useful, not only because of its obvious practical significance, but also because (as will become clear shortly) it can inform our thinking about political integrity as well.

Consider again, then, the case discussed in Chapter 1, of a corporate executive who has to decide whether to bribe foreign officials in order to secure major government contracts. When introducing this case, I argued that there is moral value in this executive unconditionally rejecting bribery as a means of doing business. More specifically, I argued that, as with many other unconditional moral commitments, the unconditional rejection of bribery would pre-empt the ubiquitous psychological tendency to engage in self-deception and self-seeking rationalizations. If this executive rejected bribery only conditionally, it would be all too easy for him to rationalize bribery of foreign officials as benefiting all relevant parties, including even vulnerable populations in the relevant foreign countries.

Now, a proponent of the self-absorption charge would insist that in circumstances where the vulnerable genuinely stand to gain from such a dirty deed, then it is simply self-indulgent to pay much attention to the thought that bribery is incompatible with one's own integrity. If the alternative to our protagonist paying the bribe *really* is that a competing firm will win the relevant government contracts and only provide worse services to the population, then it is morally dangerous to get squeamish about this bribe. This insistence, however, reflects an impoverished understanding, not only of how self-seeking rationalizations operate, but also of how several other psychological dynamics bear on the issue.

One way to see this point is the following. In many cases, it is going to be far from easy for an executive in a case such as this to acquire firm knowledge of how his decisions about bribery will really affect the interests of vulnerable people on the other side of the world. Even in cases where such information could in principle be attained, actually obtaining and processing this information is quite likely to cost non-trivial amounts of time and money. These, of course, are costs that integrity calls on corporate executives to accept. But market competition generates significant pressures that go against a steadfast willingness to absorb costs for the sake of one's moral principles. These market pressures make it

---

'integrity' becomes a form of narcissism. The question [this view] would keep in the forefront of our minds is always 'how do I come out of this looking?' There certainly are people like this, but the idea that we should be expected to admire them seems to me bizarre." Barry, *Democracy, Power and Justice* (Oxford: Clarendon Press, 1989), 340.

tremendously tempting for the executive to convince himself that he either "does not need any research" to know how his decisions are going to affect foreign populations, or to satisfy himself with only the most superficial, in-house research, clearly doctored to provide him precisely with the news he wants to hear.[22]

I am assuming that this description of an executive's likely reasoning, though obviously stylized, is sufficiently plausible, and disturbing, to make at least some ethicists uneasy. But the sad fact is that even this description is extremely *rosy* in comparison to what robust empirical evidence suggests about corporate executives' ethically fraught choices. For one thing, the pace and automatic routines of corporate life hardly provide opportunities for the kind of "slow thinking"[23] that social psychologists and behavioral economists have long shown is needed for serious deliberation.[24] Furthermore, extensive empirical evidence suggests that, precisely because of familiar psychological factors, corporate executives rarely if ever spend any serious amount of time thinking about distant victims of their decisions. The result is a fundamental divide between modern corporate executives and the business managers of the past, whose knowledge of those affected by their decisions was—typically—far more intimate. One scholar of white-collar crime describes this divide as follows:

Harmful conduct committed by an executive was no longer against a specific group of individuals known to the executive, but, instead, against an ill-defined and little-known mass. This not only increased the magnitude of the harm that the executive had the capacity to inflict but it also *fundamentally shifted the psychology of harm*. By divorcing executives from contact with the individuals directly impacted by their actions, executives were shielded from experiencing the emotional feedback that arose from their decisions ... with the harm neither

---

[22] For striking parallels between such corporate dynamics and political decision making, including in cases (such as the Vietnam War) on which I touch below, see Anna Elisabetta Galeotti, "Liars or Self-Deceived? Reflections on Political Deception," *Political Studies* 63 (2015): 887–902; see also Galeotti's *Political Self-Deception* (Cambridge: Cambridge University Press, 2018).

[23] See, e.g., Daniel Kahneman, *Thinking, Fast and Slow* (New York, NY: Farrar, Straus and Giroux, 2011).

[24] "Much managerial activity," as business scholar Eugene Soltes points out, "consists of sets of routinized activities ... that promote mindlessness." See his *Why They Do It: Inside the Mind of the White-Collar Criminal* (New York: Public Affairs, 2016), 154. Soltes has conducted extensive interviews with scores of corporate executives convicted of financial crimes, including with Dennis Kozlowski, the Tyco CEO who spent more than eight years in prison for misusing more than a hundred million dollars in company loans. Soltes notes Kozlowski's self-serving description of his "routine of signing documents"—including the ones that landed him in prison: "[t]wice a month I had folders with yellow stickies that were this big," Kozlowski recalled as he spread his arms wide to indicate the immense stack awaiting his signature. "I signed everything, but it was the same thing that I had been doing since 1976 ... I had the company tell me what it was and I signed it. So how's that criminal?" Reflecting on Kozlowski's rationale, Soltes observes: "with decades of mindless signatures behind him, Kozlowski never thought to stop and carefully consider whether, even if he could sign a document, doing so was appropriate use of his authority ... Kozlowski signed papers without carefully considering how others, including some members of his own board, would perceive the forgiveness of millions of dollars in loans."

present nor visible, the affective system does not whirl into gear to promote avoidance of harmful action. There isn't an internal signal that warns "Stop!" and prompts the executive to choose a different course of action.[25]

Once we consider these ubiquitous psychological phenomena, it should become apparent that, at least in the significant case of corporate executives' ethical decision making, integrity talk does not represent a surrender to any psychological urges to neglect others. The opposite is the case: integrity, both as a moral factor and as a broader moral framework, crucially guards *against* some of the most pernicious psychological pitfalls that predictably lead us to neglect others.

We can further bolster this contention by noting another key point, which sets corporate executives apart from ordinary individuals. As philosophers writing on global poverty have long noted, the psychological effects of distance manifest themselves in the thinking of ordinary individuals in much the same way that they affect the titans of industry.[26] But the leaders of major corporations obviously face different ethical situations when compared with ordinary individuals. This is not only because the impact of their everyday decisions on the lives of distant others is so much greater. It is also because of their central fiduciary responsibilities toward investors and shareholders. These responsibilities, in turn, open the way to a whole slew of additional self-seeking rationalizations for ethically dubious conduct, especially when executives are not accountable in any way to the distant victims of this conduct. If ascertaining the effects of questionable conduct on distant others requires expensive research, and if the law does not require such research, then it is clearly psychologically easy for corporate leaders to convince themselves that they are merely abiding by the best interests of their investors and shareholders by refraining from such research. In fact, such corporate executives may even convince themselves that they are doing the mature, responsible thing: they do not let any inappropriate squeamishness about their own integrity get in the way of their fiduciary duty to maximize shareholder value.[27] And finally, they can always remind themselves that if they do not treat this duty as overriding, eventually they will be replaced by someone who will.

Viewed from outside the corporate bubble, however, it seems plain that all of these forms of reasoning only further buttress, rather than undermine, integrity's moral significance. We should indeed worry about psychological traps that cause

---

[25] Soltes, *Why They Do It*, 124.

[26] Thus Thomas Pogge, for instance, writes: "We live in extreme isolation from severe poverty. We do not know anyone earning less than $30 for a 72-hour week of hard, monotonous labor. The one-third of human beings who die from poverty-related causes includes no one we have ever spent time with. Nor do we know anyone who knows and cares about these deceased—someone scarred by the experience of losing a child to hunger, diarrhea, or measles, for example." Pogge, *World Poverty and Human Rights* (London: Polity, 2002), 4.

[27] One would expect neo-classical economists to support this reasoning. See for example Milton Friedman, *Capitalism and Freedom* (Chicago, IL: University of Chicago Press, 1962), 133.

practical indifference to the fate of vulnerable others, especially distant others. But the key example of corporate business suggests yet again that, in many crucial cases at least, integrity is not a cause of this worry, but rather a key part of the remedy.

3.5 From the Corporate to the Political Realm (I): Who Sets Up Binary Choices?

I have elaborated on the case of corporate decision making partly because it has various implications for how the self-absorption charge fares in the political context. One way to see these implications is to consider another dimension of ethical decision making that is especially salient in the political realm, yet that the self-absorption charge again ignores. By framing ethical situations as a matter of a binary choice between our own purity and others' practical needs, the self-absorption charge artificially ignores the question of who supplies the information that leads us to conceptualize our relevant choices in such binary terms. When it comes to political decision making bearing on global affairs, the answer to this question is often "global corporations." Indeed, the main reason why we are so familiar with binary understandings of global reform proposals is that corporations have been extremely successful in shaping policy discourse about these proposals. And their success has arguably been a major cause of why policy alternatives that go beyond simple binary choices are so frequently overlooked.

In order to see how this misleading binary setup bears on global policy issues involving integrity, let us consider two specific components of global trade that play a significant role in the economies of many liberal democracies: customary purchases of sweatshop goods, and customary transactions in natural resources controlled by kleptocrats. In both of these cases we can identify clear victims of customary practices—whether sweatshop workers whose labor rights are grossly violated, or peoples whose ownership of state resources is ignored by strongmen abusing public coffers. Yet in both of these cases, it is also not obvious that enacting legal prohibitions against customary trade will improve the lot of its current victims. Therefore, at least some of the relevant victims might accordingly prefer customary trade to continue. Even if sweatshop workers believe that their employers are violating their rights, it does not necessarily follow that they also believe liberal democracies should prohibit their companies from dealing with their employers, or that such prohibitions would improve their circumstances. Similarly, many populations living under autocrats may agree that customary oil trade, for example, allows their rulers to systematically steal publicly owned wealth;[28] but it does not necessarily follow that these populations would actually

---

[28] See, e.g., Pogge, *World Poverty and Human Rights*, chap. 6; Leif Wenar, *Blood Oil* (Oxford: Oxford University Press, 2016). See also my "Democratic Disengagement: Towards Rousseauian Global

want liberal democracies to prohibit oil corporations based in their jurisdictions from trading with these rulers, or that such a prohibition would make the peoples living under autocrats better off.[29]

How, then, should we think about these cases? One powerful answer is suggested by what I called in Chapter 2 the global integrity test. This test alerts us to the fact that the laws of affluent liberal democracies are involved in the relevant customary practices. The laws—simply through their silence—allow the purchases of the relevant resources. Moreover, whether considering natural resource transactions or sweatshop goods purchases, it is clear that if the relevant foreign practices were enacted *within* the borders of liberal democracies, their identity-grounding institutions would be distorted beyond recognition. Legalizing child labor in sweatshops, for example, would take affluent liberal democracies back to Dickensian realities they had left behind almost two centuries ago. Even more obviously, institutionalizing at home the practice that allows de-facto rulers to treat state property as their own personal property would fatally undermine the foundational commitment of liberal democracy to the sovereignty of the people— and particularly to the idea that the sovereign people, rather than those who wield effective political power, owns state property.[30] These points suggest that inhibition regarding liberal entanglement in such foreign practices is well captured in terms of a threat to liberal integrity—a threat that is amplified given that all of these cases involve repeated interactions rather than "one-off" departures from liberal commitments.

Now, proponents of the self-absorption charge are likely to respond that this reasoning only reinforces their concerns about integrity's self-indulgence: if the victims of customary trade will be best served by continuing this trade (and if they accordingly favor its continuation), then it would be profoundly self-indulgent of liberal democracies to refuse to engage in this trade in the name of their own purity. The problem with this response, however, is that it ignores how the corporations who benefit from customary trade get to shape the causal premises that underlie policy debates concerning reforms to this trade.[31] And we have no reason to think that corporations wield this power in a way that is truly driven by

Reform," *International Theory* 3 (2011): 355–89; "Rigorist Cosmopolitanism," *Politics, Philosophy & Economics* 12 (2013): 260–87; "Environmental Reform, Negative Duties, and Petrocrats: A Strategic Green Energy Argument," *The Journal of Politics* 77 (2015): 914–27.

[29] For some elaborate (if at times overstated) pessimism on this score, see Chris Armstrong, "Dealing with Dictators," *Journal of Political Philosophy* (forthcoming).

[30] Though I argue elsewhere that this idea has been heavily under-theorized. See my "The Idea of Public Property," *Ethics* 129 (2019): 344–69, as well as *The People's Duty*, chap. 2.

[31] For corporate impact on policy premises regarding trade in sweatshop goods in particular, see the essays in Yossi Dahan, Hanna Lerner, and Faina Milman-Sivan (eds.), *Global Justice and International Labor Standards* (Cambridge: Cambridge University Press, 2016). On corporations' pervasive impact on U.S. policy premises more generally, see Lee Drutman, *The Business of America Is Lobbying* (New York: Oxford University Press, 2015).

the best interests of the victims of customary trade. When oil corporations, for example, defend their dealings with some of the world's most brutal and corrupt dictators by appealing to the danger that divestment will pose to the victims of these dictators,[32] we have ample reason to suspect that their real concern lies not with these victims but with profit-making. When corporations that rely on sweatshop labor argue that they are in fact helping sweatshop workers, we similarly have good grounds for questioning whether the welfare of these workers is a genuine corporate priority.[33]

Once we bear in mind these simple yet salient facts, it should once again become clear how often integrity serves as a defender of the vulnerable. If they are to act with integrity, liberal democracies must demand that corporations actually explain why the only alternative to their customary business practices are grave threats to the most basic interests of millions abroad. Liberal democracies ought to demand of oil corporations, for example, to explain what would be wrong with measures such as legislation that freezes bank accounts, denies visas, and prevents business opportunities for senior figures in foreign dictatorships that are credibly associated with theft of their peoples' natural resource wealth.[34] Liberal democracies similarly ought to demand of corporations reliant on sweatshop labor to show precisely why alternatives such as a global minimum wage are not within our reach.[35] In other words, by capturing the moral duty not to accept self-serving binary presentations of policy choices at face value, the claims of integrity can make a practical difference *alongside*, rather than at the expense of, attention to serious costs that policy changes might involve for the world's most vulnerable.

3.6 From the Corporate to the Political Realm (II): National Security and the Moral License of Fiduciary Obligations

Having seen how the self-absorption charge can be resisted in one global policy area, I now want to turn to another such area, where this charge may initially seem especially powerful: national security. Here as well, our earlier discussion of corporate executives and their personal failures of integrity suggests some important lessons. This is particularly true with regard to the notion of fiduciary obligations that plays a key role not only in corporate but also in political decision making.

---

[32] See for example Steve Coll, *Private Empire* (New York: Penguin, 2011), e.g. at 521.
[33] See, e.g., Michael Kates, "The Ethics of Sweatshops and the Limits of Choice," *Business Ethics Quarterly* 25 (2015): 191–212.
[34] "The Magnitsky Act" that was passed by U.S. Congress in late 2012 with regard to corrupt Russian officials is a good example. See http://www.gpo.gov/fdsys/pkg/PLAW-112publ208/html/PLAW-112publ208.htm.
[35] For a defense of this alternative see Ian Shapiro, *Politics Against Domination* (Cambridge, MA: Harvard University Press, 2016).

Politicians' fiduciary obligations loom especially large when national security is at stake. That is a key reason for why it may initially seem especially inappropriate for politicians to prioritize their own integrity when dealing with national security. The pursuit of national security, after all, routinely involves dirty deeds—from cooperation with extremely unsavory allies, to a variety of forms of deception and coercion. In turn, it is natural to think that political leaders who prioritize their discomfort with such deeds over national needs are betraying crucial fiduciary obligations, which literally involve matters of life and death. Hence the intuitive claim that political leaders ought not to get squeamish when national security is on the line.

Now, it is true that political leaders have important fiduciary obligations toward their own citizens, and it is also true that we expect of our leaders to prioritize fulfillment of these obligations over their own psychological well-being. If it is obvious that a certain policy serves a crucial public end, but elected leaders simply feel too distraught about this policy to carry it out, then this does give us strong grounds for voting them out of office. In practice, however, the real causes for concern are overwhelmingly cases of the opposite sort. In these cases, the worry is not that "squeamishness" will prevent our leaders from "dirtying their hands" for the greater good. The far more common danger, especially when national security is involved, is that a variety of all-too-predictable psychological dynamics will push leaders to vastly exaggerate their moral license to engage in dirty deeds for the public good. And in *this* context—just as in the corporate example discussed earlier—we should view integrity as contesting, rather than facilitating, the most morally dangerous psychological phenomena.

We can start to unpack this claim with the following observations. Even if we grant that elected leaders have important fiduciary obligations to advance the national interest, it is plainly implausible to say that elected leaders ought to be willing to inflict even the most severe harms on outsiders for the sake of trivial gains to their own citizens. There clearly are moral constraints on what may be done to foreigners in the name of "the national interest." However, there is considerable psychological temptation for elected leaders to heavily underestimate the weight of these constraints in their decision making, or even to ignore these constraints altogether, particularly in the name of national security.

This temptation, in turn, is so potent partly because of obvious self-interest: since their compatriots can vote them out of office while foreigners cannot, it is natural for elected leaders to convince themselves that even limited security gains for their own citizens justify policies imposing massive harms on foreigners. But the psychological temptation to underestimate the weight of moral constraints protecting foreigners also stems—just as in the corporate case—from the psychology of distance. It is too easy for elected leaders to view distant foreigners—especially ones with whom they share no bond of ethnicity, language, religion, or culture—as once again an "ill-defined and little-known mass" whose rights and interests count for little when national security is in any way involved.

As a result of all this, the most common moral danger in the design of national security policies is not that of insufficient willingness by elected leaders to "dirty their hands" for the greater good. Rather, the common danger has to do with excessive such willingness. More specifically, the danger is excessive willingness to engage in dirty deeds without pursuing the morally essential inquiries on which integrity insists. Far too often, there is no serious attempt by decision-makers to verify that dirty deeds massively harming foreigners will actually be effective in advancing national security plausibly interpreted. Nor is there a serious attempt to research alternatives that might spare foreigners of the relevant harms. In fact, in extreme cases, sheer indifference to the fate of distant others might push political leaders to simply dismiss the very idea that such research should affect their decisions at all, let alone constrain them in any fundamental way. Three American examples, in chronological order, will help to illustrate these worries.

3.6.1 Vietnam

Consider, first, the "domino theory" which shaped so much of U.S. foreign and national security policy during the Cold War in general, and with regard to Vietnam in particular. According to the domino theory, a communist victory in virtually any given country posed a grave risk of a snowball effect, sweeping multiple other countries in its wake, in a way that would ultimately risk American national security. Presidents Eisenhower, Kennedy, Johnson, Nixon, and Reagan were all firm adherents to the domino theory, as were many of their key officials.[36] Yet the theory was a monumental failure, both in general and specifically when applied to Vietnam. Jerome Slater, for example, concludes his detailed study of the domino theory with regard to Vietnam as follows:

> There was an inverse correlation between the plausibility of the domino theory and its relationship to vital American interests: The theoretically most dangerous threats were least likely to occur, while the events that were most likely to occur were of little or no concern to genuine U.S. national interests. As a result, even [if] it had been true, the domino theory (in its even minimally plausible versions) would have been irrelevant, for communist domination over Southeast Asia was not a sufficient threat to vital U.S. interests or national security to justify a major war ... the United States went to war in Vietnam ... in order to preempt a range of theoretically possible but highly unlikely future threats, few of which were

---

[36] Jerome Slater, "The Domino Theory and International Politics: The Case of Vietnam," *Security Studies* 3 (1993): 186–224, passim.

genuinely critical and all of which could have been met by a variety of much less costly means if they had actually occurred.[37]

These grave mistakes were intertwined with a recurring failure by policy makers to properly assess the domino theory in general, and the stakes posed by Vietnam in particular. This failure, in turn, was not merely something that could be identified only retrospectively. An essential part of what made the Vietnam War a monumental example of "folly," as Barbara Tuchman famously put it, was precisely that the fatal flaws of the premises on which it relied were evident *at the time*.[38] Even during the Cold War, it was never clear who precisely was supposed to be the aggressor behind the falling "dominos," how exactly the dominos were supposed to be linked, what made the process irreversible, and why it posed a real threat to U.S. national security. Thus the Vietnam War was "an intellectual as well as a military, political, economic, and moral catastrophe, for the domino theory that drove it was...a house of cards built on sand":

> It is astonishing that there was such a breakdown of intelligence at every level of the American government over such a long period, and that there was such vagueness and inconsistency on the central components of the domino theory...The premises underlying the domino theory were rarely systematically reassessed, even during the critical policy reviews undertaken precisely in order to re-examine the basis of American policy in Vietnam before embarking on a new escalation...successive major policy reassessments simply repeated the litany: revolution is a new form of aggression; if one domino goes, they all will go; not only Southeast Asia, but all of the Third World, all the Pacific nations, Latin America, the Middle East, and even Europe is endangered.[39]

What were the causes of this spectacular intellectual failure? One natural answer is that "the United States unconsciously had become an imperial power"—that just as with past empires, "American interests had become defined in increasingly extravagant fashion."[40] But alongside this answer, there is also another, painfully simple fact. For all of the human and economic toll that blind adherence to the domino theory took on American society itself, the theory's most disastrous costs were borne overwhelmingly by numerous *foreign* countries, not only in Indochina, but also in the Middle East, in Africa, and in Latin America. During the Cold War, the United States repeatedly supported corrupt and brutal dictatorships in all of these regions—in many cases at the expense of elected

---

[37] Slater, "The Domino Theory and International Politics," 216.
[38] See Barbara Tuchman, *The March of Folly* (New York: Alfred A. Knopf, 1984), part five: "America betrays herself in Vietnam."
[39] Slater, "The Domino Theory," 217–18.   [40] Slater, "The Domino Theory," 218.

governments it overthrew—simply in order to prevent them from aligning with "the eastern bloc," despite the lack of any proof that such alignment was either forthcoming or posed any meaningful danger to U.S. national security.[41] Apparently, the sharp contrast between the miniscule probabilities which ostensibly justified this support and the enormous harms it imposed on the victims of these dictatorships rarely occurred to American decision-makers. Consequently, little if any thought was given to less dirty alternatives that would help to achieve the same national security goals without imposing such massive harms on some of the world's most vulnerable people.

3.6.2 The Bush "War on Terror"

Having considered one example of the kind of political oversight that integrity criticizes in the making of national security decisions, let us now turn to a second example: the national security policies of the George W. Bush administration. Consider, for instance, the administration's infamous "1 percent" doctrine. According to this doctrine, "if there was even a 1 percent chance of terrorists getting a weapon of mass destruction—and there has been a small probability of such an occurrence for some time—the United States must now act as if it were a certainty."[42] Vice-President Dick Cheney—the man most associated with this doctrine—described it as entered not on "our analysis" but on "our response."[43] This "standard of action," as Ron Suskind put it, "would frame events and responses from the administration for years to come":

> The Cheney doctrine. Even if there's just a one percent chance of the unimaginable coming due, act as if it is a certainty...Justified or not, fact-based or not, "our response" is what matters. As to "evidence," the bar was set so low that the word itself almost didn't apply...a key feature of the Cheney Doctrine was to quietly liberate action from such accepted standards of proof, and it was effective. Suspicion, both inside America and abroad, became the threshold for action.[44]

The implications of this doctrine were drastic. It meant that even the most morally fraught means of pursuing national security were not going to be treated as a last resort, to be taken only after careful study of possible alternatives that might minimize harm. Instead, even the dirtiest means—including, for example,

---

[41] See, e.g., Stephen Kinzer, *Overthrow: America's Century of Regime Change* (New York: Times Books, 2006).
[42] Ron Suskind, *The One Percent Doctrine* (New York: Simon and Schuster, 2006), 62.
[43] Quoted in Suskind, *The One Percent Doctrine*, 62.
[44] Suskind, *The One Percent Doctrine*, 62, 163.

torture—could function as a *first* resort.[45] More generally, it is not clear how seriously (if at all) Cheney or other administration officials took *any* moral limits on the harms that may be inflicted on foreigners in the name of a 1 percent probability of disaster for the United States—whether coming from terrorists or from "rogue regimes."[46]

Now, it should be plain that these policy premises were morally indefensible, even on the most expansive interpretation of leaders' fiduciary obligations with regard to national security. No one would argue that parents' fiduciary obligations toward their children, for example, justify them in "pre-emptively" assaulting strangers if there is a "1 percent probability" that these strangers will threaten the safety of their children.[47] But simple observations of this sort did not give the Bush administration any pause. Moreover, the administration did not consult policy experts, or engage in serious review of its favored drastic measures, to examine whether these were in fact necessary.[48] In fact, it seems safe to say that *none* of the dirty measures pursued by the Bush administration—from its surveillance programs to its "enhanced interrogation techniques"—were based on any serious assessment of their efficacy and necessity.

3.6.3 Tracking bin-Laden

For a final example of dirty national security measures pursued without the inquiries that integrity mandates, consider the U.S. effort to track down Osama bin-Laden. This effort resulted in Navy SEALs killing bin-Laden in a compound in the Pakistani town of Abbottabad, in May 2011. In order to ascertain that the mysterious man living in the compound was in fact bin-Laden, the CIA set up a vaccination scheme in Abbottabad, aiming to extract DNA samples from what were suspected to be bin-Laden's family members. This "ruse," as the *Guardian* put it, "has provided seeming proof for a widely held belief in Pakistan, fuelled by

---

[45] See, e.g., Conor Friedersorf, "Dick Cheney Defends the Torture of Innocents," *The Atlantic*, December 15, 2014, at https://www.theatlantic.com/politics/archive/2014/12/dick-cheney-defends-the-torture-innocents/383741.

[46] Thus, for example, when Bush administration officials discussed the danger of Saddam Hussein using weapons of mass destruction as a justification for pre-emptive war, "at least some of them may have been insensitive to the magnitude of this possibility; what mattered was its very existence." Robert Jervis, "Understanding the Bush Doctrine," *Political Science Quarterly* 118 (Fall 2003): 365–88, at 373. Cheney's amoralism in particular was apparent in his dismissal of moral language by other politicians, including Bush administration allies such as Tony Blair—whom Cheney mocked as a "preacher on a tank." See, e.g., David Runciman, "Preacher on a Tank," *London Review of Books*, October 7, 2010, at https://www.lrb.co.uk/v32/n19/david-runciman/preacher-on-a-tank.

[47] See in the same spirit John Allen Paulos, "Who's Counting: Cheney's One Percent Doctrine," *NBC News*, July 2, 2006, at http://abcnews.go.com/Technology/story?id=2120605.

[48] See Suskind, *The One Percent Doctrine*, passim, e.g. at 226–7. See also Suskind's *The Price of Loyalty* (New York: Simon and Schuster, 2004).

religious extremists, that polio drops are a western conspiracy to sterilize the population."[49] The negative consequences have been dramatic:

> After nearly half a century of vaccinating children and adults around the globe, international health workers finally had cornered the polio virus in a few remaining pockets in northern Nigeria, Afghanistan, and Pakistan... But [the killing of] Osama bin Laden... and the subsequent fallout in Pakistan and the surrounding region... allowed the virus to fight back. Almost four years later, polio remains a significant threat in Pakistan, which reported 327 new cases in 2014, 60 percent of the world total.[50]

A major part of the problem was that once rumors spread that the Pakistani doctor who led the vaccination scheme was linked to the CIA—rumors eventually confirmed by the U.S. government—"every vaccination worker in Pakistan," as *National Geographic* put it, "fell under suspicion."[51] Consequently, in June 2012, the Taliban started to "systematically kill polio workers":

> When the polio teams started using police escorts, the Taliban set off hidden roadside bombs that would wipe out an entire convoy. Clinics were bombed or set afire. The attacks occurred in Karachi, Peshawar, and throughout the tribal borderlands until the Pakistani health authorities, the WHO, Rotary International, and UNICEF halted all vaccinations... By that point, says Dr. Elias Durry, the WHO's emergency coordinator for polio eradication in Pakistan, "we'd pretty much given up all hope of eradicating polio from Pakistan." Meanwhile, the number of polio cases in Pakistan rocketed.[52]

These severe consequences were joined by further downstream repercussions from the CIA operation—including the further global spread of polio, following the arrival of militants from the same polio-contaminated area in Pakistan to fight in Syria's civil war.[53]

In light of these costs, it is natural to ask: why did U.S. decision-makers take this particular path to tracking bin-Laden? Was there really no other way, apart from a vaccination scheme, of confirming bin-Laden's whereabouts without

---

[49] Saeed Shah, "CIA Tactics to Trap Bin Laden Linked with Polio Crisis, Say Aid Groups," *The Guardian*, March 2, 2012, at https://www.theguardian.com/world/2012/mar/02/aid-groups-cia-osama-bin-laden-polio-crisis.

[50] Tim McGirk, "How the bin Laden Raid Put Vaccinators Under the Gun in Pakistan," *National Geographic*, February 25, 2015, at https://news.nationalgeographic.com/2015/02/150225-polio-pakistan-vaccination-virus-health.

[51] McGirk, "How the bin Laden Raid Put Vaccinators Under the Gun in Pakistan."

[52] McGirk, "How the bin Laden Raid Put Vaccinators Under the Gun in Pakistan."

[53] See Jason Motlagh, "Fighting Polio Amid the Chaos of Syria's Civil War," *National Geographic*, March 5, 2015, at news.nationalgeographic.com/2015/03/150305-polio-syria-iraq-islamic-state-refugees-vaccination-virus-jihad.

compromising the operation? Given the staggering array of U.S. military tech-nologies, this is hard to believe. It is much more plausible to think that in their zeal to track bin-Laden, U.S. decision-makers, including decision-makers in the Obama administration, simply failed to take any account of Pakistan's already-entrenched culture of suspicion toward vaccinations. According to policy experts cited by the *National Geographic*, at least, "it is unlikely that the administration considered the consequences the raid would have on the fight against polio."[54]

3.6.4 National Security and Collective Integrity Failures

Integrity, to reiterate my basic claim in this section, requires a thorough assess-ment of the consequences and efficacy of different policy options as a precondi-tion for "dirty" measures. This requirement, far from leading to any kind of self-absorption that comes at the expense of vulnerable others, protects the most likely and most vulnerable victims of dirty measures. And it is therefore violations of this requirement that should be our focus if we are concerned about the vulner-able's practical needs, rather than any "squeamishness" ostensibly associated with integrity.

This contention is vividly illustrated by the aforementioned examples—one reason why I chose them. But another reason why I deployed these particular examples is that they implicate not only the integrity of individual decision-makers, but also the polity's collective integrity.

We can see this point by examining again each of the three examples, in reverse order. Consider the case of the bin-Laden operation. President Obama's announcement that bin-Laden had been killed triggered nation-wide celebrations. In multiple cities throughout the United States, thousands gathered spontaneously to mark the occasion.[55] More than 56 million Americans watched the President's announcement—his largest audience since election night.[56] More than 4,000 tweets were posted on Twitter during every second of the President's speech.[57] "U-S-A" chants took over different sports events, from a nationally televised baseball match in Philadelphia to a boxing match in Florida.[58] Thousands of

---

[54] Alexander Mullaney and Syeda Amna Hassan, "He Led the CIA to bin Laden—and Unwittingly Fueled a Vaccine Backlash," *National Geographic*, February 27, 2015, at https://news.nationalgeographic.com/2015/02/150227-polio-pakistan-vaccination-taliban-osama-bin-laden.

[55] See, e.g., Emily Babay and Brian Hughes, "Crowds Rejoice at White House After News of Bin Laden's Death," *The Washington Examiner*, May 2, 2011.

[56] Sam Schechner, "Obama Drew Big TV Crowd," *Wall Street Journal*, May 4, 2011, at https://www.wsj.com/articles/SB10001424052748703834804576301821550865988.

[57] Craig Kanalley, "Twitter Reactions to Osama Bin Laden's Death (Tweets)," *The Huffington Post*, May 2, 2011, at https://www.huffingtonpost.com/2011/05/02/osama-bin-laden-death-tweets_n_856119.html.

[58] See, e.g., "Wrestler's Bizarre Declaration of Osama bin Laden's Death," *The Telegraph*, May 3, 2011, at http://www.telegraph.co.uk/news/newstopics/howaboutthat/8490123/Wrestlers-bizarre-declaration-

university students—from Ohio, through Indiana, to California—set off a wide range of celebrations.[59] Yet none of this collective pride was matched by any clear instance of collective shame, or any other form of collective reckoning, when it became clear what harms the operation had inflicted on numerous innocent polio victims.

In fact, when news broke out about the details of the CIA scheme to identify bin-Laden, public response was conspicuously absent. While a number of health organizations and public health schools protested the CIA's use of health workers, and while a few media outlets covered the story, ordinary American citizens registered little by way of protest at the CIA's methods. Not a single rally, spontaneous or planned, gathered to hold decision-makers to task. No sports event or student group sought to raise attention to the grave effects of these methods for polio victims in Pakistan or any other foreign country. How many ordinary Americans—of those who even bothered to inform themselves about these effects—approved of the CIA's methods (even if only retroactively)? In the lack of reliable survey data, we cannot tell. But it is sensible to suspect that such approval was far from uncommon.

If this is right, then the operation to track bin-Laden implicated not only individual decision-makers, whether in the CIA or in the Obama administration. It also implicated ordinary Americans—a fact that the idea of collective integrity captures quite forcefully. As I argued in Chapter 2, just as there is moral value in ordinary citizens identifying with the polity's fundamental moral struggles, so there is moral value in citizens incorporating their polity's moral failures into their identity—feeling appropriate shame about these failures, and, to the degree that they can, seeking to prevent their recurrence. None of this happened in the case of the bin-Laden operation.

A similar thought applies, even more broadly, to the measures pursued by the Bush administration in its "war on terror." Especially in the immediate aftermath of the September 11 attacks, dissenters who questioned the administration's favored dirty means, including even the most drastic provisions of the PATRIOT Act, were seen by many as "distasteful at best and traitors at worst."[60] In their haste to rally behind the flag, both congress and the media firmly sided with the administration's agenda, as did the general public, almost 90 percent of which approved of President Bush's policies following the terrorist

---

of-Osama-bin-Ladens-death.html; Adam Rubin, "Phillies Crowd Erupts in 'U-S-A' Cheers," *ESPN*, May 2, 2011, at http://www.espn.com/espn/print?id=6463361&type=story.

[59] See "How Did Students Respond to Osama's Death at Different Colleges?" *Huffington Post*, May 2, 2011, at https://www.huffingtonpost.com/nextgen-journal/bin-ladens-dead-college-s_b_856162.html.

[60] Ion Bogdan Vasi, "The New Anti-War Protests and Miscible Mobilizations," *Social Movement Studies* 5 (2006): 137–53, at 139.

attacks.[61] The same rabid, unreflective nationalism made the Iraq War initially palatable to large swaths of Americans, who clearly took little effort to distinguish between Al Qaeda and Saddam Hussein.[62] If a sufficient number of ordinary Americans had bothered to learn that the "alliance" trumpeted by the administration between Al Qaeda and Saddam was even less plausible than Saddam's alleged possession of weapons of mass destruction, the numerous calamities of this supposedly "necessary" war may well have been averted. To the extent that this is true, we can say that it is not only public officials but also large portions of American society who failed to do their morally essential homework. Notwithstanding the administration's numerous lies, these citizens were *culpably ignorant* of the most basic issues pertaining to their country's "war on terrorism." This ignorance meant that many ordinary citizens had clearly neglected their role as the ultimate authors of their society's collective project. And this neglect, in turn, meant that the blatant moral failures of the Bush years not only implicated the integrity of individual government officials. These failures also compromised the moral integrity of American society writ large.[63]

Much of the same can be said, finally, with regard to the Vietnam War and the domino theory. For one thing, notwithstanding the place of the Vietnam War protests as a key moment in modern American history, American society has made little effort to incorporate into its identity the memory of the wrongs done to millions of innocents in Indochina during the war. Despite the extraordinary number of monuments to American soldiers who died in Vietnam, one struggles to find anywhere in the United States (let alone in nationally prominent sites) any kind of collective commemoration of the suffering that the U.S. military brought upon untold millions in Indochina. The marked absence of such commemoration cannot be attributed solely to individual politicians: once again, this is, at least in part, a *collective* failure.

A parallel collective failure applies to the "domino theory" more generally. There has been little if any collective reckoning in the United States with this theory's calamitous effects for numerous foreign nations, despite its pervasive impact over American foreign policy throughout the Cold War. Moreover, much of the intellectual laziness that enabled the rise of the domino theory continues

[61] See http://users.hist.umn.edu/~ruggles/Approval.htm; see also David Domke, Erica S. Graham, Kevin Coe, Sue Lockett John, and Ted Coopman, "Going Public as Political Strategy: The Bush Administration, an Echoing Press, and Passage of the Patriot Act," *Political Communication* 23 (2006): 291–312.

[62] See, e.g., "Poll: 70% Believe Saddam, 9-11 Link," *USA Today*, September 6, 2003, at www.webcitation.org/5PplzWLGL?url=http://www.usatoday.com/news/washington/2003-09-06-poll-iraq_x.htmat; Dana Milbank, "Bush Defends Assertions of Iraq-Al Qaeda Relationship," *The Washington Post*, June 18, 2004, at http://www.washingtonpost.com/wp-dyn/articles/A50679-2004Jun17.html.

[63] The utterly unjustified invasion of Iraq—especially given the lies on which it was based—could have provided sufficient grounds for impeaching Bush. Instead, the invasion's immediate impact was a massive (albeit temporary) spike in Bush's approval ratings. See http://users.hist.umn.edu/~ruggles/Approval.htm.

unabated not only in American policies after the Cold War, but also in widespread societal attitudes toward these policies.

Of particular significance here has been the ubiquitous tendency to implausibly lump together all foreign societies that share certain characteristics perceived as "dangerous." During the Cold War "socialism" was the suspect characteristic, leading both ordinary American citizens and policy makers to flatly ignore crucial differences across "socialist countries."[64] In the twenty-first century, "Islam" has become the key suspect, similarly leading to a blatant refusal to consider simple facts concerning a variety of differences across Muslim countries. This refusal—by individual politicians and by many of their supporters—seems like the only possible explanation for abhorrent policies such as the Trump administration's travel ban. This ban—egregiously upheld by the Supreme Court at the end of 2017—targets nationals of multiple foreign countries whose only "relevant" sin is being predominantly Muslim.[65] It is hard to see how such a reprehensible measure could have even been seriously considered—let alone given Trump political momentum—had a sufficient portion of ordinary Americans bothered to acquire minimal levels of information about numerous salient distinctions across different Muslim societies.[66] This is yet another case where sizeable portions of the general public fail, just like its leaders, in pursuing even a modicum of the due diligence that integrity mandates, opting for ignorance instead.

We can now sum up this section with a sad but crucial observation. Proponents of the self-absorption charge may fear that integrity routinely gets in the way of helping the vulnerable. But, to paraphrase Marx, it is ignorance that integrity castigates, rather than integrity itself, which typically hinders help to the vulnerable.

3.7 In Lieu of a Conclusion: When the Conflict Is Real

I have spent this chapter trying to combat the appeal of the self-absorption charge against integrity. But for all of my efforts here, it is possible that certain readers will remain unswayed. Such readers might point out that my arguments do not remove the possibility that our own integrity will in fact conflict with the needs of

---

[64] Slater, "The Domino Theory," passim.

[65] See Ariane de Vouge, "Supreme Court Lets Full Trump Travel Ban Take Effect," December 5, 2017, *CNN*, at http://www.cnn.com/2017/12/04/politics/supreme-court-travel-ban/index.html.

[66] Then again, it is also quite hard to imagine another society where the resident ambassador of the Czech Republic would feel compelled to respond officially to popular anger confusing his country with Chechnya. But this is exactly what happened in the aftermath of the attack on the Boston Marathon by U.S. citizens of Chechen origins. See, e.g., Charlie Campbell, "Czech Republic Forced to Remind the Internet That Chechnya Is in Different Country After Boston Bombing," *Time*, April 23, 2013, at http://newsfeed.time.com/2013/04/23/czech-republic-forced-to-remind-the-internet-that-chechnya-is-a-different-country-after-boston-bombing.

vulnerable others; and whenever that conflict is real rather than illusory, it still seems as if focusing on our integrity is objectionably self-absorbed.

I have postponed this trenchant objection to the very end of the chapter for two reasons. First, although it would indeed be self-absorbed to see integrity as *always* trumping any other moral consideration, it should be abundantly clear by this point that my account of integrity steers well clear of such lopsided conclusions. Arguing that integrity is an independent and non-trivial moral factor is not the same as arguing that it is always a decisive factor. To reiterate, we can and should recognize—as I have been recognizing throughout this chapter and Chapters 1 and 2—that there are circumstances where the claims of integrity will be out-weighed by countervailing moral considerations.

Second, once we see that the conflict between our own integrity and the needs of vulnerable others arises only in a much smaller range of cases than we may initially think, we should also be able to see an important affinity between integrity (or, at least, the theory of integrity offered here) and other theories that fall squarely within the "moral mainstream." Take for example deontological rights theories that insist on respect for constraints associated with others' rights, even when such respect would set back the rights-bearers' interests. Theories of this sort seem at least as open to the charge of neglecting others' needs as are integrity arguments.[67] In fact, even rule-consequentialist theories—insofar as they may be unwilling to bend the rules in the slightest to attend to exceptional need in particular cases—may be thought to be guilty of a similar neglect. That is precisely why, whereas integrity arguments might be accused of fetishizing our own purity, and certain deontological theories of fetishizing rights, many rule-consequentialist views have been accused of "fetishizing rules."

The problem, however, is that in order to adopt such a critical stance toward *all* of these established bodies of moral thought, one must adopt a very particular act-consequentialist position that is itself extremely controversial. This point is especially important given that the initial appeal of the self-absorption charge, as I pointed out earlier, came in part from its seemingly ecumenical character. Therefore, if it is the case that in order to endorse the objection one has to adopt a very specific—and highly contested—act-consequentialist view, this is already a significant finding. It might be possible to construct a coherent position that demands of one to make every single conduct decision in a way that would *always* prioritize the effects of one's conduct on the most vulnerable, no matter what the countervailing considerations. But if that is the view that is supposed to ground the charge of self-absorption, then it is very hard to see how the charge can generate a real following across the philosophical aisle.

---

[67] In fact, compared to integrity arguments, such deontological theories may even be more open to this charge if they assume an absolutist form.

4

"All the Demagogue's Men"

Or How a Liberal Democracy Disintegrates

Up to this point, our inquiry into the relationship between personal and political integrity has largely focused on contexts where these two kinds of integrity point in the same direction. For one thing, much of the argument (particularly across Chapters 1 and 2) has pivoted on analogies between individual integrity and the polity's collective integrity. Moreover, I have been emphasizing (especially in the latter part of Chapter 3) circumstances where personal and political integrity align in the practical steps they require and prohibit.

In contrast, my aim in this chapter and Chapter 5 is to examine important cases, featuring individual political actors, where the relationship between individual integrity and the polity's collective integrity is more complex. In Chapter 5, I show how individual and collective integrity can yield different, and sometimes conflicting, practical guidance regarding the awarding and withdrawal of political honors. In this chapter, I discuss another variant of integrity complexity, rooted in the destructive conduct of political leaders I label "media demagogues."

Though I shall say more about my definition of media demagogues in the pages that follow, we can start with an intentionally compressed description. Media demagogues are politicians who rely on their mastery of the media, and on recurrent lies, as they exploit the electorate's worst fears and prejudices to climb to the top of the executive branch. Even when they get there, however, media demagogues never let go of the media. They spend the bulk of their time portraying themselves, through every possible mass communication outlet, as rare defenders of "the people" against "the old elites." In fact, their use of the media is so incessant that they do not seem to distinguish between campaigning and actually running the country.

One central aim of this chapter is to argue that the rise of media demagogues produces integrity complexity for the political actors who surround them. These actors, in turn, include both political operatives who are considering whether to serve the demagogue, and fellow politicians, who are considering whether to ally with him. From the perspective of both of these kinds of political actors, it may appear as if integrity's dictates are *indeterminate*. This is partly because media demagogues—for reasons that I shall go on to elaborate—not only manifestly lack personal integrity, but also pose predictable threats to the integrity of liberal democracy. These threats, in turn, generate moral pressure to refuse to collaborate

Integrity, Personal, and Political. Shmuel Nili, Oxford University Press (2020). © Shmuel Nili.
DOI: 10.1093/oso/9780198859635.001.0001

with media demagogues. Yet the same threats also generate countervailing pressures to work with media demagogues, in the hope of acquiring leverage that will allow one to moderate their worst excesses.

In turn, if there is no coherent integrity path out of this dilemma—if the integrity framework cannot provide systematic guidance for potential collaborators with media demagogues—then this would be a damning result when it comes to integrity's political relevance. For one thing, such a result would reignite the suspicion that, contrary to my claims in Chapter 3, integrity talk does indeed unduly moralize politics. In particular, integrity talk improperly moralizes politics by questioning virtually every conduct option actually open to real-world political actors. Because integrity is compromised no matter what choices such actors make, integrity either seems to paralyze them—implausibly pushing them to make no choices at all—or it provides them with no useful practical guidance.

A key goal of this chapter is to forestall such concerns. I argue that the integrity framework can offer a coherent moral strategy for political actors who are facing predicaments such as those associated with media demagogues. More specifically, building on the complex relationship between integrity and clean hands outlined in Chapter 3, I argue that integrity's verdicts are not, in fact, indeterminate when it comes to collaborating with media demagogues. Ultimately, integrity considerations unequivocally condemn political operatives who dirty their hands by serving or allying with media demagogues. This is true, moreover, no matter how much such operatives tell themselves—and others—that they are dirtying their hands only in order to help protect the polity's integrity from the danger posed by the demagogue.[1]

On my way to this conclusion (which will be the focus of 4.4 and 4.5), I shall also pay a great deal of attention (4.1–4.3) to media demagogues themselves. This attention is necessary, if nothing else, because without extended background on media demagogues, we cannot have a complete picture of the moral factors bearing on the integrity-laden decisions of their prospective collaborators. However, I also believe it is important to see precisely how and why the language of integrity is well suited to the task of characterizing, and condemning, media demagogues. This thought may seem puzzling, insofar as our moral condemnation of media demagogues appears to be over-determined. Let me therefore offer, already here, four responses to this over-determination worry.

---

[1] As will become clear in the course of the chapter, the relationship of individual political actors to collective institutions differs from the people's relationship to these institutions. This difference is very much in line with a key point I stressed already in the Introduction: that we should expect the idea of collective integrity to play different roles in different contexts. More specifically, we should not expect collective integrity to play the same analytical role in individual-level contexts, as it does in collective cases of the kind highlighted in the preceding chapters. But these shifting roles should not prevent us from discussing problems centered on individual political action. On the contrary: it is essential to examine how the argument might bear on such problems, if it is to give us a truly holistic picture of the pertinent political issues to which we naturally expect it to apply.

First, even if alternative moral views can condemn media demagogues just as forcefully, there is still value in having a systematic account of precisely why media demagogues conspicuously lack integrity. If nothing else, such an account will allow us to further reduce the force of the familiar suspicion that the language of integrity is fundamentally ill suited to the dirty realities of politics.

Second, to reinforce what I said above, if it turned out that the integrity framework yields counter-intuitive implications with regard to media demagogues, then this would be a significant objection to the framework. Therefore, the discussion of media demagogues has, among other things, an important "defensive" function. This, at least, is the case if one grants (given the preceding chapters) that the integrity framework offers multiple positive contributions to our moral and practical thinking. If that is true, then there is value simply in checking that the framework's gains in some areas of moral and practical inquiry are not offset by implausible implications in other important areas. But in order for the integrity framework to pass this "safety check," it is not necessary to show that integrity arguments provide the *only* way to reach intuitively attractive conclusions. It is therefore not necessary to show that integrity arguments provide the only way to condemn media demagogues.

Third, at least in some cases, it matters not only that we get to the right conclusions, but that we get to them *promptly*.[2] And, when it comes to media demagogues, that is not always easy to do. After all—as I will highlight in a moment—media demagogues share all sorts of suspect characteristics with run-of-the-mill politicians. It is therefore not a trivial matter to be able to quickly pinpoint exactly why media demagogues are nonetheless set apart, morally speaking, from so many contemporary politicians.

Finally, related to several of these points is an observation about the link between contemporary media and "attacks on our integrity," as these have been understood in canonical essays in contemporary moral philosophy. Specifically, consider again Bernard Williams' seminal charge that utilitarianism constitutes an "attack on personal integrity." When leveling this charge, Williams had in mind the image of utilitarianism bombarding us with ever-shifting demands, and, consequently, preventing us from retaining our focus on any fundamental commitment or project that endures over time. There is, I think, a remarkable affinity between this image and the effect that telecommunications exert on our lives in the twenty-first century. Many of us (both inside and outside the ivory tower)

---

[2] This point can be seen as a natural corollary of an observation that both critics and adherents of integrity talk have recognized. Discussing the classic case of a lie told to a murderer to protect his prospective victim, Brian Barry, for example, observed that any view that requires a tortuous path to justify such a lie should be suspect, simply because it could only arrive so slowly at the only plausible result (see Barry, *Democracy, Power and Justice*, 339–41). If we have reason to be dissatisfied with an account that is too slow to arrive at the obviously correct result, then we also have reason to be satisfied with an account that reaches the correct result especially quickly.

might be immune to the abstract charms of utilitarian moral doctrine. But few if any of us are completely immune to the ubiquitous, immediate, and frantic contemporary telecommunications scene. Most of us simply take it as a given that this scene—from social networks to email, from globally available phones to constant texting, from incessant internet updates to a never-ending list of TV channels—disrupts our ability to concentrate on any project, no matter how important to us. But if this disruption is merely a source of (self-) frustration in the everyday life of ordinary individuals, its costs are of a different magnitude altogether when those who are being constantly distracted occupy the most powerful position in the land. This "anti-integrity" image of constant distraction, I want to show, has to be central in any persuasive account of media demagogues—and ultimately, in any account of the integrity-laden choices facing those political actors who are considering associating with such demagogues.

4.1 The Integrity of a Politician

With these motivations in mind, let us start by considering the reference—ubiquitous in everyday democratic discourse about public affairs—to elected politicians' (lack of) "integrity."[3] When an elected politician is praised for his or her integrity, or, much more commonly, derided for lacking integrity, what is typically at issue?

One natural answer points to truthfulness. Even if we are not naïve enough to expect our politicians to always tell the truth, we do have good reasons to expect that our politicians will not *constantly* lie. And it seems quite clear that truthfulness is usually involved when "integrity" is invoked to discuss our politicians. However, we should be careful not to treat common talk about politicians' "integrity" as interchangeable with talk about politicians' truthfulness. If that were the case, there would be no reason for "integrity" references to thrive in everyday discourse, favoring as it does simpler terms over their more highbrow relatives.

This point suggests that our constant talk about politicians' "integrity" connotes a grander expectation than just truthfulness. The relevant expectation, I suggest, is that politicians will *genuinely stand for some—morally viable—policy commitments*. In this section, I first elaborate on the main ways in which elected politicians commonly fail this expectation (4.1.1). I then explain why the pervasive impact of mass media on contemporary politics makes such failures ubiquitous (4.1.2), and particularly manifest in the case of media demagogues (4.1.3).

---

[3] This pervasive discourse is emphasized, for example, in Edward Hall's "Integrity in Democratic Politics," *The British Journal of Politics and International Relations* 20 (2018): 395–408.

4.1.1 "Standing for Something" in Politics

Williams famously argued that without fundamental commitments or projects, individuals may lack a reason to "go on."[4] Whether or not one thinks that this claim is true in general, a parallel claim applies even more forcefully, and with more specific implications, to any individual who pursues public office in a liberal democracy. Any such individual ought to be able to identify public projects or commitments that motivate his or her quest to secure or keep a formal public role: without this ability, one has no defensible reason to "go on" in politics. "I want to stay in office because I never get tired of the attention" or "I want to be in office because my father wanted me to be a senior politician" are clearly not tenable answers. Electoral doom is surely the only morally appropriate fate of any candidate for highest office who is unable to articulate a public-oriented answer to the most basic question: "why do you want to lead the country?"

Yet politicians in a liberal democracy clearly ought to do more than merely articulate a public-oriented answer to this classic question. For one thing, the public vision they offer must be at least minimally plausible. This is true in practical terms: a presidential candidate in an extremely poor nation that has barely functioning electricity, for example, better not promise to turn the country into a global tech leader within one year in office. But every politician's public vision must also be at least minimally *morally* plausible: a candidate in a national election who promises to solve an economic crisis through a series of predatory wars meant to take over the precious resources of neighboring countries, for instance, is ignoring the core moral values of liberal democracy in a way that should disqualify him from contention just as immediately as he should be disqualified if his "public vision" consisted of nothing but himself at the center of a society-wide personality cult.

Very often, however, even politicians who pass these basic tests do not succeed in convincing us—or at least, *should* not succeed in convincing us—that they genuinely stand for something in public life. The reason, in turn, will likely have to do with the following issues.

First, we may accuse a politician of "not really standing for anything" because this politician is not *steadfast* in holding any particular policy commitments. In the classic case, this politician's past votes and public pronouncements strongly suggest that she disavows any policy position the moment it seems unpopular. This evident lack of steadfastness should make us question whether she really has any substantive policy commitments.

Second, we may question whether a given politician genuinely stands for something if the policies for which he advocates seriously lack in *coherence*.

---

[4] See, e.g., Williams' "Persons, Character and Morality," in *Moral Luck* (Cambridge: Cambridge University Press, 1981), 12.

Take, for instance, a politician who proposes a variety of disjointed public measures, without any rationale that unites them or explains why they these particular measures should be prioritized, given so many other demands on public attention and resources. Such a politician may not be as obvious a target for criticism as the politician who shifts her policy "commitments" with the latest opinion poll. But it nonetheless makes sense to say that the former, just like the latter, does not really stand for any collective project. His public policy views are far too scattered to really amount to any clear *vision*.

Third, the charge that a given politician does not "genuinely stand for any-thing" also seems appropriate when we suspect that this politician has failed to engage in any serious reflection on the policies to which he pledges support. This suspicion has clear parallels in everyday life. When an acquaintance lectures to us at length about his "profound commitment" to some principle of personal con-duct, for example, only to reveal at the end of his lecture that he only first thought about the relevant principle the day before, we have ample grounds for doubting the depth of his attachment to this principle. When a politician does something similar, however, we have ample grounds not just for doubt but also for anger. Given what is at stake in the making of public policy, it is profoundly wrong of politicians to attach themselves to any particular policy principles without at least a modicum of reflection on whether and why these principles are justified.[5]

Now, these three complaints—regarding a lack of steadfastness in endorsing public policy principles, the absence of a coherent public vision, and a failure to actually reflect on the policy principles one espouses—can be made independently of one another. But these complaints very often go together. The politician who constantly shifts his "cherished principles" to always fit the direction of the popular wind is very likely to end up without any recognizable public vision, and with little by way of reflection on whatever principles he is trumpeting at any given point in time. Such a conclusion, in turn, is not only alarming in and of itself, but is also disturbing given the fear it fuels: namely, that the only real motivation driving this politician is simply the pursuit of power. Insofar as this pursuit is detached from any public interest, it renders hollow the politician's pronouncements of fidelity to the public good: such pronouncements turn out to be nothing more than repeated acts of deception.

Once we combine these elements—lack of steadfastness, incoherence, lack of reflection, and systematic deception—we can see why it makes sense to identify the charge of "not really standing for anything" with the language of integrity. Although integrity talk is not necessary in order to accuse someone of each of

---

[5] One way to capture the problem here is to return to the terminology suggested in Chapter 1. Politicians cannot treat their substantive policy commitments in a manner akin to the normally passive commitments of personal decency, which individuals typically incorporate into their identity without any sustained contemplation.

these moral failures in particular, the idea of integrity provides a powerful unifying framework, simultaneously contesting *all* of these failures. The charge of a "manifest lack of integrity" is a powerful way to capture the serious shortcomings of ever-shifting politicians who make unreflective, incoherent, and deceitful pronouncements about their "commitments."

4.1.2 Failures of Integrity and the Media

The next step in our inquiry is to examine how the multiple moral failures I have just brought under the integrity umbrella relate to a phenomenon that has profoundly altered public affairs in contemporary democracies—namely, the "mediatization" of politics. Following a leading scholar of political communication, I take this concept to refer to "a process whereby politicians (and by extension other opinion advocates) tailor their message to the perceived news values, newsroom routines and journalism cultures prevalent in their societies."[6]

Three aspects of the mediatization process are particularly pertinent for our purposes. The first has to do with media assumptions, derived from commercial imperatives, as to what politics are "newsworthy." Commercial media outlets, as John McManus put it, "compete with each other to offer the least expensive mix of content that protects the interests of sponsors and investors while garnering the largest audience advertisers will pay to reach."[7] These commercial considerations mean that the media typically opts for political stories that fit the requirements of "infotainment"—tales of personal conflict that are simple in form, bounded in time, and have a clear bottom line. So in order to fit the media's expectations, politicians routinely have to pretend that public policy issues are less complicated and more personal than they actually are. Politicians similarly have to pretend that these issues involve much shorter time horizons than they actually do, and that these issues can be resolved—immediately and perhaps even permanently—if only "the right people" get to control decisions. A more honest politician, who insists on paying attention to the complexity and time horizons of real policy problems, will fail to get much media traction. "We need to reflect on this issue more seriously" is a far less attractive media statement than "I can solve this tomorrow."[8]

---

[6] Jay G. Blumler, "Mediatization and Democracy," in Frank Esser and Jesper Stromback (eds.), *The Mediatization of Politics* (London: Palgrave, 2014), 31–41, at 33–4.

[7] John McManus, *Market-Driven Journalism: Let the Citizen Beware?* (Thousand Oaks, CA: Sage, 1994), at 85.

[8] There is obviously a collective action problem lurking in the background. If a critical mass of senior politicians openly admitted to the electorate that, on the vast majority of significant public issues, there are no simple solutions, only difficult choices among competing values and priorities, then it would clearly be easier for other politicians to do the same. And if, under such conditions, significant portions of the electorate still fell for simplistic, empty slogans as substitutes for serious reflection on political affairs, then a key part of the moral blame for the resulting failures of public policy would lie with the electorate. However, to the extent that senior politicians (typically) don't even try this kind of

Second, very much related, the *pace* of the media similarly pressures politicians to ignore the need for serious reflection—as well as for coherence and steadfastness with regard to their public commitments. For one thing, the immediacy and extraordinarily short shelf-life of the typical news story offers little time to reflect on one's policy pronouncements before making them. A politician who restrains herself from pronouncing judgment on topics she has not yet examined in detail—one who always responds to breaking news stories by saying, "I haven't yet had time to properly study this issue"—is unlikely to remain a viable public figure for long. Politicians, in other words, often have strong media reasons to say *something*—virtually anything—over saying nothing. Consequently, they often end up with a set of meaningless platitudes, or with a multitude of scattered policy statements, each of which is given on the basis of fleeting considerations of exigency, but with few (at best) connected by any kind of coherent philosophy.

Along the same lines, the frantic pace of the news cycle creates strong incentives against steadfast attachment to any particular policy commitments. This is especially true for those commitments that revolve around long-term visions, since such visions are often obscured or cast as irrelevant by stories of dramatic failures that dominate the short-term, and that are amplified by the media, focusing as it does on "bad news."

However, the media's frenzied pace threatens politicians' steadfastness not only by pressuring them to sacrifice the future for the sake of the present. This pace also undermines steadfastness by relegating even policy statements from the recent past to the realm of distant memory, making it easier for politicians to zig-zag at will. This too is a predictable result of the "'here today gone tomorrow' rhythm" that characterizes "much news production":

> Since news feasts on "the new," all involved in its making are drenched in the fluid immediacy of events and their coverage. For their part, politicians...often seem impelled to keep up with and respond to the news on its terms and in its time. This may result in ill-considered ploys, sloganizing and news-steered gimmickry...The fact that what is highlighted in the news at one time is off the radar at others may be consequential in other ways. Attention to even important issues...may follow a "now you see it, now you don't" pattern. Politicians who have made policy commitments in response to a propitious

honesty, the main moral responsibility for public policy failures continues to lie largely with them, insofar as they fail to live up to what their positions of leadership require. For claims in similar spirit, see Eric Beerbohm, "Is Democratic Leadership Possible?" *American Political Science Review* 109 (2015): 639–52. For quite a different view see Judith Shklar, *Ordinary Vices* (Cambridge, MA: Harvard University Press, 1984), chap. 2, where Shklar simply takes it as a given that elected politicians will try to hide gaps between democratic ideals and democratic realities.

news environment at a particular time may disregard or flout them when the agenda has switched gear, moving to different topics and concerns later on.[9]

The third aspect of the mediatization of politics that is central for our purposes is closely related to the previous two. The "juicy," simplified, personalized stories that the media treasures, and the relentless pace with which it shifts from one story to another, play a pivotal part in the elevation of style over substance in contemporary democratic politics. Catch-all slogans take the place of substantive policy. Electoral candidates know that rather than winning policy battles, by proving to the public the superiority of their favored policy measures, it is usually far more important to win the "personality battle" against their opponents—to "look more presidential," for example. In turn, once politics takes this personal-ized form, and is compressed into soundbites, it is not hard to see how serious deliberation about public affairs suffers. A politician who conveys a powerful "presidential air" and who becomes identified with a few catchy slogans, for instance, is overwhelmingly likely to be the favorite in a media-saturated compe-tition for office against someone who lacks such charisma and slogans, even if the latter has virtually all the facts on her side, and even if the former's "substantive" agenda consists of misleading appeals to emotions rather than any kind of sober reasoning.[10]

Although scholars of political communication sometimes debate the best labels for these processes, their existence and importance are rarely questioned. Moreover, whether one chooses to speak of the "personalization" of political discourse, of "fragmentation" and "simplification" of political speeches, or of "the soundbite effect,"[11] the basic point remains the same: once the media replaces political substance with personal style, little room is left for serious reflection on substantive public issues, for a steadfast commitment to public policy principles backed by facts, or for the articulation of any coherent public vision. These are some of the key reasons for why media-saturated politics is generally inhospitable to people of integrity—and why even those people who do enter the political arena with their integrity intact quickly confront tremendous pressures to compromise it.

---

[9] Blumler, "Mediatization and Democracy," 35.

[10] For similar observations about how the media turns "political leaders and aspirants" into "char-acters in a soap opera," see Williams' "Truth, Politics, and Self-Deception," *In the Beginning Was the Deed*, 154–64 (especially 161–4). In the same pages, Williams interestingly (if briefly) ties these observations to the possibility of collective self-deception regarding public affairs, enabled by the media. Although I think that the idea of collective integrity has important implications for collective self-deception, in this book I largely put this issue aside. I say more about it in *The People's Duty*, chap. 3.

[11] See, e.g., Gianpetro Mazzoleni, "Mediatization and Political Populism," in *The Mediatization of Politics*, 43–4.

4.1.3 Media Demagogues

It would be naïve—partly for the reasons just given—to view any of our elected leaders as paragons of integrity. But even if none of our leaders fully satisfy the requirements of integrity, some are still special, in the wrong sense: they fail these requirements to a remarkable extent. Moreover, even within the universe of such "ignobles," a specific subset of cases stands out. This subset includes elected leaders who share the following features.

First, these leaders are *populists*: they portray themselves as political outsiders, the only genuine representatives of "common people" battling "the old elites," depicted in turn as ossified and corrupt.[12] Second, these leaders are *demagogues*. They constantly lie (not least with regard to their representation of "the common people"). They promise the impossible. And they systematically exploit and cultivate irrational reactions by key parts of the electorate—especially fear of exaggerated or imaginary threats.

However, third, while such techniques have been deployed by demagogues since antiquity, the present-day demagogues in which I am interested are set apart—from their predecessors as well as their contemporaries—by the nature of their dependence on mass media. Like all successful modern politicians, these demagogues are savvy media operators: they make full use of their telegenic qualities; they craft effective messages fit for mass-media transmission; they are adept at constantly seizing the media initiative away from their opponents, and at minimizing public attention to their constant zig-zags. But these demagogues do not just have formidable media skills. Rather, their political existence is *inter-twined* with the mass media in a much deeper way: their media performances, rather than any substantive public agenda, are the real core of their political activity. Any serious observation of these politicians strongly suggests that, insofar as they are concerned, actual government is decidedly secondary to—if not simply subsumed by—constant media posturing.

Now, why do media demagogues warrant special attention? One key reason is that examples of such leaders are not only abundant already, but are also bound to multiply further in the coming years. At the very least, this is what we can expect if the waves of popular disillusionment with established democracies' elites and institutions continue unabated, and if democratic politics remains so thoroughly "mediatized." Under such conditions, the most unscrupulous populists—those most willing to contradict their previous policy pronouncements, to scapegoat, and to lie whenever doing any of these things confers electoral benefits—are going to enjoy a systematic advantage in electoral competition.

---

[12] All central themes, for example, in Jan-Werner Müller's *What Is Populism?* (Philadelphia, PA: University of Pennsylvania Press, 2016).

There is also, however, another important reason to pay close attention to media demagogues. This reason has to do with the direct and foreseeable link between such demagogues' manifest failures of personal integrity, and the threats they pose to the integrity of liberal democracy. I now turn to elaborate this link.

4.2 Media Demagogues' Integrity Failures and the Integrity of Liberal Democracy

The link between media demagogues' failures of integrity and the danger they pose to collective integrity merits sustained discussion. Accordingly, my discussion of this link proceeds gradually. In this section, I lay out some of the general dangers that the lure of individual power poses to the integrity of liberal democracy, and explain why these dangers are especially salient, and predictable, when it comes to media demagogues (4.2.1). I then illustrate these dangers by examining two of the most widely discussed media demagogues in contemporary democratic politics—Silvio Berlusconi and Donald Trump (4.2.2). In 4.3, I discuss a different sort of media demagogue—Benjamin Netanyahu—in order to better illustrate the full extent of the danger that media demagogues pose to the integrity of liberal democracy.

4.2.1 The Corrupting Effects of Political Power and the Integrity of Liberal Democracy

Any politician who climbs to the top faces the risk of losing any genuine public commitments on the way there. Even individuals who seek highest office with the best of intentions and with meaningful, substantive public policy commitments in mind may very well forget—or at least effectively relinquish—these commitments in the struggle to achieve and retain power, as power increasingly becomes not a means, but an end in itself.

This sadly familiar danger, in turn, poses multiple threats to the identity-grounding institutions of liberal democracy. For one thing, once elected leaders effectively relinquish any substantive policy commitments, the resulting vacuum is often filled by their (more or less) naked pursuit of self-interest. This pursuit, in turn, is most visible in straightforward instances of corruption—of the abuse of public office for private gain. But the pursuit of self-interest also has broader dangerous ramifications, which are especially manifest in those circumstances where elected leaders seem to lose the ability to *distinguish* between the public interest and their own private interest.

Elected leaders may lose this ability because they convince themselves that the democratic mandate they have received legitimates their efforts to tame any meaningful institutional constraints on their power, melding together their personal interest in power with the very expression of "the public interest." Moreover, elected leaders (especially those who have been at the apex of power for an extended period of time) may convince themselves that their very survival in power is vital to "the national interest"—meaning that by serving themselves they are necessarily "serving the nation."

Finally, very much related to these dynamics is the more general blending of private and public. Those elected leaders who manage to cement their hold on political power often come to think that there is no wrong involved in either symbolic or practical fusion of their private persona and their public role. They may come to regard it as natural that various means of symbolic public deference—even veneration—toward their office increasingly take the form of deference and veneration of them as individuals. Similarly, it may also come to seem natural to them that the public carries the costs of their private lifestyle choices—a fitting tribute to the unique service they render to the public through their very perseverance in office. Moreover, when faced with any countervailing pressures on such issues—and especially with institutional pressures, for instance from legal officials—elected leaders who have lost the distinction between private and public may very well push back. Instead of mending their ways, they will oppose any institutional checks that prevent them from treating the country as their own personal fiefdom, and portray such checks—to themselves and to others—as ungrateful and undemocratic.

Now, all of these dynamics can, in principle, occur in any electoral political system in which formal institutions and the informal collective ethos allow them to emerge. And this fact alone should remind us of the general hazards involved, for example, in an overly subservient citizenry, and perhaps even in formal regulations that do not impose any limits on how long any given individual can hold the country's highest elected office. Yet there is nonetheless ample reason to think that such pernicious dynamics represent an especially acute and especially predictable danger when the relevant leaders are media demagogues.

This is so for at least three reasons. First, media demagogues' elevation of style over substance, emphasized above, means that they will have fewer meaningful public commitments *ab initio*. Moreover, the primacy of style over substance, combined with the sheer pace of media demagogues' lies and zig-zags, means that these demagogues will be especially quick to shed whatever limited substantive commitments they do have once in office, replacing them with a core commitment to their own private interest.

Second, media demagogues are especially likely to engage in self-interested behavior once in office, because the general fusion of public and private interest is especially likely in their case. If nothing else, this is because such a fusion rests, as I noted above, on *self-deception*—that is, on leaders convincing themselves that their private interest is inseparable from the public interest. And media demagogues are especially likely to convince themselves that this is indeed the case.

Media demagogues are, first and foremost, gifted salespeople—and they tend to be gifted to an extent that leads them to buy their own product. This result is only natural if we consider the extent to which media demagogues immerse themselves in the virtual reality of the mass media they manage and manipulate so skillfully. After repeatedly telling the entire world, in numerous ways, that they alone can "save the nation," and after working time and again to present the appearance of a fusion between themselves and the state, media demagogues quite predictably come to believe their own rhetoric. That is why "the state is me" is considerably more likely to become a genuine mindset for the media demagogue than for any other kind of elected leader.

Finally, elected leaders who are media demagogues stand out in comparison to their peers when it comes to the likelihood that they will disrupt the normal workings of institutions of liberal democracy meant to check their power in general, and their ability to pursue their private interest in particular. This is true, if nothing else, because a key part of media demagogues' rise to power, as stressed above, revolves around their self-portrayal as an antithesis to the "corrupt elites" that shape and staff these institutions. The implications of this fact are particularly grave with regard to core *legal* institutions of liberal democracy. When their self-interested behavior predictably leads media demagogues to clash with legal authorities, media demagogues are more likely than other elected leaders to challenge these authorities and to try to undermine their public legitimacy, casting their own legal travails as nothing but the result of "political persecution" that conflicts with "the will of the people."

4.2.2 Trump and Berlusconi

Two elected leaders—current U.S. President Donald Trump, and former Italian Prime Minister Silvio Berlusconi—provide an especially vivid illustration of how media demagogues' multiple failures of personal integrity combine to threaten the integrity of liberal democracy.

Both men's credentials as media demagogues are impeccable, as we can evince by recalling the three aforementioned characteristics of such demagogues. Consider, first, media demagogues' self-portrayal as representatives of "the common people" battling corrupt elites. Trump's self-portrayal, as a political outsider fighting for "the common man" against "the swamp" of Washington DC, has been pivotal to his presidential campaign, as well as to his time in the White House, in much the same way that Berlusconi rose to power portraying himself as an alternative to the corrupt political establishment that was brought down by Italy's "clean hands" investigations of the early 1990s.

Now consider the second feature—recurrent use of lies and exploitation of irrational impulses in the electorate. The pace of Trump's exploitation of irrational fears and prejudice (not least against Hispanic migrants) has been matched only by the sheer pace of his distortions of the truth. The *Washington Post*, for example, documented 2,140 false or misleading claims made by Trump during his first year as President—a number that had already doubled by August 2018;[13] as of October 2019, the number stood at almost 13,500 false or misleading claims, an average of about fourteen such claims a day.[14] Berlusconi, during his heyday, was not far behind: repeatedly warning his electorate of utterly fanciful "communist plots" against him personally and the nation as a whole; routinely castigating, and in some cases even actively ensuring the sacking of, journalists who published inconvenient facts concerning his personal and political conduct; and at one point even going so far as to create a fake city for international media consumption, proclaiming that "fiction is better than reality."[15]

Finally, both Trump and Berlusconi provide textbook examples of media demagogues' fusion with the media. Berlusconi's media empire, which has towered over the Italian media market, has been at the very heart of both his commercial and political prominence. Trump does not own a media empire, but it is nonetheless true that Trump, in the words of the *New York Times*' White House correspondent, "does not exist without the media."[16] As Michael Wolff writes, already decades prior to entering politics, "The story of Trump was the story of how he tried to make himself a story."[17] Moreover, during the decades in which both tycoons constantly strived to make themselves a story, they cultivated a similar penchant for showmanship and sheer bravado. In both cases, this bravado would come to dominate their style as politicians, representing a (supposed) alternative to any serious political program.

These commonalities were not lost on political observers. As Trump began his unlikely political rise as a presidential contender, various pundits noted his striking resemblance to the Italian media demagogue who preceded him. The *New York Times*' Frank Bruni, for instance, spoke in 2015 of "Trumpusconi":

> They're both after omnipresence, and they both understood early on how crucial television was to that...They're priapic twins, identical in their insistence on being seen as paragons of irresistible lust. If hideously sexist utterances ensue, so be it...Trumpusconi is a study in the peril and pitfalls of unchecked testosterone and tumescent avarice...The two billionaires' tasteless words are

---

[13] Glenn Kessler, Salvador Rizzo, and Meg Kelly, "President Trump Has Made 4,229 False or Misleading Claims in 558 Days," *Washington Post*, August 1, 2018.

[14] Glenn Kessler, Salvador Rizzo, and Meg Kelly, "President Trump Has Made 13,435 False or Misleading Claims Over 993 Days," *Washington Post*, October 14, 2019.

[15] Maurizio Viroli, *The Liberty of Servants* (Princeton, NJ: Princeton University Press, 2011), 31.

[16] Tim Hains, "NYT's Maggie Haberman: Trump Thought the Presidency Would Be Like Being Mayor of New York," *RealClearPolitics*, February 1, 2018, at https://www.realclearpolitics.com/video/2018/02/01/nyts_maggie_haberman_trump_thought_presidency_would_be_like_being_nyc_mayor_in_the_1980s.html.

[17] Michael Wolff, *Fire and Fury: Inside the Trump White House* (New York: Hanry Holt, 2017), 74.

so interchangeable that it's sometimes hard to tell who said what...Both men have learned that they can turn such cloddishness to their advantage, by casting it as unvarnished candor. Sloppy talk becomes straight talk. Insult becomes authenticity, even if it's pure theater and so long as it's a hell of a show. And self-regard goes a long, long way. It can be mistaken for wisdom. It can masquerade as vision. With enough of it, the clown transforms himself into a ringleader.[18]

The same year, Rula Jebreal, writing for the *Washington Post*, presciently warned that under-estimating Trump's "calculated buffoonery" would be just as dangerous as was the case with Berlusconi's:

Berlusconi presented himself as Italy's strongman, speaking like a barman, selling demonstrably false promises of wealth and grandeur for all...Like Trump, Berlusconi [was] using his ugly gaffes as an effective, disruptive campaign strategy to distract both from his lack of well-thought-out policy ideas, as well as his dangerous ignorance on foreign policy. That seems to be Trump's plan, too...

Trump's political path has been carved by a media culture that favors entertainment over news. Political debate and discussion on TV have been reduced to mud-wrestling...Berlusconi's opponents fell into his PR trap in the same way in Italy, rushing to condemn his gaffes and his deliberately provocative statements calculated to rouse the far right...It is precisely that authoritarian demagoguery wrapped in comedy that Trump has brought to American politics...So it's now urgent that America learns the lessons taught (and havoc wrought) when Italy's political and media establishment underestimated Berlusconi. They viewed him as a joke, an ignorant buffoon, and he was widely dismissed as a comical figure, unfit to lead a serious country. None of that stopped him.[19]

[18] Frank Bruni, "La Dolce Donald Trump," *New York Times*, June 18, 2015.
[19] Rula Jebreal, "Laughing at a Buffoon Won't Stop Him From Having an Impact on Politics," *The Washington Post*, September 21, 2015. Weeks before the presidential elections that Trump won, *The Guardian* similarly observed that "the parallels between Berlusconi and Trump are striking": "Beyond wealth, Berlusconi, like Trump, always painted himself as an outsider, as anti-establishment, even when he was prime minister. And, like Trump, Berlusconi's appeal was populist and linked to his individual personality...his electoral campaigns were all about him. Nothing else mattered. He dominated the agenda from start to finish...He was also reluctant to accept the verdict of the electorate as final when he lost. He would make frequent (and unsubstantiated) claims of electoral fraud and ballot-stuffing. Remind you of anyone? He also created a set of enemies against which he could mobilise his followers: the judiciary, the media (despite owning much of it), politics itself, Communism, women (he often commented on the appearance of female opponents) and the EU and the euro. He presented himself as a victim of political correctness gone mad, an ordinary/extraordinary man speaking his mind. He promised the world, and it mattered little if he was quickly proved wrong, or had no intention of fulfilling any of his promises." John Foot, "We've Seen Donald Trump Before—His Name Was Silvio Berlusconi," *The Guardian*, October 21, 2016.

While many of the commonalities between Trump and Berlusconi warrant attention, here I wish to highlight two shared features in particular. The first is the extraordinary ease with which both men, always on the lookout for an immediate "media win," have been willing to contradict their own previous public pronouncements, no matter how recent, whenever doing so seemed beneficial from a PR point of view. During Trump's 2016 campaign, for example, he "committed" himself to the deportation of immigrants, even though in 2012 he poured scorn on Mitt Romney's self-deportation proposal as causing republicans to "lose everybody who is inspired to come into this country."[20] Trump similarly had little trouble completely changing his stance on abortion rights or on universal health care (vehemently endorsed in the past, but opposed once associated with President Obama). Even the "nationalist" label that Trump has often touted has carried no stable meaning—nothing by way of a stable political vision.[21] Trump's conduct as President, as I will go on to note below, has scarcely been different.

What about Trump's Italian counterpart? According to Jebreal, at least, Berlusconi's zig-zags "may have been even more shameless." She recalls the following encounter with Berlusconi as Prime Minister:

In 2005, I was one of five journalists from the Middle East invited to brief Berlusconi on how to improve his relationship with the Muslim world—whose civilization he had dismissed as inferior and backward. Berlusconi feared that Italy would be targeted for terrorist attacks similar to those seen in London and Madrid... My journalist colleagues and I unanimously advised him to distance himself from the Iraq invasion, of which he had been an enthusiastic backer. The following day, Berlusconi appeared on my TV news show and proceeded to deny having *ever* supported the Iraqi war... *If necessary to avoid a potential pitfall, Berlusconi was willing to deny in the evening precisely what he had stated that same morning.*[22]

Bearing such zig-zags in mind, let us consider a second key feature of Trump and Berlusconi's political conduct: the extraordinary degree to which both of these demagogues have refused to distinguish between the public interest and their own

---

[20]   Michael Kranish and Marc Fisher, *Trump Revealed* (New York: Scribner, 2016), 310.

[21]   As Joshua Green put it: "Trump doesn't believe in nationalism or any other political philosophy—he's fundamentally a creature of his own ego. Over the years, Trump repeated certain populist themes: the United States is being ripped off in trade deals by foreign competitors; elites and politicians are stupid crooks. These were expressions of an attitude—a marketing campaign—rather than commitments to a set of policies. When Trump sensed nationalism was no longer generating a positive response for him, he abandoned it, announcing... 'I'm a nationalist and a globalist,' as if the two weren't opposed. At heart, Trump is an opportunist driven by a desire for public acclaim, rather than a politician with any fixed principles." Joshua Green, *Devil's Bargain: Steve Bannon, Donald Trump, and the Storming of the Presidency* (New York: Penguin, 2017), 241.

[22]   Jebreal, "Laughing at a Buffoon."

private interest. This refusal has been manifest in both demagogues' fusion of their private persona and their public role. Thus, for example, just as Berlusconi made it a point to repeatedly hold state receptions in his private mansions, so Trump himself, and other members of his administration, have repeatedly used state occasions to advertise various aspects of the Trump family's various private business ventures, and in many cases advanced these ventures directly through state functions. More generally, both men have clearly considered it natural that various forms of symbolic public deference—even veneration—toward their office increasingly take the form of deference and veneration of them as individuals: if Berlusconi was keen to use every symbol of the state as "a gaudy throne and an adoring mirror,"[23] the same has been true for the American President—as evident, for example, in his transformation of presidential medallions, formerly commemorating the institution of the presidency and the national motto (E pluribus unum), into a presentation of the President's private estates.[24]

These symbolic transgressions upon the basic norms of liberal democracy have been accompanied by a fusion of private and public with tangible practical implications. Thus, for example, given that Trump has refused to divest from his business empire upon becoming President, it was all too predictable that claims about this empire reaping massive profits from his presidency, and about his private business partners exerting far-from-innocent influence on his policies, would proliferate.[25] On this as on so many other fronts, Trump is following Berlusconi's "shining" example. The Italian media mogul not only refrained from even the thought of divestment. As the *Economist* observed in yet another profile noting the profound similarities between Trump and Berlusconi, "ad-personam laws" were a Berlusconi trademark during his reign.[26]

However, the most important aspect of "Trumpusconi's" fusion of public and private, and the one that has posed the greatest danger to the integrity of liberal democracy in their respective countries, concerns their personal clashes with the law, and their sustained, explicit attempts to place themselves above the law. These attempts, in turn, are linked directly to both media demagogues' marked absence of personal integrity—an absence that made their clashes with the law predictable, arguably even over-determined.

[23] Bruni, "La Dolce Donald Trump."

[24] Kenneth P. Vogel, "Trump Leaves His Mark on a Presidential Keepsake," *New York Times*, June 24, 2018.

[25] "Take any hot-button issue of the past year, and there's a good chance Trump's tenants lobbied the federal government on it, either in support of or in opposition to the administration's position," *Forbes* noted in February 2018, adding that "at least three dozen known Trump tenants have meaningful relationships with the federal government, from contractors to lobbying firms to regulatory targets." See Dan Alexander, "Trump's Biggest Potential Conflict of Interest Is Hiding in Plain Sight," *Forbes*, February 28, 2018, at www.forbes.com/sites/danalexander/2018/02/13/trump-conflicts-of-interest-tenants-donald-business-organization-real-estate-assets-pay/#592cf2848f97.

[26] See, e.g., "What Donald Trump and Silvio Berlusconi Have in Common," *The Economist*, November 10, 2016.

One way to evince this point is to consider the intimate link between Trumpusconi's personal struggles with the law and the pair's marked lack of any public vision—a lack I identified above as a quintessential integrity failure for any public figure. In Berlusconi's case, this failure was all too apparent from the outset. It is "an open secret," as one scholar put it to *NPR* in 2011, that Berlusconi "entered politics to avoid trials and safeguard his empire."[27] When one's basic reason for becoming a politician to begin with has nothing to do with the public—when it entirely concerns one's private desire to escape the grip of the law—then it should not come as a shock when one proceeds to do what Berlusconi actually did time and again: to craft laws that would retroactively de-criminalize grave offenses for which he was convicted, or shield him from prosecution while in office.[28]

In Trump's case, the lack of any serious public commitment has been manifest in the marked absence of even minimal study and reflection on public affairs. This absence directly conflicts with the aforementioned requirements of personal integrity in a politician: a U.S. President who has not bothered to master even the U.S. constitution fails integrity's requirements of reflectiveness to a truly extraordinary extent.[29] But the fact that Trump has failed to engage in even the most rudimentary study of his public role and its legal foundations has also been intimately connected to the legal problems that have dogged his presidency from the very beginning. Trump's failure to grasp that his firing of FBI director James Comey could easily be interpreted as an attempt to halt FBI investigations, and therefore as an impeachable obstruction of justice, was only one prominent example of this connection.

Such failures, it should be emphasized, are not incidental to Trump's media demagoguery, any more than they were with Berlusconi. It is *not* the case that Trump is a media demagogue who "also happens" to fail to reflect on the basic institutional setup surrounding the public office he holds. Rather, this failure to reflect—or at least *refusal* to reflect—has been at the heart of Trump's media-driven campaign, a campaign that remained fundamentally unaltered

---

[27] Sylvia Poggioli, "How Berlusconi Created a Country in His Own Image," *NPR*, November 13, 2011, at https://www.npr.org/2011/11/13/142278142/how-berlusconi-created-a-country-in-his-own-image.

[28] Appointing his personal lawyers as parliament members was only one way to achieve the desired result. In those cases where Berlusconi was unable to wiggle his way out of conviction by grinding the legal procedure to a near halt and enjoying the benefits of statutes of limitations, his lawyers were also sent to finish the job as legislators. As Maurizio Viroli fumed during Berlusconi's last term in power, "the trusted right-hand men of the signore are at the same time legislators and his defenders. If their skill at defending him from the laws proves inadequate, then they will arrange to defend him by passing new laws." Viroli, *The Liberty of Servants*, 73–4.

[29] See, e.g., Ted Barrett, "Pol: Trump Defended Articles of the Constitution That Don't Exist," *CNN*, July 8, 2016, at https://edition.cnn.com/2016/07/08/politics/sanford-questions-trump-constitution-gaffe/index.html.

upon his entrance into the White House.[30] Thus, for example, it is partly because he has consistently refused to engage in serious reflection on any policy topic that he would always be ready with a quick statement, however ill thought, that would allow him to seize the media initiative away from his opponents, while casting their comparative slowness not as a matter of minimal reflection on the fundamental issues at stake in public life, but rather as simply "low energy."[31] In much the same way, Trump's carefree dismissal of any kind of study and expertise on substantive issues as "overrated" was part of his electoral appeal as a supposed "fresh voice" that would not get bogged down in dreary policy debates that often yield uninspiring results. Deferring to experts and getting stymied by the complexity of facts, after all, was what "politicians" do, whereas Trump's populist appeal lay precisely in his "not being a politician."[32] Much like Berlusconi, he was supposed to be the supremely self-confident businessman, who by dint of his "pure instinct" would succeed where all the timid, gray bureaucrats have failed before.

Now, the preceding paragraphs should not be taken to suggest that, simply in virtue of their shared media demagoguery, Trump and Berlusconi's respective personal clashes with the law were bound to be entirely identical. But I do want to stress the extent to which their shared media demagoguery has made it predictable that both men would respond to their personal legal travails in very similar fashion. Rather than moderate their exercise of power in response to their legal troubles, both media demagogues pursued the opposite path—doubling down in their attacks on the "corrupt system" that is supposedly haunting them, and constantly striving to place themselves above the law. Thus Trump proudly announced that he has the power to pardon himself,[33] sent his lawyers to explain that the President "cannot obstruct justice" since he is "the chief law enforcer of the United States,"[34] and asked the FBI to investigate itself in order to undermine the special counsel appointed to investigate him.[35] Berlusconi opted for legislation

[30] See, e.g., Mark Landler, "On Foreign Policy, President Trump Reverts to Candidate Trump," New York Times, April 3, 2018.
[31] See, e.g., Ashley Parker, "Jeb Bush Sprints to Escape Donald Trump's 'Low Energy' Label," New York Times, December 29, 2015.
[32] Thus Wolff, for example, suggests that for Steve Bannon, at one point Trump's chief strategist, "Trump's hyperbole, exaggerations, flights of fancy, improvisations, and general freedom toward and mangling of the facts, were products of the basic lack of guile, pretense, and impulse control that helped create the immediacy and spontaneity that was so successful with so many on the stump." Wolff, Fire and Fury, 45.
[33] Kevin Breuninger, "Trump: 'I Have the Absolute Right to Pardon Myself '," CNBC, June 4, 2018, at https://www.cnbc.com/2018/06/04/trump-i-have-the-absolute-right-to-pardon-myself.html.
[34] Steve Benen, "Trump Lawyers Not Done Suggesting the President Is Above the Law," MSNBC, December 5, 2017, at http://www.msnbc.com/rachel-maddow-show/trump-lawyers-not-done-suggesting-the-president-above-the-law.
[35] David Leonhardt, "Trump's Attacks on the Rule of Law Reach a New Level," New York Times, May 21, 2018.

that will shield him from criminal prosecution ex-ante—a "monstrosity,"[36] as one angry commentator put it, that was only blocked by Italy's supreme court after being in place for a year. When that happened, Berlusconi, just like Trump, reverted to his well-worn strategy of casting legal authorities as politically biased; in 2009, for example, when forced once again to answer to legal charges concerning bribery, Berlusconi proclaimed: "The real Italian anomaly is not Silvio Berlusconi but communist prosecutors and communist judges in Milan who have attacked him again and again since he entered politics and decided to attack the power of the communists."[37] Substitute "liberal" for "communist" and the statement would very likely match many of Trump's recurrent grievances.

All of these aggressive reactions, in turn, have been predictable in at least two ways. First, these reactions represent a natural continuation of both demagogues' electoral campaigns: it is only natural for demagogues who vow to "clean up the swamp" to proclaim that "the swamp is fighting back" by fighting them personally. Second, in both cases, their ability to deceive themselves predictably led both Trump and Berlusconi to portray the personal legal challenges they face as nothing but an illegitimate "witch hunt."[38] Having told the entire world, time and again, that these challenges are themselves illicit, both demagogues have clearly come to "buy" their own message—believing that the "legal persecution" they have suffered is rooted in various lies and in a simple desire to destroy them personally.[39] Furthermore, both media demagogues have managed to convince themselves that the personal challenges they have faced—whether coming from critical media or from legal authorities—are fundamentally *undemocratic*, insofar as these challenges overlook the "mandate to rule" they have received from the people.[40]

What all of these points suggest is that the failures of personal integrity that are central to the conduct of media demagogues such as Trump and Berlusconi not only lead them, quite directly and predictably, to personal clashes with the law. To make things even worse, these failures of personal integrity—not least those associated with self-deception—also mean that media demagogues will *not*, of their own accord, back away from these clashes. This means, among other things,

---

[36] Foot, "We've Seen Donald Trump Before."
[37] Philip Pullella, "Silvio Berlusconi Says Communist Judges Out to Destroy Him," *Reuters*, October 28, 2009, at https://www.reuters.com/article/us-italy-berlusconi/silvio-berlusconi-says-communist-judges-out-to-destroy-him-idUSTRE59R1JX20091028.
[38] See, e.g., "Victim of Witch-Hunt, Says Berlusconi," *Sydney Morning Herald*, September 27, 2012; John Schoen, "Trump Is Tweeting 'Witch Hunt' a Lot More Than He Used to, as Mueller Probe Grinds on and Manafort Goes on Trial," *CNBC*, August 1, 2018, at https://www.cnbc.com/2018/08/01/trumps-witch-hunt-tweets-are-getting-more-frequent-as-mueller-probe.html.
[39] See, e.g., Richard Owen, "Sick Silvio Berlusconi Phones TV Show to Rant at 'Conspirators'," *The Times*, October 29, 2009, at https://www.thetimes.co.uk/article/sick-silvio-berlusconi-phones-tv-show-to-rant-at-conspirators-fb2j6sjl2c6.
[40] See, e.g., Michael Shear, "'I'm President and They're Not': Trump Attacks Media at Faith Rally," *New York Times*, July 1, 2017; Elisabetta Povoledo, "Berlusconi Calls Italian Judiciary a 'Cancer of Democracy'," *New York Times*, June 25, 2008.

that other political actors, as well as ordinary citizens, must firmly back the legal system as it examines the conduct of media demagogues. With such backing, there is *some* chance that these demagogues will be restrained. Very late in the day, this was (to an extent) the case with Berlusconi, whose never-ending political ambitions, even as an octogenarian, were hampered when the Italian Senate banned him from holding public office for six years following his irrevocable conviction for tax fraud.[41] It remains to be seen whether this will also be the case with Trump, who, in the words of the *New York Times*, "has attacked the law enforcement apparatus of his own government like no other president in history, and who has turned the effort into an obsession."[42]

4.3 The Subtler Demagogue: The Case of Benjamin Netanyahu

Having canvassed some of the central dangers that media demagogues' failures of personal integrity pose to the integrity of liberal democracy, I now want to further sharpen these dangers by illustrating just how broad is their scope. I wish to show that even elected media demagogues who, unlike Trump and Berlusconi, have had serious substantive policy commitments and who are far from buffoons predictably come, over time, to share many core attributes with their far less reflective counterparts. Taken together, the corrupting influence exerted by long-held political power, and the self-deception that is made so much easier by an entire life spent in virtual, media-generated reality, ultimately lead even intellectually accomplished media demagogues to conduct themselves in a manner that strongly resembles those media demagogues who are far less intellectually gifted.

I devote this section to a vivid Israeli example of these dynamics: Benjamin Netanyahu. My discussion of Netanyahu's case will be longer than the survey of Trump and Berlusconi offered above. One reason has to do with the difference in the global visibility of Italian and especially American politics on the one hand, and Israeli politics on the other. This difference means that a longer exposition is therefore in order with regard to Netanyahu (or, as he is more commonly known, "Bibi").[43]

---

[41] See, e.g., "Italy's Senate Expels Ex-PM Silvio Berlusconi," *BBC*, November 23, 2013, at https://www.bbc.com/news/world-europe-44092700. True to form, Berlusconi responded by labeling the Senate's decision a "day of mourning for democracy." Equally true to form, Berlusconi also fought on in the European Court of Human Rights, and was eventually able to get the ban scrapped, although without returning to the premiership (as of the time of writing). See "Silvio Berlusconi: Ban on Former PM Holding Office Scrapped," *BBC*, May 12, 2018, at https://www.bbc.com/news/world-europe-44092700.

[42] Mark Mazzetti, Maggie Haberman, Nicholas Fandos, and Michael Schmidt, "Intimidation, Pressure and Humiliation: Inside Trump's Two-Year War on the Investigations Encircling Him," *New York Times*, February 19, 2019.

[43] Those readers who are familiar with Netanyahu's zig-zags, self-seeking rationalizations, and self-deception, and with the ways in which all of these feed into the threats he poses to the most fundamental liberal institutions in Israel, can skip ahead to 4.4.

Another reason to discuss Netanyahu in special detail is that, in contrast to both Trump and Berlusconi, no one—not even the many critics who disdain Netanyahu—has ever labeled him a "buffoon" or a "joke" of any sort. On the contrary: Netanyahu is routinely described, even by his most ardent detractors, as a talented, intellectually sophisticated man.[44] This marked difference may generate—among other things—the expectation that the kinds of policy zig-zags with which Berlusconi and Trump have been identified will not be present in Netanyahu's case. Yet a key part of what I want to show—in some detail—is that Netanyahu's overwhelming focus on the media has made him just as prone to zig-zags as has been the case with "Trumpusconi."

Finally, it is important for my purposes to show the extent to which Netanyahu, while differing from Berlusconi and Trump insofar as he has actually held serious policy commitments, has also predictably relinquished those commitments under the pressures of the corrupting effects of long-held power. This process, combined with a remarkable degree of self-deception, has led to Netanyahu's fusion of the public interest with his own private interests. All of these, in turn, have been greatly amplified by the media reality in which Netanyahu has come to live. The result has been a *functional equivalence* between Netanyahu's conduct and that of elected leaders of the "Trumpusconi" variety. This functional equivalence reveals the force—and the extent of the danger—that the "mediatization" of politics poses not only to the integrity of elected leaders, but through them to the integrity of liberal democracy.

The roots of this functional equivalence lie with Netanyahu's long-standing refusal to distinguish between media management and substantive political work. Netanyahu's own writing has reflected this refusal,[45] but his adherence to this "fusion of media and politics"[46] has also been documented by scores of observers—journalists, academics, advisers, and fellow politicians.

One key piece of evidence, abundantly clear already during Netanyahu's first term as Prime Minister (1996–9), was the sheer amount of time that Netanyahu spent on dealing with the media. Seeing as Netanyahu spent hours upon hours talking to them or to the cameras, journalists had started—half-jokingly,

---

[44] One key detractor and biographer, whom I will cite here at length, says of Netanyahu: "He is a leader blessed with talents and abilities... He is quick on the uptake and has substantial analytical skills... incomparable verbal abilities and the properties of a superlative politician." Ben Caspit, *The Netanyahu Years* (New York: St. Martin's Press, 2017 [trans. Ora Cummings]), 158.

[45] In a book he had written Netanyahu implicitly revealed the extent to which he was influenced by American media culture: "It might have been expected that Israel would recognize the fact that one cannot separate policy from explanation. But this is not the case [while] in other countries it is taken for granted. U.S presidents and most world leaders do not usually make important decisions without examining the probable reactions to these decisions in public opinion... The decision making process includes a detailed discussion of how the decision will affect the public, and what should be done to elicit a positive reaction." Quoted in Yoram Peri, *Telepopulism* (Palo Alto, CA: Stanford University Press, 2004), 192.

[46] Peri, *Telepopulism*, 101.

half-seriously—to ask each other if and when Netanyahu actually governed. It only gradually transpired that for Netanyahu there was no "real government" that is distinct from the media. The style—the appearance, the presentation of politics—had actually replaced the substance. As Yoram Peri put it:

> If in his first months in office it seemed as if the television appearances were designed to explain, or complement, his political action, it later appeared that the many press conferences, photo-ops, political spectacles and media events were designed to replace political action—that they themselves *were* the political action.[47]

The same "pseudo-politics" has remained with Netanyahu ever since, including throughout the decade (2009–19) during which his hold on the Prime Minister's office has been virtually unchallenged. To be sure, in recent years, Netanyahu has dramatically decreased his press interviews (outside of election seasons). But that is a merely cosmetic change. Instead of interviews, Netanyahu constantly uses his surrogates, as well as recorded messages and social media—much like Trump—to shape public discourse, bypassing journalists and directly addressing his supporters.

In light of all this, it is far from surprising that, much like Berlusconi and Trump, Netanyahu has emphasized short-term media "achievements" throughout his political career, even when these achievements are based on (more or less blatant) lies. At the turn of the millennium, Dan Meridor, a veteran politician unusual in his reputation as a principled man, captured the problem in the following words:

> Bibi behaves as if he could cheat all over again every day. His stage is television, and there it all starts and ends. Bibi understood one of the central things in the modern world, and that's mass media . . . With Bibi, the whole emphasis [is] only on image—not reality. For him the world's a screen, and reality has no consequence—only the reality you produce on the screen matters. Bibi went into it big time, and he deals with media image incessantly . . . For him, the essence of policy is to sit in the morning with some advisors and phrase the "line of the day," a sentence to be repeated endlessly in every radio and television . . . He understands reality isn't relevant to his re-election, and then creates a reality that suits his needs . . . Bibi is a liar who upgraded lying into an art.[48]

---

[47] Peri, *Telepopulism*, 179.

[48] Quoted in Orli Azoulay-Katz, *The Man Who Defeated Himself* (Tel Aviv: Yediot Ahronot, 1999) (Hebrew), 113–16 (all Hebrew translations are mine unless noted otherwise). These remarks were made in the late 1990s. Meridor resigned from Netanyahu's first government in 1997, after serving as Treasury Secretary for a year. In a 2017 book on Netanyahu's media tactics, Israeli media scholar Baruch Leshem quotes several media advisers who have worked with Netanyahu over the years, all of

In turn, Netanyahu's media-infused short-termism, and his willingness to lie repeatedly to achieve even the most fleeting media advantages, led to constant zig-zags in his policy pronouncements. This has been the case even with regard to the most macro-level, fundamental questions in Israeli public life, such as those of the Israeli-Palestinian conflict. Thus, for example, in June 2009, once again Prime Minister, Netanyahu formally announced for the first time his acceptance of the idea of a Palestinian state. But since then, Netanyahu has been constantly twisting his message—assuring the right-wing that his "vision" for a Palestinian state is intentionally conditioned on terms that he knows the Palestinians will never accept, while simultaneously insisting to foreign leaders angry about his deceit that he is always willing to negotiate for peace in good faith.[49]

Things look no better with regard to more minor public issues. In 2011, for example, multiple newspapers united in ridiculing Netanyahu's "zig-zags" on a motley crew of policy issues, most of which should have been too small to attract the attention of a Prime Minister, but all of them taken up by Netanyahu in pursuit of short-term media gains—whether concerning small new taxes, military appointments, or even the location of the emergency room at a specific hospital in Israel's periphery. In each of these instances, Netanyahu declared a new policy with great pomp and circumstance, only to retreat at the first sign of media or public opposition.[50] The prominent political pundit Ben Caspit crisply summarized both Netanyahu's lack of vision and his profound lack of steadfastness as follows:

> Israel's incumbent Prime Minister is Benjamin Netanyahu. This is a hollow title. Netanyahu holds the title. But he refuses the position. For two years he has not made a single significant decision. For two years it has yet to happen that Bibi encountered public, media, or political pressure, or simply difficulty, and did not immediately change his mind, regret, zig-zag, sometimes even choose a double somersault, until he escaped to some feeble compromise and continued from it straight to the next entanglement...the man who serves as Israel's Prime Minister has no idea what he wants to do. He has no plan. He has no goal. He has no agenda. There is no government action, however simple, that does not, under his hands...turn into an embarrassing farce.[51]

---

whom repeat Meridor's basic view. See Leshem's *Netanyahu: Master of Political Marketing* (Tel Aviv: Matar, 2017) (Hebrew), at 371.

[49] "He will always be ready to meet with [Palestinian Authority President] Abu-Mazzen in any place of Abu-Mazzen's choosing, to continue peace negotiations. To world leaders he will make clear, in case peace talks break down, that he has more ideas to advance them up his sleeve...the balls he juggles in the air, like a skilled magician, must never drop to the ground, not even for a moment. Leshem, *Netanyahu*, 258.

[50] See, e.g., Nadav Peri, "King Zag-Zag," *Globes*, July 24, 2012, at https://www.globes.co.il/news/article.aspx?did=1000768483 (Hebrew).

[51] Ben Caspit, "Dr. Benjamin and Mr. Netanyahu: Two Years of Zig-Zag," *Maariv*, February 10, 2011, at https://www.makorrishon.co.il/nrg/online/1/ART2/210/529.html?hp=1&cat=479 (Hebrew).

Fast forward from these 2011 remarks to the present, and very little has changed. Netanyahu, for example, has long opposed a law pushed by the radical right, to officially confiscate Palestinian lands in the West Bank, only to flip under pressure and support the law, while simultaneously telling foreign leaders that he hopes Israel's Supreme Court strikes the law down.[52] In April 2018, in the course of less than forty-eight hours, Netanyahu made multiple contradictory statements regarding his "solution to the crisis" of African refugees in Tel Aviv—unable to decide whether to concede to the extreme right demand to force more refugees to leave, or whether to allow more refugees to stay, in line with Israel's international obligations.[53] In July 2018, Netanyahu formally announced his support for the inclusion of LGBT couples in a new law making provisions for parenthood through surrogacy, only to flip days later under the threat of ultra-orthodox politicians leaving his coalition in case of such inclusion. Many more examples could be given along similar lines, but the basic point should be clear. To put it mildly: steadfastness in general, and promise-keeping in particular, are require-ments of integrity that Netanyahu fails to an extent that sets him apart even from many other politicians.

What exactly is the cause of these recurrent failures of personal integrity? Why is it that Netanyahu is always so willing to make new promises, or to bend to the demands of the relevant audience, even if he made diametrically opposite prom-ises and concessions to another audience the day before? The most common explanation, advanced by many observers over the years, has been that Netanyahu's zeal for power is his only real political commitment.[54] This explan-ation is obviously true to a significant extent. But three further points are import-ant in any complete picture of the motivations driving the man's political conduct.

The first point is that, arguably in contrast to Berlusconi and Trump, Netanyahu really *had* certain substantive policy commitments that were the result

---

[52] See Yehonatan Lis, "Knesset Approves Law Confiscating Palestinian Lands," *Haaretz*, February 7, 2017, at http://www.haaretz.co.il/news/politi/1.3630778 (Hebrew); see also Ian Fisher, "Israel Passes Provocative Law to Retroactively Legalize Settlements," *New York Times*, February 6, 2017; Barak Ravid, "The Israeli Response to Foreign Criticism of the Confiscation Law: The High Court Might Strike It Down," *Haaretz*, February 7, 2017, at http://www.haaretz.co.il/news/politics/.premium-1. 3658137 (Hebrew); Shai Nir, "Regulation—Till the Judges Decide: The High Court Continues to Freeze the 'Regulation Law'," *Davar Rishon*, December 5, 2017, at http://www.davar1.co.il/97796 (Hebrew).

[53] See, e.g., "Netanyahu Is Zigzagging: Freezing the Agreement on Asylum Seekers," *Calcalist*, April 2, 2018, at https://www.calcalist.co.il/local/articles/0,7340,L-3735429,00.html (Hebrew).

[54] Doron Rosenblum, a veteran political pundit known for his acerbic wit, went so far as to cast, in multiple columns over the years, "Netanyahu's desire to be Prime Minister" as an independent agent, casting its shadow over the real Netanyahu, whether or not the latter is actually Prime Minister. In one such column, Rosenblum invoked Gogol's tale of the nose: "Netanyahu sits at home or comes up the stairs for some meeting—but 'Netanyahu's desire to be Prime Minister' is riding in a carriage at the same time through Nevsky Prospect, ceremoniously dressed...Netanyahu is leafing through the budget books in his office—but 'Netanyahu's desire to be Prime Minister' is up and about in the foyer, sweaty and restless; looking for opportunities, exchanging secret whispers...". Doron Rosenblum, "In General," *Harretz*, June 2, 2004, www.haaretz.co.il/misc/1.971405 (Hebrew).

of serious reflection. As the years passed, however, these commitments were increasingly eroded, becoming secondary to his political survival.

The sharpest example of this erosion concerns Netanyahu's views with regard to the appropriate response to terrorism. Many commentators have pointed out that Netanyahu would have probably never entered politics to begin with, had his admired older brother not been killed while commanding a famous counter-terrorism military operation. An uncompromising stance against terrorism has accordingly been essential to the younger Netanyahu's public activity, going all the way to international policy conferences he organized in his brother's memory, to the early books he wrote, and to his diplomatic work during the 1980s. It is therefore not hard to believe that, throughout the decades in which Netanyahu repeatedly opposed concessions and negotiations with terrorists, he was express-ing genuine political convictions. These convictions led him, more specifically, to oppose the release of terrorists in exchange for kidnapped Israeli soldiers. As Leader of the Opposition, for example, Netanyahu vehemently protested govern-ment decisions to release "murderers for nothing," arguing that such concessions would only incentivize "further acts of terrorism." But in 2011, back in the Prime Minister's seat, Netanyahu, desperate to divert attention from massive protests over socio-economic issues, left all this legacy behind: he led his government to release more than a thousand terrorists, including dozens sentenced to life in prison, in exchange for the release of one Israeli soldier, Gilad Shalit, who was kidnapped five years earlier and held by Hamas. Caspit describes Netanyahu's decision as follows:

> It was classic Bibi. After having "educated" the world not to surrender to terror
> and never negotiate with terrorists, after writing books and convening congresses
> and delivering hundreds of speeches and berating all the prisoner-exchange deals
> made by Israel over the years under other prime ministers, he was the one to cave
> in to terror, carrying out one of the most shameful incidents in Israel's
> history...He had set aside historic principles, all his beliefs and doctrines, for
> political profit...[55]

How could a Prime Minister who clearly detests compromises with terrorists justify such a deal? This question takes us to a second key feature of Netanyahu's endless political zig-zags: the centrality of self-deception and self-seeking ration-alizations. To the extent that Netanyahu has been able to rationalize his betrayal of his most firmly held policy convictions for the sake of surviving as Prime Minister, this is largely because, over time, Netanyahu has convinced himself that his private interest in power is *intertwined* with the public interest. In

---

[55] Caspit, *The Netanyahu Years*, 247.

Netanyahu's own eyes, whenever he compromises to maintain his grip on the Prime Minister's office, he is—*ipso facto*—benefiting the people: he serves the people by serving himself.[56]

The same self-deception has led Netanyahu to convince himself even of various easily disproven falsehoods that he has uttered in pursuit of a sharp "media effect." Thus, for instance, Netanyahu waxed poetic about his childhood trips through British-mandate Jerusalem, even though he was only born a year after the British mandate ended. Netanyahu also eulogized Rehavam Zeevi, an extreme right-wing leader who was assassinated in 2001, as a member of his government, even though Zeevi never served in any of his governments. In both—widely publicized—instances, though he was promptly rebutted by mocking critics, Netanyahu refused to concede. Instead, he chose, in the words of one of his former media advisers, to "rationalize things that did not happen, and to believe they had actually occurred."[57] Netanyahu, in other words, has a remarkable ability to believe his own rhetoric. And if this is the case with falsehoods that are so easily disproven, then it should be even less surprising that Netanyahu would be able to convince himself that it is a vital public interest that he continues to hold ever-increasing power.[58]

Netanyahu's self-seeking rationalization of his political survival as intertwined with the very survival of the state, combined with the erosion of his substantive policy commitments over time, connect to a third central feature of his conduct: the increasing, and predictable, threat that this conduct poses to the integrity of Israel's liberal democracy.

The criminal charges now hanging over Netanyahu's head, especially those that concern the freedom of the press, make this threat particularly manifest. One

---

[56] "'Without Bibi, Israel is doomed,' Sara [Netanyahu] would repeat to her interlocutors in the years when her husband was pushed into political exile, and even subsequently upon his return to government. He himself would say that he had to come back 'To save the country'... This messianic conception is what drives the couple's desperate need to hold on to power at any cost. They are firmly persuaded that their struggle is not for their own benefit; it's for the sake of the people and the state. [That is why]... they are amazed at criticism of trivialities like the massive expenses incurred by the prime minister's residence, their luxurious lifestyle, and their hedonistic extravagances." Caspit, *The Netanyahu Years*, 436.

[57] Quoted in Leshem, *Netanyahu*, 371.

[58] This is especially true with regard to Iran, Netanyahu's prime obsession. Caspit (*The Netanyahu Years*, 178–9) describes Netanyahu's mindset concerning "the Iranian issue" after his loss in the 1999 general elections as follows: "Iran was already building its nuclear program and Netanyahu was building a model of the approaching catastrophe. 'No one understands the danger,' he thought, 'better than I do.' He truly believed no one but him had the historical, intellectual, and mental attributes to bring together all the sane forces in the world to stop the second Holocaust." The many fallacies in this reasoning warrant a much longer treatment than I can offer here; only some of these fallacies were noted in the scathing critique of Netanyahu by Meir Dagan, the former head of Mossad (Israel's national security agency charged with handling Iran's nuclear project), who was directly subordinate to Netanyahu for several years. See, e.g., "Meir Dagan: Netanyahu Brought the Greatest Strategic Damage to Israel on the Iranian Issue," *Haaretz*, February 27, 2015, at https://www.haaretz.co.il/news/politics/1.2576367 (Hebrew).

example, featuring a criminal indictment for fraud and breach of trust, concerns negotiations between Netanyahu and the publisher of one of Israel's largest newspapers, who offered Netanyahu friendlier coverage throughout his media empire, in exchange for a new law that will limit the circulation of his most significant competitor, *Yisrael Hayom*, a newspaper widely seen to be under Netanyahu's control.[59] Another example concerns a criminal charge for bribery: according to this charge, Netanyahu, who appointed himself Communication Secretary, made policy decisions that conferred enormous financial benefits on Israel's largest telecommunications company (to the tune of at least half a billion dollars), in exchange for favorable media treatment secured by the company's owner, who also owns one of Israel's largest web portals.[60]

As the criminal allegations against him have gathered pace, Netanyahu's attacks on law-enforcement authorities, and his broader attempts to dismantle institutional checks on his power, have intensified markedly. In August 2017, for instance, Netanyahu announced to a crowd of virulent supporters that "the people are tired of the recruited media" which is "contemptuous of the people's choice," branded as "leftist" the anti-corruption protests targeting him, dismissed as "fake news" many of the "alleged facts" presented against him, and proclaimed: "the left, and the media, and they're the same thing... [are]... on an obsessive, unprecedented hunt against me and my family to carry out a regime change," because they "know they will keep losing in the polls, because our support only keeps increasing."[61] The fact that the Chief of Police and the Attorney General are his own appointees evidently did not lead Netanyahu to hesitate to portray the criminal allegations surrounding him as a left-wing conspiracy.

The same trends were evident even more recently. Clearly believing that electoral victory is his best bet of escaping his legal predicaments, Netanyahu crossed whatever few red lines he may have had left in the run-up to Israel's April 2019 elections. Desperate to maximize the size of his right-wing bloc, Netanyahu culti-vated a union among fringe right-wing parties, one of which is so extremist that its head was denied a U.S. visa because of his affinity with what the U.S. state department officially considers a Jewish terrorism organization.[62] To add insult to

---

[59] The following, matter-of-fact description from *The Economist* ("A Tough Deal to Swallow," April 8, 2015) is one telling example: "*Yisrael Hayom* is a freesheet owned by Sheldon Adelson, a casino mogul and supporter of Benjamin Netanyahu, Israel's prime minister. Its headlines are routinely approved by the prime minister's office."

[60] For a complete English translation of the full set of the criminal charges against Netanyahu, see "Full Text: The Criminal Allegations Against Netanyahu, as Set Out by Israel's AG," *The Times of Israel*, May 9, 2019, at https://www.timesofisrael.com/full-text-the-criminal-allegations-against-netanyahu-as-set-out-by-israels-ag.

[61] See, e.g., Raoul Wootliff, "At Netanyahu's Chilling Rally, Echoes of Trump's War on the Media," *Times of Israel*, August 10, 2017.

[62] As pointed out, for example, in Noah Siegel, "Otzma Party Is Dangerous. I Know Because I Banned Its Leader from the U.S.," *Jerusalem Post*, February 26, 2019.

injury, Netanyahu's party also pursued unprecedented vote repression tactics targeting Israel's Arab citizens.[63] Immediately following the elections, Netanyahu, directly contradicting his earlier denials, devoted himself to securing Berlusconi-style executive immunity protections, which would shield him from prosecution so long as he remains in office[64]—only to discover at the very last minute that he is unable to assemble a parliamentary majority for a new government. In response, Netanyahu effectively forced an unprecedented snap election, rather than allow his main opponent a chance to form a government, in blatant contradiction of the spirit of the law. In turn, during the run-up to those elections (September 2019), Netanyahu, his cronies, and his campaign staff further intensified attacks on "witch-hunting" legal authorities and on Israel's Arab minority. When this second national vote also proved inconclusive, Netanyahu used his iron grip on Israel's right-wing bloc to effectively force a third election (March 2020), which again left him short of an immunity-providing parliamentary majority. As this book goes to print (early May 2020), Netanyahu, weeks away from the commencement of his criminal trial, is widely seen as seeking a fourth election. He appears constitutionally unable to even contemplate resigning from office.

One could offer many more examples of Netanyahu's obsession with power. But the basic point should already be clear: the different threads of Netanyahu's media demagoguery and his multiple failures of personal integrity all reinforce each other, in a vicious cycle that predictably endangers the integrity of Israeli liberal democracy. Netanyahu's willingness to abandon his few policy commitments generated a vacuum that was predictably filled with his own private interests, while his obsession with controlling the media has been a key cause of the criminal charges that he is now facing. Netanyahu's never-ending quest for power, which may have been a "mere" obsession in previous decades, is now a personal necessity. And so, as Netanyahu's self-deception and the abandonment of any substantive policy beliefs intensify, it is not only Netanyahu who loses any shred of (personal) integrity. The integrity of (whatever remains of) Israeli liberal democracy is bound to suffer as well.

---

[63] See, e.g., Megan Specia, "Israel Voting Cameras Lowered Arab Turnout, Netanyahu Backers Claim," *New York Times*, April 10, 2019.

[64] See, e.g., "Opposition Lambastes Netanyahu After Report Says He Will Push for Immunity Law," *Times of Israel*, May 16, 2019. Integral to the realization of this goal, in turn, is a sustained effort to abolish the Supreme Court's power to strike down laws passed by parliament, including any law that will spare Netanyahu of a criminal trial or conviction. See, e.g., Raoul Wootliff, "Unbridled Government: How Netanyahu's Purported Plan Will Cripple the High Court," *The Times of Israel*, May 15, 2019. Had a small right-wing party garnered 1,300 (!) additional votes in the April elections, it would have crossed the electoral threshold, handing Netanyahu his coveted immunity majority, while effectively abolishing the Supreme Court. It is hard to overstate just how narrow was the escape of Israeli democracy, or how deeply it would have sunk following such "reform."

4.4 Integrity and Media Demagogues' Servants:
Returning to "Dirty Hands"

So far, I have spent the bulk of this chapter on the link between media demagogues' lack of integrity and the threat they pose to the integrity of liberal democracy. My aim in the remainder of the chapter is to examine how this link bears on the integrity of those who choose to serve or ally with media demagogues—a choice that, I assume, necessarily involves "dirty hands."

There are three main reasons why I wish to scrutinize this choice. First, such scrutiny should bring into view further implications of the important and complex relationship between integrity and clean hands outlined in Chapter 3. Second, the arguments I will develop here should also contribute more generally to political theory's discussions of "clean hands." Whereas these discussions have traditionally focused exclusively on leaders at the apex of political power, I hope to illustrate here the philosophical and practical significance of reflecting also on those surrounding such leaders. Finally, the discussions of "dirty hands" that have been most influential in political theory still exhibit a structure inherited from authors who have written centuries ago—from Machiavelli to Weber.[65] In contrast, I hope to help update scholarly accounts of the problem of dirty hands, by highlighting the shifts in its structure brought about by contemporary media.

With these goals in mind, I proceed as follows. In 4.4.1 and 4.4.2, I focus on media demagogues' servants. I seek to show that, possible appearances to the contrary notwithstanding, such servants cannot rationalize their service by invoking integrity. Instead, they "acquire" the integrity failures—including, crucially, the self-deception—of the media demagogues for whom they work. I then argue (in 4.4.3) that the same predicament befalls those who ally with media demagogues. In the next, final section (4.5), I use the topic of media demagogues' allies in order to dispel yet another classic fear about "integrity solutions" to dirty hands problems: namely, the fear that such solutions lead to dangerous fanaticism.

4.4.1 Media Demagogues' Servants: The Basic Problem

When speaking of media demagogues' "servants," I have in mind individuals who serve media demagogues as political operatives—"strategic advisers," spokespersons, and the like—rather than career government officials. These officials' public service typically precedes the demagogue's time in office and will often continue after the demagogue has left office. Not so for the political operatives on whom I focus in this section: they are the demagogue's personal appointments,

---

[65] See, most famously, Michael Walzer, "The Problem of Dirty Hands," *Philosophy & Public Affairs* 2 (1973): 160–80.

and once he leaves office, they should expect to have to do so too. The main question I want to pose with regard to such political operatives is simple in form. Can their integrity align with them serving media demagogues who have conquered highest office?

The best way to begin addressing this question is to make explicit two assumptions that make it a live issue. The first assumption is that by serving media demagogues, the relevant political operatives are dirtying their hands, and know themselves to be dirtying their hands. Such servants predictably become complicit in a variety of wrongs perpetrated by their boss: scapegoating of vulnerable minorities, cynical exploitation of fears and bigotry more generally, and, once again, a whole slew of blatant lies. The "stock figure" of the dirty hands literature, as Michael Walzer put it, is the lying leader.[66] But in most political circumstances, leaders do not lie alone. Their operatives also lie for them, repeatedly.

My second assumption, however, is that there are obvious reasons not to leave media demagogues alone with the power of highest office. If nothing else, this is because the very same integrity failures that are their key assets in the media-saturated competition for office become their key liabilities once *in* office. The degree to which their policy "commitments" shift with the popular wind, the ease with which they dispense with serious policy deliberation, and the extent to which they eschew any coherent governing plan may all be advantageous when campaigning, but they make it extremely difficult for government to function effectively, let alone well.

Given these problems, it is quite tempting for political operatives to think that even if serving media demagogues requires "dirtying hands," this is the right thing to do, and indeed the proper thing to do even in *integrity* terms. Such advisers may have very little appreciation for their boss' substantive policy skills, but precisely because these skills are so limited—the advisers might say—it is crucial that they be present to offer a steady hand at the helm, steering the demagogue away from acting on some of his worst impulses. To be sure, doing so requires that they entangle themselves in various forms of behavior and posturing from which they may very well recoil privately, and which in an ideal world they would have nothing to do with. But if they prioritize a commitment to the common good over such private feelings, are they not in fact acting in accordance with integrity's requirements—steadfastly incurring personal costs for the sake of morally crucial principles with which they identify?[67]

---

[66] Walzer, "The Problem of Dirty Hands," 163.

[67] That, for example, was the view of none other than Trump victim James Comey. When, for instance, the then-Homeland Security Secretary John Kelly revealed his intention of quitting after hearing of Comey's firing, the former FBI director strongly dissuaded him, arguing that "the country needed principled people around this president." See James Comey, *A Higher Loyalty* (New York: Macmillan, 2018), 264.

Although this reasoning is tempting, I believe that it is ultimately misleading. The integrity of political operatives is incompatible with them serving media demagogues. The main reason goes back to the relationship I outlined in Chapter 3 between integrity and clean hands. In that chapter, I suggested that this relationship is mediated through causal inquiries. One must identify plausible causal connections between dirty deeds and the promotion of fundamental moral commitments or projects. These connections, in turn, must be sufficiently clear, and sufficiently likely to materialize. Whenever this is not the case, integrity strongly pressures one to keep one's hands clean.

This understanding of the link between integrity and clean hands bears directly on whether political operatives' integrity can align with them serving media demagogues. If such service necessarily means dirtying one's hands, as I am assuming, then a political operative cannot serve media demagogues while also preserving a fundamental commitment to serve the common good. This is because any sensible political operative should know that she has extremely limited prospects of reliably steering a media demagogue toward policies that will advance the common good. One key reason, in turn, is that media demagogues are simply not the kind of leaders who can be reliably steered in *any* stable policy direction, especially over time and especially by any given political operative.

The sad paradox here is that the very same attributes which make media demagogues dangerous once in office (and that therefore ostensibly permit "dirty" service on the part of political operatives) also make it extraordinarily difficult for any given political operative to consistently push these demagogues toward certain policies and away from others. Such influence might be possible when the relevant operatives are working for a leader who espouses a systematic political vision, and who has the resolve to persist with this vision in the face of publicity costs. A leader of this sort may trust the long-term advisers that helped to build the overarching vision, may abide by their suggestions as to how to realize this vision, and may very well stick with these suggestions over the long haul, even in the face of various public relations crises.[68] However, media demagogues, almost by definition, are leaders of virtually the *opposite* sort.

Such leaders not only lack any genuine commitment to any systematic political vision worthy of the name. They also lack—in some cases *conspicuously* lack—the cool temperament that is essential for any particular adviser to be able to exert reliable influence over them. Because they live and breathe the frenzied pace of contemporary mass media—because they "see" so little apart from the next headline, spin, and soundbite—their trust in any adviser often seems to extend

---

[68] The hope for such long-term perseverance animates, for example, Andrew Sabl's discussion of "democratic constancy" in his *Ruling Passions* (Princeton, NJ: Princeton University Press, 2001). A key part of what I want to show here is that media demagogues lack such constancy to an extent that sets them apart even from the typical pandering politician.

only as far as the last PR success that this adviser has delivered, and often threatens to break down at the first PR "disaster" of which the relevant adviser is "guilty," no matter how great this adviser's level of objective expertise or knowledge of relevant facts. For the same reason, media demagogues are frequently tempted to discount the advice of any given political operative in the face of conflicting advice from others—even if this conflicting advice is far less informed—when doing so holds the promise of "winning" the next news cycle. This is true, moreover, even if all the actual facts and substantive arguments make the promise of such a "win" a distinctly hollow one.

Furthermore, media demagogues' overwhelming urge to sustain a constant media momentum frequently leads them to abandon advice they have already endorsed, whenever there are immediate publicity gains to be had. Thus, for instance, it is common for media demagogues to accept the advice of those who serve them to stand firm on a certain issue, and yet fail to act on the very same advice when the first opportunity arises to reap publicity gains from displays of flexibility.

Finally, given the sheer ubiquity of such phenomena, there is ample room to suspect that political operatives *themselves* know—if not in advance, then very shortly after starting to work for media demagogues—just how limited is their ability to influence such demagogues. Any competent observer of media demagogues—let alone anyone who has actually had an opportunity to work under them—should know that any attempt by their servants to "rein them in" is, in all probability, doomed from the start. But if this is right, then political operatives who serve such demagogues, and who try to justify this service by invoking their ability to "steer the demagogue in the right direction," are very likely to be guilty of self-deception. Such individuals are bound to know that they cannot *really* have anything like a lasting impact on their boss. Insofar as they tell themselves otherwise, they are either suffering from extraordinary hubris, or, more commonly, they are merely trying to cast a moral veneer on their self-interested pursuit of prestigious positions and the personal opportunities that come in their wake.

The ongoing travails of Donald Trump's servants provide an especially vivid example of these points. In fact, this example is so vivid that it is worth spelling out in some detail, even if many readers will already be acquainted with many of the relevant facts.

4.4.2 Trump's Servants

One of the least controversial claims one could make about the Trump White House is that Trump's concern with his media reputation has dominated his presidency. Consider, for instance, Michael Wolff's description of Trump's priorities during his first year in office:

Where past presidents might have spent portions of their day talking about the needs, desires and points of leverage among various members of Congress, the president...spent a great deal of time talking about a fixed cast of media personalities, trying to second-guess the real agendas and weak spots among cable anchors and producers and *Times* and *Post* reporters...Trump...was desperately wounded by his treatment in the mainstream media. He obsessed on every slight until it was overtaken by the next slight. Slights were singled out and replayed again and again, his mood worsening with each replay...Much of the president's daily conversation was a repetitive rundown of what various anchors and hosts had said about him.[69]

More than three years since he entered office, Trump's media obsession remains fully intact. His Twitter presidency remains in full swing, and reporters believe that Trump derives considerable pleasure from repeatedly seeing how his tweets become national headlines seconds after he releases them.[70] Trump's expectations from his staff similarly relate first and foremost to his media coverage.[71]

Trump's incessant preoccupation with the media is a key reason why he cannot be reliably contained by any political operatives serving him. One way to see this is to recall Trump's heavily documented disregard for facts, details, and expertise—all of which are deemed decidedly secondary to "media wins."[72] A political operative serving someone with such priorities cannot reasonably hope to drown out the cacophony of competing voices vying for the boss' ear by saying "I know the facts," or "I have marshalled the details and arguments," or "I have special expertise in this." This is particularly true if one is hoping to prevail over other advisers not only in a single instance, but over time.

Another, intimately related problem has to do with Trump's limited attention span and ability to focus—a limitation that clearly makes it difficult for any given political operative to consistently steer him in any given policy direction. This problem was manifest already in the 1980s, when journalist Tony Schwartz, for example, had spent the better part of a year and a half with Trump in order to ghost-write a biography portraying the businessman as an astute deal-maker.[73] Interviewed by the *New Yorker* shortly before the 2016 elections, Schwartz recalled the process of trying to elicit sustained reflections from Trump. Time and again, "after sitting for only a few minutes in his suit and tie, Trump became impatient

---

[69] Wolff, *Fire and Fury*, 197.

[70] Hains, "Trump Thought the Presidency Would Be Like Being Mayor of New York."

[71] Maggie Haberman and Katie Rogers, "An Aggrieved Trump Wants Better Press, and He Blames Leaks for Not Getting It," *New York Times*, May 17, 2018.

[72] Peter Baker, "Tips for Leaders Meeting Trump: Keep It Short and Give Him a Win," *New York Times*, March 18, 2017.

[73] An exercise that, incidentally, Schwartz still sees as having caused irrevocable damage to his own personal integrity. See Jane Mayer, "Donald Trump's Ghostwriter Tells All," *The New Yorker*, July 25, 2016, at https://www.newyorker.com/magazine/2016/07/25/donald-trumps-ghostwriter-tells-all.

and irritable. He looked fidgety...like a kindergartner who can't sit still in a classroom."[74] To Schwartz, this recurring dynamic was only one piece of evidence among many indicating that Trump "has no attention span":

> Trump has been written about a thousand ways from Sunday, but this fundamental aspect of who he is doesn't seem to be fully understood... And that is that it's impossible to keep him focussed on any topic, other than his own self-aggrandizement, for more than a few minutes... [the result is] a stunning level of superficial knowledge and plain ignorance... That's why he so prefers TV as his first news source—information comes in easily digestible sound bites... I seriously doubt that Trump has ever read a book straight through in his adult life.[75]

A direct corollary of this problem is that in order to even try to influence him, Trump's political advisers have to be *physically* near him, and because none of them can do so around the clock, none of them can have stable influence. The *New York Magazine*, for example, observed that "unlike on most campaigns,"

> Trump's managers and strategists travelled the country with him on his private Boeing 757, for fear that staying behind in the Trump Tower war room could mean losing their influence. "There is kind of a circle-the-wagons mentality, and if your wagon's out of the circle for a while because you've gotta go do something, you're out of the loop," [one] former adviser said. "In the Trump White House, that can happen to anyone the moment you're outside of the inner circle physically."[76]

Wolff's analysis of the President's advisers and their choices is strikingly similar. Considering the President's daughter, Ivanka Trump, and son-in-law, Jared Kushner, Wolff writes:

> Part of Jared and Ivanka's calculation about the relative power and influence of a formal job in the West Wing versus an outside advisory role was the knowledge that influencing Trump required you to be all in. From phone call to phone call—and his day, beyond organized meetings, was almost entirely phone calls—you could lose him... while he was often most influenced by the last person he spoke to, he did not actually listen to anyone. So it was not so much the force of an individual argument or petition that moved him, but rather more just someone's

[74] Quoted in Mayer, "Donald Trump's Ghostwriter Tells All."
[75] Quoted in Mayer, "Donald Trump's Ghostwriter Tells All."
[76] Olivia Nuzzi, "Kellyanne Conway Is the Real First Lady of Trump's America," *New York Magazine*, March 2017, at http://nymag.com/daily/intelligencer/2017/03/kellyanne-conway-trumps-first-lady.html.

presence, the connection of what was going through his mind ... to whomever he was with and their views.[77]

These enormous obstacles toward advising the President are accompanied by further difficulties deriving from his improvisational and often simply incoherent style. This style—a natural upshot of Trump's inability to focus—has made it virtually impossible for his political advisers to manage his pronouncements. This fact was evident, for instance, in Trump's speech formally announcing his candidacy. In their biography of Trump, *Washington Post* journalists Michael Kranish and Marc Fisher describe the work that Trump's then-campaign manager put into the speech, and the radically different result that actually materialized:

> From the moment Trump announced his candidacy, the standard campaign script was out of the window ... Campaign manager Corey Lewandowski, with help, had spent the previous weekend writing the announcement speech. He had reviewed it with Trump, emphasizing the main points of the message. The prepared text ran about seven minutes. Lewandowski knew it by heart, and so as Trump's remarks passed the ten-minute mark and then the twenty-minute mark and continued on for a full forty-five minutes, Lewandowski thought to himself, This was going to be a little different.[78]

The eventual content of this speech also provided an early indication of the trouble that Trump's advisers would face in containing him. Here is how the speech actually started:

> So nice, thank you very much. That's really nice. Thank you. It's great to be at Trump Tower. It's great to be in a wonderful city, New York. And it's an honor to have everybody here. This is beyond anybody's expectations. There's been no crowd like this. And, I can tell, some of the candidates, they went in. They didn't know the air-conditioner didn't work. They sweated like dogs. They didn't know the room was too big, because they didn't have anybody there. How are they going to beat ISIS? I don't think it's going to happen.[79]

Trump, as another one of his biographers observed, "spoke in such a disjointed and ungrammatical way that fact-checking his statement was an exercise in futility ... aside from his 'thank you's,' it is impossible to determine just what Trump was trying to say."[80] But this speech was far from a one-off. "The entire

---

[77] Wolff, *Fire and Fury*, 70–1.   [78] Kranish and Fisher, *Trump Revealed*, 310–11.

[79] Quoted in Michael D'Antonio, *Never Enough: Donald Trump and the Pursuit of Success* (New York: St. Martin's Press, 2015), at 345.

[80] D'Antonio, *Never Enough*, 345.

event, as Kranish and Fisher noted, "was a remarkably revealing window onto what was to come. *Trump would not and could not be handled.* He *intended* to be unpredictable. He was the ultimate improviser, supremely confident of his own gut instincts."[81]

These attributes, in turn, were still evident once Trump reached the White House. If anything, Trump's willingness to disregard any of his own previous statements, or the advice of virtually anyone around him, only became *more* evident. In the course of a single week in 2018, for example, the President, completely ignoring his political advisers, announced the imposition of sixty billion dollars' worth of tariffs on Chinese imports, replaced his national security adviser, and publicly threatened to veto a 1.3-trillion-dollar spending bill approved by Congress, only to sign the bill a few hours later.[82] *The New York Times* summarized Trump's conduct during this eventful week as a "head-spinning series of presidential decisions that left the capital reeling and his advisers nervous about what comes next":

> The decisions attested to a president riled up by cable news and unbound. Mr. Trump appeared heedless of his staff, unconcerned about Washington decorum, or the latest stock market dive, and confident of his instincts. He seemed determined to set the agenda himself, even if that agenda looked like a White House in disarray. Inside the West Wing, aides described an atmosphere of bewildered resignation as they grappled with the all-too-familiar task of predicting and reacting in real time to Mr. Trump's shifting moods. Aides said there was no grand strategy to the president's actions, and that he got up each morning this week not knowing what he would do. Much as he did as a New York businessman at Trump Tower, Mr. Trump watched television, reacted to what he saw on television and then reacted to the reaction.[83]

One can offer many more examples of Trump's fundamental unpredictability as President—from his spontaneous suggestion to re-visit the Trans-Pacific Partnership

---

[81] Kranish and Fisher, *Trump Revealed*, 311. It is worth noting that these core attributes, displayed by Trump so vividly and repeatedly, have limited his servants' influence not only directly, but also in more indirect—albeit still crucial—ways. If nothing else, Trump's continued disregard of facts, combined with the sheer incoherence and implausibility of so many of his speeches, would drastically limit his advisers' ability to remind Trump of his prior commitments as a significant constraint on his present and future conduct. Since Trump's extensive speeches have articulated few if any such commitments, he could not be kept in check by any such reminders.

[82] "In the frantic hours before the signing, two senior officials said they were uncertain whether the president would veto the measure and prompt a shutdown or ultimately relent. White House officials raced to schedule an afternoon briefing for the news media, although they had no idea what they would end up telling reporters." Mark Landler and Julie Hirschfeld Davis, "After Another Week of Chaos, Trump Repairs to Palm Beach. No One Knows What Comes Next," *New York Times*, March 23, 2018.

[83] Landler and Davis, "After Another Week of Chaos."

trade agreement from which he withdrew days after assuming office,[84] through his self-contradictions on immigration,[85] to his constant oscillation with regard to gun control policies.[86] Add to these examples the President's widely documented willingness to let his staff battle each other,[87] as well as his widely documented suspicion of any subordinate who "gets too big for his boots," and the result is predictable: an administration with the highest turnover rates in modern history,[88] and one in which no political operative can realistically hope to have enduring influence.

The normative conclusion that follows from these empirical observations is straightforward: prospective or current political appointees who choose to dirty their hands by serving in the Trump administration cannot preserve their moral integrity. There is overwhelming evidence that no amount of dirty deeds that such appointees may perform for the President will allow them to reliably steer him toward the common good—or even just away from "the common bad." Given that this is so, prospective and current appointees have only two options, neither of which aligns with the preservation of moral integrity. First, such appointees can simply admit that their service for the President flatly contradicts basic commitments of decency—that they are dirtying their hands without moral justification, merely for amoral if not immoral gains. Alternatively, such appointees can persist in telling themselves that their serving the President ultimately derives from their fundamental commitment to the common good. The preceding paragraphs, however, should make clear that this rationale cannot succeed without a considerable amount of self-deception. Insofar as many appointees—repeatedly—engage in such self-deception, the reason, it is safe to assume, is that their desire to see themselves as "helping the country" has conveniently aligned with their much more mundane desire to help themselves.

The case of Kellyanne Conway, a prominent spokesperson for Trump who has held a formal advisory role in the White House, illustrates the first strategy. In March 2017, Joe Scarborough and Mika Brzezinski, the co-hosts of a popular morning show in which Conway was often interviewed, blasted her for the marked discrepancy between her defense of Trump on-air and her scorn for Trump once off the air. *The Hill* reported the pair's remarks as follows:

[84]   Ana Swanson, "Trump Proposes Rejoining Trans-Pacific Partnership," *New York Times*, April 12, 2018.

[85]   Tal Kopan, "Trump Contradicts Self Repeatedly in Immigration Meeting," *CNN*, January 9, 2018, at https://edition.cnn.com/2018/01/09/politics/donald-trump-immigration-contradictions/index.html.

[86]   See, for example, D'Antonio, "Trump: A Profile in Cowardice," *CNN*, July 16, 2018, at edition. cnn.com/2018/07/16/opinions/donald-trump-profile-cowardice-russia-dantonio/index.html.

[87]   Mark Landler and Maggie Haberman, "Trump's Chaos Theory for the Oval Office Is Taking Its Toll," *New York Times*, March 1, 2018.

[88]   See, e.g., Eli Stokols, "Trump White House Saw Record Number of First-Year Staff Departures," *Wall Street Journal*, December 28, 2017; Dareh Gregorian, " 'Off the Charts': White House Turnover Is Breaking Records," *MSNBC*, September 23, 2019, at https://www.nbcnews.com/politics/white-house/charts-white-house-turnover-breaking-records-n1056101.

"This is a woman…who came on our show during the campaign and would shill for Trump in extensive fashion and then she would get off the air, the camera would be turned off, the microphone would be taken off and she would say 'bleeech I need to take a shower,' because she disliked her candidate so much," Brzezinski said…Scarborough backed [Brzezinski] up…"'I'm just doing this for the money, I'll be off this soon,'" he said, imitating Conway. "I don't know that she ever said, 'I'm doing this for the money,' but this is just my summer vacation, my summer in Europe. And basically, I'm gonna get through this."[89]

The second self-deception strategy is illustrated by two Goldman-Sachs executives, Gary Cohn and Dina Powell, who both agreed to serve as part of Trump's economic team, each lasting about a year in the White House. Cohn served as the head of the President's National Economic Council. Powell acquired economic as well as security policy roles. The pair's reasons for joining the Trump administration were described as follows:

> For Cohn and Powell, the offer to join the Trump administration was transmuted beyond opportunity and became something like a duty. It would be their job…to help manage and shape a White House that might otherwise become the opposite of the reason and moderation they could bring. They could be instrumental in saving the place—and, as well, take a quantum personal leap forward.[90]

If the claims of the preceding paragraphs are cogent, however, in reality, the "quantum personal leap forward" had to be *far more* than a secondary consideration for such individuals, merely following after the primary aim of "saving the place." Given the speed with which it became clear that no political appointee could really "save the place"—or, more precisely, save the President from himself—the "personal leap forward" provided the only real reason to be in the White House. Any attempt to convince oneself otherwise would have amounted to nothing more than self-deceit.

It is not easy to say whether it was recognition of this fact that ultimately drove Cohn and Powell—and various other individuals—to leave Trump's White House, or whether it was simply the fear that an extended stay would damage their own personal prospects. What *is* clear, however, is that with each additional staff departure, the moral justifiability of new individuals filling in the vacated roles continues to diminish. Each such departure, as the *Washington Post* fumed

[89] "'Morning Joe' Hosts: Conway Secretly Hates Trump," *The Hill*, March 15, 2017, at thehill.com/blogs/blog-briefing-room/333396-morning-joe-hosts-kellyanne-conway-secretly-hates-trump.
[90] Wolff, *Fire and Fury*, 146.

following Cohn's resignation, should further "dispel some of the self-delusions with which Trump enablers have been trying to soothe themselves—and us... whatever information-process, rules-of-access and paper-flow controls that his staff can devise, they do not take the place of a disciplined, knowledgeable and temperamentally sound president."[91]

4.4.3 Netanyahu's Allies

The example of the Trump White House, which I just deployed to illustrate my claims against working with media demagogues, may strike some readers as misleading, or at least as limited in scope. Such readers might think that, even in the context of media demagogues, the Trump presidency is *sui generis*—a case so extreme that it is without any real parallels. It is partly because of such concerns, however, that I sought, earlier in this chapter, to show that even media demagogues who are far more competent, "disciplined, and knowledge-able" than the current American President may end up, by dint of a similar media obsession, conducting themselves in markedly similar ways. Accordingly, I wish to end this section by returning to my example of precisely such a demagogue—Benjamin Netanyahu.

More specifically, I wish to suggest that those politicians who work with Netanyahu commit integrity mistakes, and engage in self-deception, in ways that are quite parallel to the mistakes and self-deception of those who choose to serve Trump. Moreover, in Netanyahu's case—as in Trump's—the relevant mistakes become increasingly grave over time, as the scope of the threat that the media demagogue poses to collective integrity becomes clearer.

A sharp illustration of these points is provided by the multiple politicians who have allied with Netanyahu at different points since 2009, despite personal and political grievances with regard to his conduct. Initially, it may seem as if such politicians can try to justify their alignment with Netanyahu as a matter of integrity, following very similar reasoning to the one presented earlier with regard to media demagogues' servants. If, in virtue of their clout and bargaining power, Netanyahu's potential allies can push him to enact better (or, at least, less bad) public policies, is that not, after all, what their integrity as public figures requires? Should they not put their proper commitment to the public before their personal dislike of the man?

I believe that prospective Netanyahu allies cannot cling to such reasoning to keep their integrity intact. This is easiest to see in the case of those Netanyahu allies who repeatedly promised not to join any Netanyahu coalition, only to do

---

[91] Jennifer Rubin, "Five Lessons from Cohn's Exit," *Washington Post*, March 7, 2018, at washingtonpost.com/blogs/right-turn/wp/2018/03/07/five-lessons-from-gary-cohns-exit.

exactly that at the first possible opportunity. It is not difficult to argue that such politicians were driven to join Netanyahu simply because of their own ambition, rather than because of any public commitment.[92]

The same conclusion, however, may very well apply to politicians who managed to convince themselves that "this time Netanyahu will be different." One variant of this approach was exemplified in the conduct of those who clearly wanted to believe Netanyahu when the latter attempted to present himself as a "reformed," "mature" leader who has "learned from the past." The aforementioned Dan Meridor, for example, notwithstanding all of the harsh criticism he leveled at Netanyahu in 1999 (the gist of which I quoted above), chose to realign with Netanyahu and re-join the Likud party in 2009. When confronted with his 1990s critiques of Netanyahu's credibility, Meridor responded that "in the years that passed we have learned from experience. We matured."[93] Yet this was a chronicle of disappointment foretold: prior to the 2015 elections, Meridor forcefully attacked both Netanyahu and his Likud party, announcing that he refuses to "serve as the Likud's laundry detergent," and that he will not even vote for the party, given its increasing neglect of basic liberal values.[94] Since then, Meridor has returned to criticizing Netanyahu for "failing to lead," and for placing his interests in political survival over the most fundamental public interests.[95] Given his intimate knowledge of Netanyahu over decades, the only surprising element of this process was that Meridor actually managed to convince himself, for however brief a period, that Netanyahu had truly changed for the better.

A similar example concerns Tzipi Livni, a prominent figure of Israel's center-left. Between 2009 and 2012, Livni, as the Leader of the Opposition in the Knesset, vehemently attacked Netanyahu's government on virtually every possible issue. Yet in 2013, Livni announced that she is joining Netanyahu's new government, having been persuaded by Netanyahu that he will not only entrust her with the role of managing Israeli-Palestinian negotiations, but that he is genuinely eager to pursue peace. Following extensive discussions to mend their personal relationship, Livni announced to the media that she is "convinced" that she will have full authority to negotiate with the Palestinians, that the Prime Minister too recognizes the "necessity" of reigniting the peace process, and that she will not be a

---

[92] A prime example is former defense minister Shaul Mofaz, who joined Netanyahu's government in May 2012, having proclaimed only two months earlier that there is no way that he would join the "bad, failing, and obtuse" government, and that Netanyahu is a "liar." See, e.g., Harriet Sherwood, "How Likud-Kadima Deal Strengthens Netanyahu's Hand," *The Guardian*, May 8, 2012, at https://www.theguardian.com/world/2012/may/08/likud-kadima-deal-strengthens-netanyahu-hand.

[93] See, e.g., Mazal Mualem, "Meridor Upon Returning to Likud: We Learned and Matured," *Haaretz*, November 9, 2008, at https://www.haaretz.co.il/news/politics/1.1359298 (Hebrew).

[94] "Meridor: 'Likud Is Nationalist, I Will Not Be the Party's Laundry Detergent'," *Haaretz*, December 18, 2014, at https://www.haaretz.co.il/news/elections/1.2515890 (Hebrew).

[95] See, e.g., "Dan Meridor Attacks Netanyahu: Not a Leader. Politics Before National Security," *Marriv*, May 29, 2016, at http://www.maariv.co.il/news/politics/Article-543555 (Hebrew).

mere "fig leaf" in Netanyahu's government.[96] All of these hopeful pronouncements were falsified, one by one, during Livni's short stay in Netanyahu's government. Insofar as the end result was predictable, the entire dynamic represented
a serious failure of integrity on Livni's part, even if—and partly *because*—she
deceived herself at least as much as she deceived others. At the end of 2014, a
month before Netanyahu fired Livni from his government and initiated new
elections, one political commentator observed:

> Livni can only blame herself... she always knew who she's dealing with. During
> her opposition days, between 2009 and 2012, she gave fiery speeches against
> Netanyahu's reticence. She was right in every single one of them. Netanyahu does
> not want, is not able, and does not believe in any solution vis-à-vis the
> Palestinians, territorial or otherwise. Livni knew that Netanyahu did not change
> in the slightest even when she joined his government in early 2013. She got power
> and in exchange gave Netanyahu quiet at the center of the political map,
> diplomatic support, and international legitimacy. In other words; Livni sacrificed
> the peace process at the altar of comfort and personal interest... over the last
> term Livni blinded us, hugged Netanyahu, and briefed whoever was needed to
> say that Netanyahu is on the verge of transformation, personal and diplomatic.
> Only towards the end of the term she reminds us that the world is different.[97]

What is true for these cases is also true for those politicians who may have wanted
to believe that by joining Netanyahu's coalition, they can implement some of the
substantive policy commitments that Netanyahu himself once had. Thus, for
example, the same 2013 Netanyahu coalition that Livni chose to join was also
joined by Yair Lapid, another centrist politician, who was appointed Treasury
Secretary by Netanyahu. The flagship issue for Lapid's party has been curtailing the
excessive privileges accorded by the state to ultra-orthodox Jews—not least in the
form of state subsidies that effectively allow many of the ultra-orthodox to refrain
from work throughout their adult lives.[98] Netanyahu himself had sought to reduce
these subsidies during his own term as Treasury Secretary a decade before, only
to promise to the ultra-orthodox parties that he will significantly increase the
very same subsidies, as part of the political deal that allowed him to return to
the premiership. Lapid, who made the absence of the ultra-orthodox from
Netanyahu's coalition a condition of his party's entrance into the government,

---

[96] Yehonatan Lis, Yair Etinger, and Yossi Verter, "Livni in an Interview with Haaretz: Netanyahu
Realized That We Must Start a Peace Process," *TheMarker*, February 20, 2013, at https://www.
themarker.com/wwwMobileSite/1.1933770 (Hebrew).

[97] Shalom Yerushalmi, "Netanyahu and Natural Selection: The PM Returns to His Allies,"
NRG, October 30, 2014, at www.makorrishon.co.il/nrg/online/1/ART2/638/874.html?fb_action_ids=
805520399489570&fb_action_types=og.comments (Hebrew).

[98] For a detailed discussion of ultra-orthodox privileges in Israel, see *The People's Duty*, chap. 5.

may have tried to convince himself that he can remind the Prime Minister of his lost convictions: that he can re-enact in 2013 the same reforms that Netanyahu pursued in 2003, but ensure that these reforms would remain in place. None of this happened; instead, Lapid was fired by Netanyahu at just the same time as Livni was,[99] and all of Lapid's reforms were promptly canceled once Netanyahu assembled yet another government in 2015, this time with the ultra-orthodox instead of Lapid's party as coalition partners.[100]

Note, finally, that whatever limited moral plausibility there might have been to aligning with Netanyahu in years past has surely evaporated as the criminal investigations surrounding him came into full view. Livni and Lapid, at least, seemed to realize this. In March 2018, for example, Netanyahu was obliged by Knesset regulations to attend a formal parliamentary session devoted to the charges of personal corruption against him. Neither of his former coalition partners minced words during the session. Livni began by pillorying Netanyahu for seeking early elections prior to the Attorney General's decision whether to indict him:

Prime Minister, you want elections before the public will know the truth about your personal corruption, before people who know you will tell the truth—and they are the truthful ones. To hide truth you will again take the hatred and the persecution out of the same old pocket, to pit some against their brothers. You feed on the hatred that you spawn. Your term will end at some point. I don't know when it will happen, I hope it happens quickly. The only question that remains open is to what extent you will ruin by then the foundations on which the state of Israel was founded as a democracy. I know that you want the history books to say that you've defended Israel, I suppose that you'll talk as always about how strong the country is thanks to you, [but] that is not so. The rot of your corruption is what's destroying us from the inside.[101]

Lapid was equally trenchant in his criticism of Netanyahu:

Prime Minister, I have been following everything that you've been saying over the last few weeks. Your main claim is that several sources, gathered in some dark room, have colluded and jointly decided to bring you down. These are the sources that you tell us "cannot be trusted": the TV, the radio, the newspapers,

<hr/>

[99] Yehonatan Liss, "Netanyahu Fired Ministers Lapid and Livni," *Haaretz*, December 2, 2014, at https://www.haaretz.co.il/news/politi/1.2502416 (Hebrew).
[100] See, e.g., Yaki Adamkar, "'We Promised, and Kept Our Promise': Here Is How the Haredi Succeeded in Erasing 'Lapid's Legacy'," *Walla*, July 25, 2016, at https://news.walla.co.il/item/2982068 (Hebrew).
[101] Quoted in "Netanyahu: If There Would Be Elections, We'd Win: We Are Not There Yet," *Calcalist*, March 12, 2018, at https://www.calcalist.co.il/local/articles/0,7340,L-3733868,00.html.

the chief of police that you appointed yourself, the attorney general and state prosecutor that you appointed yourself, the state comptroller that you appointed yourself. I only have one question—why?

... A Prime Minister in Israel who has a shred of responsibility left cannot say on Facebook that state prosecutors and the police are pressuring state witnesses to lie. He cannot say that legal authorities cannot be trusted ... if God forbid a terrorist attack happened tomorrow, would you not go to the police? What is most evident in all of these [corruption] cases is your endless and obsessive preoccupation with one exclusive topic—yourself and your fate, what is good for you. For the good of the country, it is your time to step off the stage.[102]

Speeches such as these express quite sharply the threat that Netanyahu poses to the integrity of liberal democracy. But these speeches impose a particularly heavy burden of personal integrity—on those who make them as well as on any other Israeli politician in a position of real influence—not to ally with Netanyahu in the future, no matter how many promises Netanyahu makes with regard to any policy area.

4.5   In Lieu of a Conclusion: Media Demagogues, Integrity, and Fanaticism

In 4.4, I argued that media demagogues' prospective allies and servants cannot rationalize their work with such demagogues in integrity terms, because, at least over time, they have no realistic hope of reliably steering such demagogues in any particular policy direction. Because their failure to do so is eminently predictable, integrity firmly pushes prospective allies and servants *away* from dirtying their hands for media demagogues. In lieu of a conclusion, I want to use this final section to make one more argument buttressing the same integrity verdict.

According to this argument, even in those rare instances where media dem-agogues' prospective allies actually *do* have sufficient clout to reliably advance particular policy goals by supporting the demagogue, they must also take into account the much broader threat that the demagogue poses to the integrity of liberal democracy. No matter how deep is one's attachment to any specific policy, aligning with the demagogue in order to advance this policy, in a way that is entirely oblivious to the damage that the demagogue inflicts on the identity-grounding institutions of liberal democracy, is not a mark of personal integrity. Rather, it is a form of fanaticism.

One way to appreciate the significance of this point is to temporarily step back from the very concrete political dynamics that have occupied us in this chapter,

---

[102] Quoted in "Netanyahu: If There Would Be Elections."

and return to the more abstract, foundational discussion of integrity in the book's opening part. Specifically, we can return to the opening part's claims in favor of a conception of integrity that excludes commitments that are clearly morally untenable. In Chapter 1, I argued that commitments can be morally untenable not only when they are repugnant, but also when they reflect a *fanatic ordering* of moral values. That chapter used the example of fanatical private conduct (recall the proponent of animal rights who murders numerous human beings to save a single non-human animal). But the same idea applies to public life. A person (or group) with a "tunnel vision" commitment to a single public value or policy—one that pays virtually no heed to how the relevant value or policy bears on other moral values in public life, no matter how basic—cannot plausibly be considered a paragon of integrity. This is especially easy to see, moreover, when the fanatic form of commitment threatens the integrity of liberal democracy. When that is the case, it seems plausible to say that the relevant agent, far from being "the embodiment of integrity," is acting in ways that are antithetical to integrity.

To see the relevance of all this for thinking about political alliances with media demagogues, consider again the case of Silvio Berlusconi. More specifically, consider the de-facto alliance that the Vatican had formed with Berlusconi during his time as Prime Minister.[103] Senior officials of the Catholic Church routinely—even if implicitly—encouraged Catholic Italians to vote for Berlusconi, who was deemed a reliable guarantor of the Church's favored policies on its "core issues," such as gay marriage, in vitro fertilization, and abortion.[104] The Church's support for Berlusconi represented, in my view, a form of fanaticism, insofar as it paid no heed to the structural damage that Berlusconi was inflicting on the very foundations of Italian liberal democracy.

We can evince this point especially clearly by considering the many sex scandals in which Berlusconi has been embroiled. Berlusconi was actually accused, for example, of having sex with an underage prostitute and then abusing his authority to protect her from allegations of theft, as well as of a broader scheme to recruit and pay young women to attend parties at his villas.[105] But imagine that the allegations against Berlusconi had gone even further. Suppose, for example, that Berlusconi had been accused of rape while serving as Prime Minister. Suppose, moreover, that Berlusconi had tried to hide behind immunity laws enacted solely to shield him

---

[103] For a detailed account of this alliance see Massimiliano Livi, "The Ruini System and 'Berlusconismo': Synergy and Transformation between the Catholic Church and Italian Politics in the 'Second Republic'," *Journal of Modern Italian Studies* 21 (2016): 399–418.

[104] See, e.g., "Abortion Big Issue In Italy Elections," *Associated Press*, February 12, 2008, at https://www.cbsnews.com/news/abortion-big-issue-in-italy-elections. One way to assess this choice by the Church is to ask whether the policies it wanted Berlusconi to enact or retain—with regard to abortion, marriage, euthanasia, and other issues—are actually morally appropriate even when considered apart from any other policy choices. But we can bracket this question here.

[105] See, e.g., Peter Walker, "Ruby Rubacuori Could Finally Bring Down Silvio Berlusconi," *The Guardian*, January 14, 2011.

from prosecution for other grave criminal offenses. Now suppose that the Vatican commented on this state of affairs along the following lines: "the Church condemns both the Prime Minister's private conduct, and his attempt to shield this conduct from the reach of the law. The Church sees rape as one of the greatest wrongs that a human being can perpetrate. And yet, the Church still believes that crucial public policies endorsed by the Prime Minister override all of these concerns."

Now, I think it is fair to say that, in the twenty-first century, no Church representative would utter such a statement, for fairly obvious reasons. But if that is true for this hypothetical case, then why should we not reach the same conclusion when assessing the Church's alliance with Berlusconi under actual conditions? Why should we think that there is a qualitative difference between this hypothetical case and the Church's actual willingness to look the other way when Berlusconi sought immunity from criminal prosecution that will place him above the law? The Church's acceptance (however tacit and passive) of Berlusconi's "sultanistic" ambitions, simply in order to preserve "non-negotiable" Catholic values, represents the same kind of moral failure: no matter how much this acceptance relies on deeply held convictions, it is not an expression of integrity. Rather, it is a quintessential expression of fanaticism.

A parallel example of the crucial difference between integrity and fanaticism is given by the alliance that Israel's ultra-orthodox ("haredi") parties have forged with Netanyahu. The ultra-orthodox never had any illusions about the depth of Netanyahu's personal attachment to Jewish religion—widely known to be non-existent. Yet recent times have forced them to confront head-on a more dramatic problem. On the one hand, by serving as Netanyahu's crucial coalition partners, they are preserving his hope of escaping his legal predicaments through political means. On the other hand, Netanyahu represents the ultra-orthodox's own best hope of sustaining their most cherished public policies. Netanyahu has given the ultra-orthodox renewed hope of preventing the enforcement of core curricula— even of basic competence in English or math—as part of ultra-orthodox schooling. Netanyahu has guaranteed ever-increasing state subsidies for hundreds of thousands of yeshiva students dedicating their life exclusively to Torah study. Netanyahu has also brought back generous child benefits supporting extraordinarily large haredi families; and has promised continued exemption of the ultra-orthodox community from military service. Next to all this, the "tiny" fact that Netanyahu's conduct threatens Israel's very existence as a liberal democracy seems paltry, entirely insignificant to many of the ultra-orthodox. In January 2018, for example, Yisrael Cohen, a haredi pundit writing in one of Israel's major dailies, reminded the haredi community of the setbacks to their cherished policies during Lapid's time in government, their gains since those "dark days," and the threat of renewed setbacks if Netanyahu loses power to Lapid:

> Lapid hurt the yeshiva budgets, cut the child benefits, pushed for the enforcement
> of core curricula and for mandatory recruitment of yeshiva students, and that is

merely a small portion of the "edicts" that came out of his rule over the treasury and education ministries. Today the wheel has turned, and the haredi once again have the upper hand. The yeshivot budgets have been restored, the child benefits issue has been solved, the independence of haredi education has been more or less preserved, the conscription law is being taken care of... there is no doubt that this is the golden age of haredi Jews... and so the ultra-orthodox must not, under any condition, bring down the government. The ultra-orthodox must turn a blind eye to the bribery and fraud investigations and stand by Netanyahu's side...[106]

Following precisely this reasoning, the leaders of the haredi parties in Netanyahu's coalition were the first to come out and announce their "support of the Prime Minister" once the police publicly announced its recommendation to indict him on multiple criminal charges. This decision, just like the Vatican's support of Berlusconi, represents another instance not of integrity but of a fanatic devotion to specific policy commitments—a devotion that is oblivious to the basic integrity of liberal democracy.

Now, although both of the examples of fanatic alliances I just outlined revolve around religious fanaticism, I should stress that the relevant fanaticism can take an entirely secular form. This point can be illustrated by looking at some of the key allies of the other media demagogue on whom this chapter has focused—Donald Trump. Of particular importance here are those Trump allies who have joined forces with him out of a single-minded devotion to the reduction of tax rates, an aim achieved with the tax reforms enacted in late 2017. Such allies cannot plausibly claim the mantle of integrity as a description of their choice, no matter how sincere and deeply held their belief in "small government" may be. Anyone who is willing to sacrifice the most rudimentary elements of American liberal democracy at the altar of lower taxes is not a person of integrity, but a fanatic. This is true for any Trump allies in Congress who have managed to convince themselves that lower taxes justify virtually any policy debacles and erosion of democratic institutions that Trump may bring in his wake.[107] And this is especially true for any libertarian Trump backer who actively relishes the institutional dangers posed by the President, seeing in them an ideological opportunity. After all, if you actively wish that trust in government would plummet, and dream that it would

---

[106] Yisrael Cohen, "Only Netanyahu Is Good for the Haredi," *Haaretz*, January 1, 2018, at https://www.haaretz.co.il/opinions/.premium-1.5563843 (Hebrew).

[107] Consider, for example, former House Speaker Paul Ryan, who "traded his political soul," according to one conservative columnist, "for...a tax cut." Quoted in Mark Leibovitch, "This Is the Way Paul Ryan's Speakership Ends," *New York Times*, August 7, 2018. More generally, Leibovitch observes that "[f]ar from any unified governing philosophy, the animating objective for much of today's Republican Party has been reduced to whatever Trump does or wants. The main goal of many elected Republicans is to curry the approval of the president, avoid provoking him (or, worse, a tweet) and thus not inflame the 'base.' Being deemed an infidel inside the Church of the Base can be lethal for even the most ensconced incumbent." Republican conduct during Trump's recent Senate trial strongly suggests that this subservient behavior will persist so long as he is in office.

"all fall down," then you have an obvious interest in installing in highest office the person with the least competence possible.[108] But if that is your mindset—if you are at best indifferent to the severe harms that an incompetent and dangerous President might inflict on an enormous number of people—then your conduct can surely be only a manifestation of fanaticism, not an example of integrity.

[108] I have in mind here the billionaire hedge-fund manager Robert Mercer, whose attitude toward Trump was summarized by one acquaintance as follows: "Bob thinks the less government the better. He's happy if people don't trust the government. And if the President's a bozo? He's fine with that. He wants it to *all* fall down." Quoted in Jane Mayer, "The Reclusive Hedge-Fund Tycoon Behind the Trump Presidency," *New Yorker*, March 27, 2017. Italics in the original.

5

Honoring Integrity?

This final chapter has two overarching aims. First, as in Chapters 3 and 4, I aim to establish that the integrity framework does not unduly moralize politics, and is in fact well equipped to deal with a variety of questions concerning the dubious place of saintliness and purity in political life. Second, as in the previous chapter, I once again wish to show how the integrity framework can deal with important political circumstances, in which different integrity considerations seem to pull in conflicting practical directions.

However, whereas Chapter 4 focused on individual decision making, this chapter will focus once again on collective policy choices. And whereas Chapter 4 pivoted around some of the most morally objectionable public figures imaginable in a democracy, my goal in this chapter is to examine how the integrity framework can guide decisions whose scope is wider. In some cases, these decisions too concern repugnant political figures, but in many other cases, such decisions concern individuals who are much closer to the opposite end of the moral spectrum. The decisions I have in mind are about the awarding and withdrawal of political honors.

Many readers may very well be aware of a variety of real-world cases that have made political honors publicly salient. Yet it may still be helpful to start by recalling some recent events, which make vivid the fact that such honors neither are, nor are they being treated as, "merely" symbolic.

On the evening of June 17, 2015, Dylann Roof, a white supremacist, murdered nine black members of Mother Emmanuel Church in Charleston, South Carolina. Photos of Roof with Confederate battle flags were published shortly after this massacre. As a result, the Confederate battle flag was taken off the South Carolina statehouse, and, according to one estimate, at least sixty other "publicly funded symbols of the Confederacy" have also been removed throughout the United States.[1] At the same time, however, heated debate about political honors to the Confederacy spread throughout the American South. A Georgia lawmaker introduced a resolution to recognize "Confederate History Month" and "Confederate Memorial Day."[2] When Louisiana's lower chamber voted to protect Confederate

---

[1] The estimate, from the Southern Poverty Law Center, is quoted in Matthew Teague, "The Civil War Over Statues in New Orleans," *The Guardian*, May 1, 2017.
[2] See Kathleen Foody, "Georgia Legislator Bids to Honor 'Confederate History Month'," *Seattle Times*, March 27, 2017.

Integrity, Personal, and Political. Shmuel Nili, Oxford University Press (2020). © Shmuel Nili.
DOI: 10.1093/oso/9780198859635.001.0001

monuments in New Orleans against the wishes of the city's mayor, the chamber's Black Caucus "literally walked off of the House floor."[3] In Arkansas, both state chambers voted, against a vocal minority, in favor of a bill separating Arkansas' commemoration of Confederate general Robert E. Lee from Martin Luther King Day. Summarizing the main opposition to the bill, a Republican representative said during the debate, "we are taking Robert E. Lee and we are putting him in the basement and we are acting embarrassed that he ever existed. It's no different than if we went out and we took that statue of the Confederate Soldiers and put it down in the basement and said nobody's going to look at it again."[4]

Many philosophers, I suspect, would say that such disputes, for all of their practical import, do not point to any moral conundrums. It is obvious that the "preservation of history" trope, so often advanced by apologists for the Confederacy, is implausible. History, after all, could be preserved equally well by moving Confederate monuments to a museum. However, even those among us who are confident that there is no moral problem whatsoever with sending monuments to Confederate generals to museums are likely to pause when considering honors to public figures whose legacy is far more complicated. The moral status of most if not all monuments commemorating Robert E. Lee may be straightforward. But this is plainly not the case for the many monuments commemorating the slave-owning founders of the United States, for example.

Moreover, the moral complexity of such honors obviously extends far beyond American public figures. Should the many societies who have honored Mahatma Gandhi re-consider any of these honors, in light of various accounts of Gandhi's highly problematic attitudes toward black Africans,[5] or toward women?[6] Should English society re-visit its monuments to many of its past heroes given their constitutive role in a colonialism that the country now disavows?[7] Should South African society re-think any of the honors bestowed on Nelson Mandela in light of changing perceptions of his legacy?[8]

My key ambition in this chapter is to examine how the ideas developed in previous chapters regarding individual and collective integrity bear on such questions regarding the morality of political honors. Understood broadly, we

---

[3] Tegan Wendland, "With Lee Statue's Removal, Another Battle of New Orleans Comes to a Close," *NPR*, May 20, 2017, at http://www.npr.org/2017/05/20/529232823/with-lee-statues-removal-another-battle-of-new-orleans-comes-to-a-close.

[4] Quoted in Colin Dwyer, "Arkansas Splits Its Holidays for Martin Luther King Jr. and Robert E. Lee," *NPR*, March 20, 2017, at http://www.npr.org/sections/thetwo-way/2017/03/20/520802543/arkansas-to-split-its-holidays-for-martin-luther-king-jr-and-robert-e-lee.

[5] See, e.g., Soutik Biswas, "Was Gandhi a Racist?" *BBC*, September 17, 2015, at https://www.bbc.com/news/world-asia-india-34265882.

[6] See discussion below.

[7] See for example Yussef Robinson, "Oxford's Cecil Rhodes Statue Must Fall—It Stands in the Way of Inclusivity," *The Guardian*, June 19, 2016.

[8] See, e.g., Norimitsu Onishi and Selam Gebrekidan, " 'They Eat Money': How Mandela's Political Heirs Grow Rich Off Corruption," *New York Times*, April 16, 2018.

can take "political honors" to refer to any form of special symbolic recognition accorded by political entities to individuals, to particular social groups, or to particular social causes. The relevant political entities, in turn, can be many. When a branch of government pays symbolic homage to key achievements of hitherto-marginalized social groups or social causes, that is a political honor. The same is true when a municipality pays tribute to the victims of past wrongs by naming streets after them; or when a regional government erects a monument to an iconic figure. These can all be seen as political honors. My primary interest here is in political honors accorded to political leaders—those individuals who are or were at the apex of power. But my approach to such individual honors will also have implications for other kinds of honors conferred by political entities.

Before I start to lay out the substance of this approach, it may be useful to remark briefly on how I understand the state of existing scholarship on political honors, and to indicate why I think the topic is an especially appropriate case study for my account of integrity. Perhaps the most striking fact about existing scholarship is the almost complete silence of normative political philosophy concerning political honors. On any plausible construal of this philosophical tradition, it has had very little to say about the topic.[9] I hope to correct this neglect here, by showing how the account of integrity developed in the previous pages can advance our thinking about the morality of political honors.

Another important feature of existing scholarship on political honors is that although this scholarship comes from diverse disciplines,[10] all of these disciplines have quite uniformly focused on the relationship between such honors and collective memory.[11] In contrast, my definition of political honors makes clear

---

[9] Although normative theorists have had much to say about more abstract topics that lie in the vicinity, such as "state speech," the moral significance of the collective "ethos," and the significance of entrenched societal practices (see, respectively, Corey Brettschneider, *When the State Speaks, What Should It Say*? [Princeton, NJ: Princeton University Press, 2012]; G.A. Cohen, "Where the Action Is: On the Site of Distributive Justice," *Philosophy & Public Affairs* 26 [1997]: 3–30; Aaron James, "Constructing Justice for Existing Practice: Rawls and the Status Quo," *Philosophy and Public Affairs* 33 [2005]: 281–316). More obviously, normative theorists have had much to say about the moral significance of desert, an issue I take up below.

[10] These disciplines include social and intellectual history, but also law, anthropology, religious studies, English, and art. See, e.g., Naomi Loraux, *The Invention of Athens* (Cambridge, MA: Harvard University Press, 1986); David Kertzer, *Ritual, Politics, and Power* (New Haven, CT: Yale University Press, 1988); Sanford Levinson, *Written in Stone: Public Monuments in Changing Societies* (Durham, NC: Duke University Press, 1998); James Young, "The Counter-Monument: Memory Against Itself in Germany Today," *Critical Inquiry* 18 (1992): 267–96; Jenny Edkins, *Trauma and the Memory of Politics* (Cambridge: Cambridge University Press, 2011).

[11] This may be partly due to the multiple forms of philosophical interest in the normativity of memory. See, e.g., Avishay Margalit, *The Ethics of Memory* (Cambridge, MA: Harvard University Press, 2002); Burke Hendrix, "Memory in Native American Land Claims," *Political Theory* 33 (2005): 763–85; Mihaela Mihai, "When the State Says 'Sorry': State Apologies as Exemplary Political Judgments," *Journal of Political Philosophy* 21 (2013): 200–20; Cecile Fabre, *Cosmopolitan Peace* (Oxford: Oxford University Press, 2016), chap. 10; Zofia Stemplowska, "Remembering War: Fabre on Remembrance," *Journal of Applied Philosophy* 36 [2019]: 382–90; Johannes Schulz, "Must Rhodes Fall? The Significance of Commemoration in the Struggle for Relations of Respect," *Journal of Political Philosophy* 27 (2019): 166–86.

that the morality of political honors is not simply reducible to the morality of collective memory. When the White House, for instance, was illuminated with "rainbow" colors to celebrate the Supreme Court's 2015 decision to legalize gay marriage,[12] this was an uplifting political honor. Or, to take a very different sort of example, an elected president who, in the manner of Brazil's Jair Bolsonaro, pays any kind of official tribute to individuals who perpetrated torture on behalf of a dictatorship is clearly conferring a profoundly wrongful political honor on such criminals—simply in virtue of the special symbolic power that is inherent in his office.[13] A compelling account of the morality of political honors should be able to say something about both of these instances of political honoring. Yet neither is really about "historical memory."

That said, I fully grant that *one* key task of a persuasive account of the morality of political honors is to capture powerful historical intuitions. And it is partly because of this central task that I believe that the topic of political honors provides fertile ground for the integrity ideas I have been exploring. After all, as I have been emphasizing since the Introduction to this book, the ability of integrity talk to capture the moral force of agents' particular histories is a key reason why this talk has such intuitive appeal. It is therefore natural to expect that an account of individual and collective integrity would have something to say about political honors.

Another important point here concerns the assessment of how honorees' private activities ought to affect honors decisions that focus on their public activities. How we should understand the divide between public figures' private and public conduct is both an important and a complex question.[14] And it is not difficult to see why any account of political leaders' integrity should have something to say about this question. After all, at its core, integrity (as I have stressed throughout the book) refers to coherence between one's convictions and one's actions. And so an account of integrity that had nothing to say about how one's private convictions—manifested in one's private activities—relate to one's public actions would surely be amiss. Moreover, even an account of integrity that did have something to say about this issue, but that turned out to be implausible in its implications for thinking about political honors, would thereby lose at least some of its overall appeal. Therefore, it is important for my purposes to show that—at the very least—my account of integrity yields no such implausible results when it comes to political honors. In particular, as in the preceding chapters, I wish to

---

[12] See "White House Lit as Rainbow After Gay Marriage Ruling," *The Guardian*, at www.theguardian.com/us-news/video/2015/jun/27/white-house-lit-up-rainbow-colours-timelapse-gay-marriage-video.

[13] As Congressman, Bolsonaro publicly dedicated his vote to impeach then-President Rousseff—who was tortured by Brazil's military dictatorship—to the head of the military torture center. See, e.g., Jonathan Watts, "Dilma Rousseff Taunt Opens Old Wounds of Dictatorship Era's Torture in Brazil," *The Guardian*, April 19, 2016.

[14] As pointed out for example in Mendus, *Politics and Morality*, passim; Richard Bellamy, "Dirty Hands, Clean Gloves," *European Journal of Political Theory* 9 (2010): 412–30.

show that the integrity framework can coherently subject both collective affairs and individual politicians to stringent moral standards, even while keeping a safe distance from implausible demands of saintliness in the conduct of political life.

My last reason for dedicating this chapter to the morality of political honors has to do with what I have called, in earlier stages of the book, the "orbiting concepts" surrounding integrity. Throughout the previous chapters, I have made extensive use of several of these concepts—self-respect, steadfastness, self-seeking rational-izations, self-deception—when elaborating and defending my ideas regarding both individual and collective integrity. I believe that the topic of political honors provides yet another context in which a similar strategy can be put to good use. In this context, however, I shall bring to the fore two further notions that are widely understood to fall within integrity's orbit. First, having devoted considerable space in preceding chapters to individual agents who deceive both others and them-selves, I wish to put center stage in this chapter the notion of *collective honesty*—of the polity, as a collective agent, avoiding deception. Second, I want to mine another natural understanding of integrity—one that focuses on *wholeness*—and see how this understanding too might yield useful practical guidance.

With these aims in mind, I proceed as follows. In 5.1, I consider, and reject, an account of political honors that focuses on political leaders' personal integrity. Such an account, I argue, cannot align with the inevitable moral deficiencies of any political leader's public record. In 5.2, I accordingly begin to develop my favored alternative, which evaluates political honors from the perspective of collective rather than individual integrity. On the collective integrity approach, decisions about the awarding and withdrawal of political honors ought to focus on the aim of marking and reinforcing appropriate moral commitments of the collective in whose name the honor is being (or has been) awarded. Elaborating this view, I suggest that political honors can often fulfill their central collectivist functions even when they involve no individual politicians—when revolving instead around "anonymous heroes," around substantive laws or policies, or even around non-human animals. I also show how the approach can account for important cases where there is a particularly firm intuition that political leaders should be at the center of political honors. In 5.3, I consider and reject an individual desert alternative to the collective integrity account. Finally, in 5.4, I argue that the collective integrity approach can provide compelling guidance with regard to the withdrawal of political honors, without falling back either on individual integrity or on individual desert claims.

5.1 Political Honors and Personal Integrity

We can delve into the substance of our inquiry by considering what we may term the *personal integrity view* of political honors. This view emphasizes the moral value of political honors that cast prominent public figures as paragons of personal integrity. The focus of political honors, on this approach, is to set up role models that will provide society with moral inspiration, not least by providing a vivid example of personal steadfastness—of considerable personal sacrifice and risk--taking—in the pursuit of moral goals.

There are several reasons why the personal integrity view represents a natural point of departure for reflecting on integrity's relationship to political honors. For one thing, any tenable view of such honors would make room for considerations involving their inspirational value. And so it is sensible to begin with a view that puts this value center stage. Furthermore, the personal integrity view clearly aligns with prevalent practices regarding political honors, which not only overwhelmingly focus on individual honorees who have achieved public prominence, but typically also portray such honorees as figures who ought to be "an inspiration for us all." Finally, the individual integrity view also does well in capturing our instinctive suspicion of honors to prominent public figures who clearly failed to live up to their public convictions in their private conduct. This is especially true, moreover, for those prominent public figures whose private failures were due to a lack of personal steadfastness.

Upon close inspection, however, the personal integrity view turns out to be less compelling than it may appear at a distance. We can start to see this by noting the following point. It is true that we may be particularly suspicious of honors to politically prominent individuals who were unwilling to pay the private costs that ought to have followed from their public convictions. And so there is value in a view that captures this suspicion in an especially immediate way. But we should not exaggerate this value. This is because, in most cases at least, the relevant suspicion can be traced simply to the private wrong in which the relevant honorees have engaged, rather than to the fact that this wrong conflicted with their convictions regarding public affairs.

The much-discussed issue of honors accorded to slave-owners is a case in point. James Madison, for instance, "insisted that enslaved Africans were entitled to a right to liberty and proposed that Congress purchase all the slaves in the United States and set them free,"[15] yet nonetheless believed he simply could not afford the financial cost involved in releasing his own slaves.[16] This manifest lack of personal steadfastness does, to be sure, give us room for pause with regard to political honors revolving around Madison. But the bulk of the moral heavy lifting here is

---

[15] Noah Feldman, "James Madison's Lessons in Racism," *New York Times*, October 28, 2017. See also Feldman's *The Three Lives of James Madison* (New York: Random House, 2017).

[16] Feldman, "James Madison's Lessons in Racism." Feldman adds: "The tension between Madison's aspirational beliefs and his highly constrained actions continues to be America's own tension. Like Madison, contemporary United States society rejects racial inequality in principle. But also like Madison, a majority of Americans—as reflected in our democratic institutions—are ultimately unwilling or unable to make the costly changes that would be necessary to achieve equality in practice." See in similar spirit Lebron, *The Color of Our Shame: Race and Justice in Our Time*, passim.

done by the simple fact that Madison held Africans as slaves, not by the fact that Madison himself recognized the wrongness of slavery. We should, after all, have the same compunction about honoring Madison as we have about honoring other political leaders who were slave-owners—including slave-owners who did *not* see their private conduct as contradicting their public views.

However, the more fatal problem for the individual integrity view lies with those political leaders whose cases initially seem less complicated. Specifically, I have in mind here iconic political leaders who not only refrained from any glaring wrongs in their private conduct, but who have clearly incurred dramatic personal sacrifices for the sake of laudable public aims. These leaders are the kinds of honorees that give the personal integrity view of political honors its pre-theoretical appeal. But I believe that once we examine such leaders in detail, we see that personal integrity considerations cannot provide stable grounds for honoring them.

The core concern here is ultimately simple. Virtually any senior political figure—any figure who has played a central role in the making of public policy—is bound to have serious moral blemishes in his or her public record. This is true even if their private record is beyond reproach, and even if they have made the most dramatic personal sacrifices for the sake of public ends that are clearly morally valuable. This point is crucial, in turn, because the individual integrity view itself should be concerned with such serious public blemishes. Insofar as integrity connotes—among other things—a certain wholeness, it does not seem very coherent to celebrate any given leader as a "paragon of moral integrity" while focusing exclusively on some elements of their public conduct, and simply "bracketing" those public issues where the leader's policies were far from morally inspirational.

As a way of making this concern more concrete, consider the case of Abraham Lincoln, and more specifically, Lincoln's policies toward Native Americans. In 2013, Sherry Salway Black, a Native American member of President Obama's Advisory Council on Financial Capability for Young Americans, and Director of the Partnership for Tribal Governance at the National Congress of American Indians, pointed out that although Lincoln may be widely celebrated as the greatest hero of American political history, he is "No hero to Native Americans." Black observed:

> Abraham Lincoln is not seen as much of a hero at all among many American Indian tribes and Native peoples of the United States, as the majority of his policies proved to be detrimental to them. For instance, the Homestead Act and the Pacific Railway Act of 1862 helped precipitate the construction of the transcontinental railroad, which led to the significant loss of land and natural resources, as well as the loss of lifestyle and culture, for many tribal people. In addition, rampant corruption in the Indian Office, the precursor of the Bureau of

Indian Affairs, continued unabated throughout Lincoln's term and well beyond. In many cases, government-appointed Indian agents outright stole resources that were supposed to go to the tribes. In other cases, the Lincoln administration simply continued to implement discriminatory and damaging policies, like placing Indians on reservations. Beginning in 1863, the Lincoln administration oversaw the removal of the Navajos and the Mescalero Apaches from the New Mexico Territory, forcing the Navajo to march 450 miles to Bosque Redondo—a brutal journey. Eventually, more than 2,000 died before a treaty was signed.[17]

Such facts regarding the Lincoln administration's treatment of Native Americans preclude, I believe, any attempt to ground honors to Lincoln in a judgment concerning his "public integrity." Any such judgment must, by its very nature, involve a holistic assessment, covering the full range of public policy issues and decisions for which Lincoln was responsible. The "inconvenient" parts of Lincoln's public record cannot be simply bracketed away.

Now, some might object that this claim sets the bar for honoring political leaders so high that it cannot count as a plausible interpretation of what the personal integrity view would require. I think this objection is misguided for several reasons, one of which is worth mentioning already here. Even if the requirements of personal integrity as I just presented them are quite demanding, they are not necessarily more demanding than the requirements that would (arguably) follow from other non-consequentialist moral and political theories applied to the same issue.

Consider, for instance, contractualist theories, which generally deny that the harms imposed on some by collective institutions can be justified by simply appealing to the benefits generated for others. Now suppose that in the immediate aftermath of the Civil War, the U.S. government would have tried to justify to Native Americans the special honors it bestowed on Lincoln by saying to Native Americans: "the wrongs that you have suffered at the hands of Lincoln's administration are outweighed by the inspiring example that Lincoln has set in guiding the Union through the many trials and tribulations of the Civil War." If we follow Rawls in thinking that society's economic institutions, for example, cannot be justified "on the grounds that the hardships of some are offset by a greater good in the aggregate,"[18] then why should we not say the same about the politics of symbolic honors? From a Rawlsian perspective—and perhaps also from other

---

[17] Sherry Salway Black, "Lincoln: No Hero to Native Americans," *The Washington Monthly*, February 2013, at https://washingtonmonthly.com/magazine/janfeb-2013/lincoln-no-hero-to-native-americans. See also Schulz, "Must Rhodes Fall?," 175. Even a sympathetic interpreter of Lincoln's views of Native Americans could not avoid recognizing that Lincoln took it for granted that Native Americans were "a foreign people that would need to be removed through purchase or conquest." See Christopher Anderson, "Native Americans and the Origin of Abraham Lincoln's Views on Race," *Journal of the Abraham Lincoln Association* 37 (2016): 11–29, at 25.

[18] *TJ*, 13.

contractualist perspectives—it seems that distinct minorities in society can rea-sonably reject honors celebrating the moral integrity of leaders who have seriously wronged *them* through certain policies.[19] This is true notwithstanding many benefits that the very same policies, or other policies pursued by the same leaders, have secured for other members of society. And if that is the case with regard to a leader such as Lincoln—as sharp an example of moral integrity in a political leader as anyone is likely to find—then it is all the more the case for virtually any other political leader.

I will have more to say below as to whether my claims set the bar of personal integrity too high for the purposes of honors decisions. But what I want to do at this point is to start developing a collectivist alternative—a conception of political honors that pivots on collective rather than individual integrity.

5.2 The Collectivist Alternative

The core idea driving the collective integrity view of political honors is simple in form. On this view, a morally appropriate honor marks and reinforces the right sort of commitments on the part of the collective in whose name the honor is accorded. In the paradigmatic case, where the honor is awarded by the state, the relevant collective is the sovereign people, understood to be acting through state institutions.

One key feature of the collective integrity view of political honors is that it rules out manipulative honors. By "manipulative honors" I mean honors that knowingly mislead—that intentionally portray their recipients as morally better than they actually are or were. Insofar as such manipulation amounts to a form of collective dishonesty, it is ruled out, *ab initio*, by the collective integrity view. This feature of the view means that it directly opposes a recurrent aspect of how political honors have actually been designed and awarded in many societies. The recurrent ten-dency to portray honorees (especially politically prominent honorees) as far better than they actually are or were, and in some cases as something close to saints, is a tendency that the collective integrity view unequivocally rejects.

The collective integrity view also leads us to re-examine a more general tendency, ubiquitous across many societies, to focus political honors on individ-uals. Consider, by way of illustration, a public monument at the site in which an epic environmental protest took place. According to the collective integrity view,

[19] In invoking "reasonable rejection" I am consciously echoing here T.M. Scanlon's *What We Owe to Each Other* (Cambridge, MA: Belknap Press, 1998), notwithstanding much-discussed difficulties in applying the moral outlook defended in this work to political affairs (see, e.g., Aaron James, "The Significance of Distribution," in R. Jay Wallace, Rahul Kumar, and Samuel Freeman [eds.], *Reasons and Recognition: Essays on the Philosophy of T. M. Scanlon* [New York: Oxford University Press, 2011], 276–304).

no moral loss follows if this monument revolves around the substance of the protest, rather than around any of its individual leaders. The former mode of honor, after all, can serve to mark and reinforce a collective commitment to environmental protection at least as well as a monument centered on prominent environmentalists. Similarly, placing a statue dedicated to environmental reform at a site where a highly polluting factory once flourished can be, at least in principle, as good a way of marking and reinforcing a collective commitment to a green agenda as is a political honor to a prominent politician who was famous for calling polluters to task.

Now, these remarks may seem to suggest that the collective integrity view simply rejects honors to individual political leaders. Yet my suggestion is *not* that such honors be avoided entirely. Rather, my suggestion is that in cases where there is a firm intuition that such honors are appropriate, this intuition can be explained through reference to collectivist considerations, rather than to the kind of considerations highlighted by the individual integrity view.

Three kinds of collectivist considerations are particularly worth highlighting here. The first has to do with what we may call *collective opposition*, an opposition that is especially evident in honors to iconic political leaders who have been assassinated. Consider, for instance, Israeli Prime Minister Yitzhak Rabin, who was assassinated at the end of a peace rally in Tel Aviv's central public square in late 1995, by a Jewish fanatic opposed to the Israeli-Palestinian peace process. The square, as well as Israel's largest highway, military headquarters, and numerous schools and streets, has since been named (or re-named) after Rabin. On the collectivist view, none of these individual honors depended for their moral force on any judgment as to Rabin's personal integrity. Thus, for example, the fact that, upon winning office in 1992, Rabin flagrantly violated some of his key campaign promises (such as his promise not to negotiate the fate of the Golan Heights with Syria[20]) did not in any way affect the profound moral value of his extensive public commemoration. Rather, this commemoration was and remains morally important as a way of marking and reinforcing precisely the core collective moral commitments that Rabin's assassin (and, to this day, Israel's radical right) firmly rejected—both a commitment to the Israeli-Palestinian peace process, and a commitment to the peaceful resolution of political disagreement more generally.

Second, it is fairly uncontroversial that—for better or worse—human beings are much more easily motivated to pursue challenging or costly actions when confronted with specific human stories, as compared to abstract reasoning. This fact about our motivational structures is evident in our amoral, everyday decisions: when we struggle to adhere to an exercise regimen that we know is good for us,

---

[20] See, e.g., "Comments by Prime Minister Rabin on Withdrawal on the Golan Heights, 8 September 1994," *Israeli Ministry of Foreign Affairs*, archived at http://www.mfa.gov.il/mfa/foreignpolicy/mfadocuments/yearbook9/pages/231%20comments%20by%20prime%20minister%20rabin%20on%20withdrawal.aspx.

abstract statistics about the resulting health benefits are always less likely to motivate us than a reminder about an inspiring role model who struggled against much greater adversity to maintain an even more demanding regimen. The same point is equally evident in our morally loaded decisions. To utilitarians' continued dismay, it is much easier to motivate us to donate funds to alleviate global poverty, for example, by presenting us with an individual human story, as compared to technical statistics about much larger populations.[21] And by the same token, it is typically easier to motivate us to support morally valuable political causes by embodying these causes in the personal tales of specific political honorees, as compared to abstract values. The motivational superiority of concrete personal narratives over abstractions can therefore provide an instrumental consideration in favor of honors that focus on specific political leaders, even when the ultimate goal of the relevant honor has little to do with these leaders, and everything to do with a collective commitment to a morally valuable cause.

Finally, it is also important to bear in mind the collective significance of a particular political language that comes to be associated with specific public figures. Part of the difficulty of making substantive moral commitments essential to a modern polity's collective identity lies in the difficulty of turning abstract moral ideas into concrete language that can actually motivate members of mass societies— can inspire them to identify with collective moral undertakings, and to engage in the collective work necessary for a more just politics. To the extent that such inspirational language comes to shape any meaningful part of public discourse, this is typically (at least in contemporary politics) because of influential political figures with whom this language comes to be identified. These figures introduce a distinct, powerful rhetoric that allows many citizens to connect to collective moral aspirations.[22] When key such aspirations become firmly attached in public consciousness to particular individuals, honors that center on these individuals make moral sense on purely collective grounds. These honors need not and should not depend on any judgment as to these individuals' personal attributes. Such honors may be nominally centered on these individuals, from statues depicting them to plaques quoting them. But it is the collective commitments that these individuals articulated, rather than the individuals themselves, that matter morally.

I should add that the three considerations I just noted—collective opposition, motivation through personification, and powerful political rhetoric—can sometimes come together. Consider, for example, the aforementioned Lincoln, and more specifically Washington DC's Lincoln Memorial. First, while this memorial is clearly morally significant, it would be mistaken to ground this significance in a judgment about Lincoln the individual politician, because of the reasons noted

[21] See, for example, Leif Wenar, "What We Owe to Distant Others," *Politics, Philosophy and Economics* 2 (2003): 283–304.
[22] For a sustained defense of the crucial role of such rhetoric, see Adam Sandel, *The Place of Prejudice: A Case for Reasoning within the World* (Cambridge, MA: Harvard University Press, 2014).

earlier. Instead, the fact that Lincoln was assassinated by someone clearly keen to preserve the subjugation of African-Americans was arguably sufficient, in and of itself, to justify a National Mall monument centered on Lincoln. If erecting a monument to Lincoln at the symbolic heart of the nation was morally essential, this was partly because of the collective message that the monument sent to anyone who shared the assassin's political views—that while Lincoln may be dead, the moral ideas that cost him his life are collectively endorsed, and will outlive him.

Second, the Lincoln Memorial's moral significance can also be traced in Lincoln's greatest texts, which are appropriately central to the monument. These texts weaved together, in a way that few before or after Lincoln had managed, some of the most evocative indictments of failures of collective integrity, from collective self-deception and hypocrisy to collective complicity, as well as some of the most stirring affirmations of the moral significance of the collective integrity of a democracy founded on equality. Consider, for example, John Burt's summary of the main tenants of Lincoln's texts, a summary striking in the degree to which it parallels the main ideas of this book:

> The great themes of Lincoln's presidential speeches and public papers are ... that the absolute cultural precondition of political freedom is the moral equality of all people; that the problem of moral equality is fraught with conflicts so deep and so intractable that the Union, whose commitment to moral equality is compromised by hypocrisy and shadowed by self-deceit, cannot be preserved or retain its freedom except through a struggle that risks its survival; that emancipation is both morally and practically the necessary precondition of restoring the Union; that conflicts over moral issues are so entangled with the weaknesses of human nature that all outcomes are tragic and no agents are pure ... [23]

Each of these themes made it eminently morally appropriate to commemorate Lincoln's most inspirational words. But it is the words—and, ultimately, the collective moral commitments that these words have marked and reinforced— that should be central, not Lincoln the man. "Canonizing" Lincoln's words, then, is morally fitting. Canonizing Lincoln the man—casting him as a secular saint—is not.

5.3 Overlooking Individual Desert?

5.3.1 A Desert-Based Account—General Objections

Having started to develop the collective integrity account of political honors, I want to pause in order to reflect on a natural individualist alternative—one

---

[23] John Burt, *Lincoln's Tragic Pragmatism* (Cambridge, MA: Harvard University Press, 2013), 649.

that focuses not on any sort of integrity as such, but simply on individual desert. Challenging a desert-based view of political honors should be useful in two ways. First, as a way of dispelling the concerns of some readers, who may have found desert conspicuously absent from the preceding discussion. Second, highlighting the difficulties with a desert-based conception of political honors will sharpen the distinctive contributions of the collective integrity account of such honors— particularly, as we shall see below, with regard to the withdrawal of such honors.

With these motivations in mind, let us consider Michael Walzer, who, as far as I am aware, is the only member of the normative tradition in political thought who has given anything like sustained attention to the morality of political honors. According to Walzer, it is quite obvious that "[T]he crucial standard for public honor is desert."[24] Walzer does not deny that instrumental considerations also play a role in the morality of political honors, but he clearly believes that this role is entirely secondary, and desert must take center stage. If it does not, the danger that political honors will be abused looms large. Thus Walzer writes:

> We could, of course, give out public honors for utilitarian reasons, so as to encourage politically or socially useful performances. Such reasons will always play a part in the practice of honoring, but I don't see how they can stand alone. *How will we know whom to honor unless we are committed to attend to personal desert?* Anyone will do, so long as the encouragement turns out to be effective. Indeed, the authorities might well think it best to invent a performance and to "frame" an appropriate performer so as to make sure that they are encouraging exactly what they want to encourage. This possibility... suggests that there are good reasons for sticking to the common understanding of individual desert. Otherwise, honor is simply available for tyrannical use. Because I have power, I shall honor so and so. It doesn't matter whom I choose, because no one really deserves to be honored. And it doesn't matter what the occasion is, for I don't recognize any intrinsic (social) connection between honor and some particular set of performances.[25]

Building on all this, Walzer discusses at length Stalin's cynical use of honors given to productive workers in the Soviet Union, as an illustration of the tyrannical dangers latent in any purely instrumental view of political honors. "In the absence of a theory of desert," Walzer accordingly concludes, any honor will be "not a recognition but an incentive, a goad, one of those offers that turns very easily into a threat."[26]

Walzer's claims may seem quite appealing at first glance. But they are vulnerable in at least three ways, all of which should push us quite firmly in the direction

---

[24] Michael Walzer, *Spheres of Justice* (New York: Basic Books, 1983), 261.
[25] Walzer, *Spheres of Justice*, 261.   [26] Walzer, *Spheres of Justice*, 261.

162 INTEGRITY, PERSONAL, AND POLITICAL

of the collectivist approach outlined above. Consider, first, Walzer's claim that instrumental considerations cannot "stand alone" when it comes to political honors. Walzer does not distinguish between importantly different ways in which instrumental considerations can "stand alone." Such considerations can "stand alone" insofar as no other considerations are thought to be relevant in *any* way to the granting of political honors. When that is the case, the danger that Walzer emphasizes, of "tyrannical use" of political honors, does indeed loom large. But there is also a much more modest—and much more morally tenable—sense in which instrumental considerations can "stand alone." Here the thought is that instrumental considerations provide the only *positive* grounds for awarding certain honors, but that this instrumental reasoning must be *constrained* by independent moral standards. There is nothing incoherent in saying that the only positive grounds we have for awarding political honors is to "encourage politically or socially useful performances," but that this encouragement cannot be based (for example) on lies, nor can it proceed through any form of intimidation. This, of course, is precisely the combination favored by the collective integrity view of political honors. But this combination can be endorsed without admitting that desert provides any positive grounds (let alone any significant positive grounds) for awarding political honors.

Second, it is problematic to assert, as Walzer does, that we will not know "whom to honor" unless we focus on personal desert. At least, this assertion is problematic if we interpret it to mean that we ought to design the institution of state honors on the basis of *pre-institutional* desert judgments.[27] This implication is difficult to accept, since it is simply not true that anyone has a pre-institutional moral claim to be honored in any special way. To be sure, *if* the practice of honoring certain kinds of individual performance has been set up, with an eye toward its instrumental benefits, and *if* the practice has been operative for a while, *then* prospective honorees will have grounds for moral complaint, in case they satisfy the relevant performance criteria but do not receive the same honor that others have received before them on account of similar performances. But the relevant moral complaint here will be best understood in terms of fairness and equality, rather than "desert"—desert as such will not be doing any independent moral work. Moreover, if the relevant practice were eventually to be abolished for compelling moral reasons—which will have nothing to do with desert—then there will be no individual with an "unmet desert" claim.

By way of illustration, imagine that at some future point, the British government breaks with centuries of tradition and adopts a highly Rousseauian view,

---

[27] Admittedly, it is not entirely clear whether Walzer sees himself as committed to a pre-institutional conception of desert. But the coherence of his position depends on such a conception: if one admits that institutions fully specify what it means to "deserve" any state honor, there is no reason to think that desert itself can provide any independent moral guidance. I say more about this in a moment.

according to which official honors are a source of social malaise and problematic hierarchy.[28] This imaginary British government accordingly follows the footsteps of countries such as Switzerland and Uruguay, and entirely abolishes official honors (as well as abolishing the monarchy).[29] If such a scenario were to materialize, no Briton would be able to say: "I *deserve* a knighthood, and so the abolition of the social practice of conferring knighthoods *wrongs* me." No individual, in other words, can claim a "natural," pre-institutional moral entitlement to political honors.[30]

With these observations in mind, we can note the third general problem with Walzer's question, which is very much related. The question "how would we know whom to honor?" presupposes an individual-desert-based account of political honors, not only in the sense I just outlined, but also insofar as this question simply ignores political honors regarding which the attribution of individual desert is fundamentally out of place. To take one example, the moral significance of monuments commemorating abstract values and their loss cannot be captured through reference to individual desert. Thus, for instance, public monuments centered on self-inflicted loss of knowledge and literary inspiration, and the acute moral dangers associated with such loss, clearly have considerable moral value (think, for example, of the monument, in the center of Berlin's Bebelplatz, to books burned by the Nazis). But it is surely far more plausible to appeal to collective commitments rather than individual desert to explain this moral value.

The same point obtains for other kinds of political honors. Monuments to service dogs killed in wartime,[31] for instance, may very well be morally appropriate for a variety of reasons, but there is no way to ground such monuments in what the dogs "deserve": after all, moral desert, as Walzer emphasizes, presupposes moral responsibility,[32] but we do not attribute moral responsibility to dogs. To take a different sort of example, it seems quite hard to explain the moral significance of monuments revolving around the anonymous through reference to individual desert: when there is no particular, reasonably identifiable individual

---

[28] One is reminded here of the immortal *Yes Minister* satire of "knights and grands," or "K's and G's," especially as these apply to the British Foreign Office, whose honors are the "Cross of St Michael and St George" (abbreviated as CMG, KCMG, and GCMG): "The foreign office is not popular throughout the rest of the Civil Service, and it is widely held that the CMG stands for 'Call Me God,' the KCMG for 'Kindly Call Me God,' and the GCMG for 'God Calls Me God.'" Johnathan Lynn and Anthony Jay, *The Complete Yes Minister* (London: BBC Books, 1989), chap. 5: "Doing the honours," 239.

[29] The Swiss and the Uruguayan (and the Irish) are admittedly special in this respect, as noted, for example, in Christopher McCreery, *The Canadian Honours System* (Toronto: University of Toronto Press, 2005), chap. 1.

[30] Notice that this narrow claim leaves open the possibility that pre-institutional desert may play an independent moral role with regard to other political issues. Here I wish to remain agnostic about this possibility.

[31] See, e.g., Steven Johnston, *American Dionysia* (Cambridge: Cambridge University Press, 2015), chapter 3.

[32] Walzer, *Spheres of Justice*, 261.

(or limited set of individuals) marked out by a political honor, collective commitments provide far more plausible grounds for the honor than individual desert.

We can, however, go even further, by seeing how even political honors that have been traditionally understood to revolve precisely around individual desert are actually better understood through reference to collective commitments. The case of honors associated with war can be used to demonstrate this point as well. Consider, then, the Medal of Honor—the United States' highest commendation for combat valor. In March 2014, President Obama awarded the Medal to twenty-four veterans who had fought in the Second World War, in Korea, and in Vietnam.[33] The ceremony was distinguished by the fact that nineteen of the recipients—African-American, Hispanic, or Jewish—were identified as having been overlooked for the Medal in the past because of racial or religious discrimination.[34]

Now, given what I said earlier, it should already be clear that on my view, the moral claim of these overlooked veterans to be honored cannot be fundamentally rooted in (pre-institutional) desert. Rather, it is rooted (at least in part) in the simple fact that the relevant veterans satisfied the criteria associated with the institution of the Medal of Honor, whose justification need not have anything to do with desert as such. These veterans have a moral claim based on simple *institutional* entitlement, to receive the same symbolic recognition that others have received before them when satisfying these criteria.

Moreover, I assume that even if all the relevant veterans—and their families—had already passed away at the time of the award, there would *still* have been considerable moral value in this ceremony. But I do not think that this value can be explained through reference to individual desert. If neither the deserving individual is still alive to enjoy their due, nor is even any descendant alive to "inherit" this due, then how can desert explain why it is so important to confer the relevant honor after so many years? More specifically, how can desert justify spending considerable public resources and more than a decade of staff work—as the U.S. armed forces did at the instruction of Congress—to review service files going all the way back to the Second World War?[35]

A better justification, I suggest, lies exactly with collective egalitarian commitments. The Medal of Honor ceremony, as President Obama emphasized in his opening remarks, provided another symbolic opportunity for American society to "confront our imperfections and face a sometimes painful past—including the

[33] See "Remarks by the President," at https://www.whitehouse.gov/the-press-office/2014/03/18/remarks-president-presentation-ceremony-medal-honor.

[34] See Scott Wilson, "Obama to Award Medal of Honor to Two Dozen Veterans, Including 19 Discrimination Victims," *Washington Post*, February 21, 2014, at https://www.washingtonpost.com/politics/obama-to-ward-medal-of-honor-to-19-soldiers-who-were-overlooked-because-of-their-ethnicity/2014/02/21/209594e8-9b10-11e3-975d-107dfef7b668_story.html.

[35] See Wilson, "Obama to Award Medal of Honor."

truth that some of these soldiers fought, and died, for a country that did not always see them as equal."[36] The award ceremony simultaneously marked this collective egalitarian commitment, and reinforced that very commitment, by offering collective encouragement to other victims of discrimination to continue to struggle to be included as equal members of society, and discouragement to those who continue to support exclusionary policies.

Now, I recognize that some readers may not be convinced by this particular example. Such readers are likely to be drawn to the thought that, when it comes to honors for extraordinary valor in combat, individual desert judgments really do have to lie front and center. Bearing such likely skeptics in mind, it may be useful to consider in brief an adjacent example, focused more directly on the Second World War. For over seventy years now, the British government has refused, notwithstanding repeated pleas by veterans' representatives, to bestow military honors on Bomber Command pilots that parallel the honors bestowed on many other units who took part in the war.[37] To my mind, it is clear that this refusal has been (and will indefinitely be) morally appropriate. But the reason for this moral judgment is not that Bomber Command pilots compared unfavorably with other military units in any measure of individual devotion or contribution to the cause of winning the war. Nor is the reason simply that Bomber Command pilots conducted missions whose moral status has long been controversial (most infamously, the bombing of Dresden). In fact, in my view, the refusal to honor Bomber Command pilots remains morally appropriate even if one grants (*arguendo*) that in the quintessentially tragic circumstances in which Bomber Command operated, all of its missions were actually appropriate, as an unfortunately necessary means of war. All of that notwithstanding, the refusal to bestow honors on Bomber Command pilots is still morally warranted, on collective integrity grounds. No matter how essential these missions may have ultimately been, and no matter how valiant were the individual pilots who executed them, taking collective pride in work such as that of Bomber Command remains incompatible with a liberal democracy's collective integrity.

5.3.2 "Desert" and Political Leaders

Having outlined several general grounds for preferring the collective integrity account of political honors over the individual desert alternative, I now want to suggest that when it comes to political leaders, we have *especially* strong reasons not to hinge our moral assessment of official honors on individual desert.

---

[36] "Remarks by the President," March 18, 2014.
[37] See, e.g.,"Campaign Medal Call for WWII Bomber Command Veterans," *BBC*, May 26, 2018, at https://www.bbc.com/news/uk-england-lincolnshire-44255399.

One problem with a desert-based view of honors to political leaders is the danger that such a view would—all too easily—feed the (self-deceptive) tendency of political leaders in general, and image-obsessed political leaders in particular, toward self-aggrandizement. Chapter 4's discussion of media demagogues' remarkably developed sense of entitlement, including the various forms of morally offensive honors and types of deference they seek, should make clear that this danger is far from hypothetical.

Even those who are not moved by this danger, however, should take seriously a different sort of problem. This problem parallels the "wholeness" that I argued must be central to an individual integrity account of political honors. Just as an individual integrity account cannot avoid assessing a leader's public record in its entirety, so an individual desert account cannot avoid making a judgment about what we may call "total desert"—that is, an assessment of whether the relevant leader's morally positive deeds "outweigh" his or her morally negative deeds, to such an extent as to make them "deserving of honor" overall.

The most obvious fact about this "total desert" assessment is that it is extraordinarily difficult to carry out, and in many cases difficult to the point of impossibility. This is true even when looking exclusively at the honoree's record as a leader (is a given prime minister's success as a military leader sufficient to "outweigh" a dismal record with regard to socio-economic policies? Does a president's contributions to healing ethnic and religious divides in a society "outweigh" environmentally dangerous policies that he or she pursued?). But the assessment of "total desert" becomes even more complicated when we incorporate other key issues into the equation.

One extremely thorny issue here has to do with the ascent of our most senior politicians. Consider a not uncommon case, where we have ample reason to accuse a politician of criminal misdeeds on the way to the top, going far beyond the customary breaking of promises and speaking half-truths. Suppose—to reprise a few examples from Chapter 4's discussion of media demagogues—that we have ample reason to accuse a leader of partaking in bribery, or of systematically cooperating with criminals, or of extreme forms of incitement against his opponents. Should we be willing to say that morally important policies enacted by this politician once he climbed to the top vindicate him retroactively, and make him deserving of honors "overall"? Or should we say that because this politician obtained office illicitly, he does not "deserve" any significant honors for how he performed once in office? Moreover, should our judgment be sensitive to whether this politician's opponents have been guilty of similar dirty deeds?

Another complicated issue here has to do with the exact motives underlying the most senior politicians' pursuit of their "signature" public policies. Suppose that we have strong reasons to suspect that an extremely morally valuable policy was pursued by a senior politician primarily in order to divert public and media attention away from credible charges that he and his inner circle have engaged in seriously corrupt behavior.[38] Does this suspicion reduce our reasons to honor this politician for the relevant policy?

Such questions, I believe, are controversial to an extent that dooms any attempt to ground honors to political leaders in desert. But one might imagine an especially trenchant desert theorist, who believes that—notwithstanding everything I have said so far—there is still room for honoring "deserving" leaders for specific elements of their public service, in a way that does not condone (or that perhaps simply brackets) any other element of their public activity. Is there anything further that might be said to such an interlocutor?

I believe so. Beyond everything that was said so far, we can also say to the proponent of the desert view that whenever the state pronounces judgment on the desert of political leaders, it is *inevitably*—even if only implicitly—pronouncing judgment on their "total" desert. The main reason why this is so is the totality of both the state's responsibilities and the responsibilities of the relevant honorees who have wielded power in the name of the state.

This point about the scope of responsibility, in turn, might be easier to see through a contrast with individual honors of a different sort—those bestowed on individuals for their performance within private organizations. Let us consider, then, a private organization in a sphere (normally) removed from the wielding of public political power—sports. To be more specific, consider the statue of Michael Jordan at the entrance to the Chicago Bulls' United Center stadium. The statue—featuring Jordan in a classic pose from his playing days—is explicitly meant to honor the sporting legacy of the Bulls' greatest ever player. Now, suppose that a Chicago charity supporting the city's poor protested this statue, arguing that the Chicago Bulls committed a moral mistake by enacting it, because Jordan did not sufficiently use his fame and riches to support Chicago's less fortunate, and he therefore does not deserve to be honored "overall"—taking his full range of activities into account.[39] To my mind, at least, it seems clear that such a complaint would be unwarranted, precisely because it mischaracterizes both the responsibilities of the Chicago Bulls as an organization, and Jordan's role within this organization. The Chicago Bulls is an organization with a very specific mandate: to compete in professional basketball. Michael Jordan's responsibility within this organization was also very specific: to play as well as he could. That is why it would have been entirely sensible for the Bulls to respond to complaints about Jordan's "total deservingness" by saying: "we take no stance on

[38] To take only one example, Ariel Sharon, Israel's Prime Minister in the early 2000s, faced such allegations regarding his commitment to the evacuation of Jewish settlements from Gaza. See, e.g., Chris McGreal, "Sharon's Son Charged in Corruption Case," *The Guardian*, February 18, 2005, at www.theguardian.com/world/2005/feb/18/israel1.

[39] This example is hypothetical. I am unaware of the actual extent of Jordan's donations to Chicago charities.

Jordan's moral desert overall. We are honoring him for his specific services to our specific causes."[40]

Such agnosticism, however, while clearly available to private organizations, is, just as clearly, *un*available to state authorities, especially when it comes to honoring those who have led them. This is because there is no sphere of public concern that falls outside these authorities' mandate, and that can be "bracketed" in the assessment of how those who lead them have performed their public tasks. A private organization such as the Chicago Bulls *might* be able to "pass the buck," and argue that the responsibility for caring for Chicago's poor (for instance) lies with public authorities. But public authorities themselves—at least nation-wide authorities with ultimate jurisdiction—cannot pass the buck in the same way. The buck, to paraphrase Truman, stops precisely with these public entities, and with those who have led them. Here any judgment about political leaders' "desert" in their public role is necessarily, even if implicitly, a judgment of their *total* desert. This judgment cannot avoid taking all aspects of public life into account, because *all* of these aspects fall within the scope of the institution's—and the honoree's—direct responsibility.

5.4 The Withdrawal of Individual Honors

Equipped with these observations, let us now turn from the awarding of political honors to their withdrawal. Here it may seem as if the collective integrity view faces special difficulties. This is because, at least in some cases, the withdrawal of honors accorded in the past seems justified precisely because of the honoree's moral shortcomings. Yet it may seem unclear how the collectivist perspective can explain this moral judgment without falling back on either personal desert or personal integrity considerations.

One way to assess this challenge is to consider individual honors given for specific public contributions, whose withdrawal seems to be justified because the honoree holds repugnant personal commitments. In my view, repugnant personal commitments will have this kind of impact only if—upon inspection—they turn out to taint collective commitments.

One way in which such tainting may come about is if the particular circumstances are such that the collective act of awarding the honor inevitably conveys *collective acceptance* of the relevant objectionable commitments. Suppose, for example, that a white soldier in the U.S. Army officially learns from his

---

[40] This is true even if the Bulls could not have said the same had Jordan, for example, been guilty not merely of failure to help vulnerable others, but of grave criminal wrongdoing (at the limit, had he been convicted of murder). Perhaps we could account for this difference by saying that actions such as murder take one out of the "moral community" in such a way as to make one ineligible for any honors, whether private or public. But I will not pursue this issue here.

commanders that he will be awarded the Medal of Honor, and then, in a press interview shortly before the award ceremony, declares, "I am saddened by the fact that I will have to receive the Medal alongside members of inferior races." In such circumstances, there is a powerful moral case for withdrawing the Medal of Honor the soldier was about to receive, simply because awarding him the medal would amount to a collective legitimization of his racism.

Another way in which repugnant personal commitments may taint the collective is if these commitments have a pervasive presence in the honoree's public activity, clearly standing in the background of any specific public contributions. Consider, for instance, the case of John C. Calhoun. Calhoun's ardent commitment to slavery was more than a personal principle relating to his private conduct and ownership of slaves. It arguably infected—directly or indirectly—virtually every aspect of Calhoun's political activity and political thought. It is hard to suggest any public view or project associated with Calhoun that was not—from Calhoun's own perspective, at least—connected in one way or another with slavery. None of Calhoun's constitutional doctrines, for example, can be detached from his desire to protect the institution of slavery. More generally, it is plausible to assume that Calhoun's stance with regard to any policy, when not directly motivated by the desire to protect slavery, presupposed either the labor of slaves, the perpetual exclusion of slaves from its intended benefits, or both.[41] Calhoun, as Harriett Martineau noted upon his death, "lived and died for the cause of slavery."[42] That is why a collective decision to retain Calhoun's political honors, no matter their direct subject, expresses a *collective* acceptance—in however reluctant, "excusing" form—of Calhoun's views on slavery. And this collective message, rather than any judgment of Calhoun's individual attributes, is the best explanation of why no political honors to Calhoun should be retained.

Moreover, it is worth noting that while this conclusion may be reasonably uncontroversial with regard to characters such as Calhoun, we only need to take a small additional step to render it quite radical. We only need to imagine the normative implications that would follow if we discovered that political leaders to whom we do not typically ascribe such all-encompassing endorsement of repugnant commitments turned out to see these very commitments as absolutely central to the meaning of their public service. Imagine, for instance, that hitherto-lost diaries by George Washington were discovered, and that in these diaries Washington explicitly said that none of his military feats or his contributions as the first president of the United States would be of genuine worth if slavery were ever to be abolished. In this kind of scenario, there would clearly be non-trivial

---

[41] For Calhoun, the country's entire "mission," as one biographer put it, "depended on the permanence of the labor system which a 'mysterious providence' had long ago wished upon the South. Slavery was the key to the success of the American dream." Irving Bartlett, *John C. Calhoun: A Biography* (New York: Norton, 1993), 227–8.

[42] Quoted in Bartlett, *John C. Calhoun*, 377.

reasons of collective integrity favoring the removal of many—perhaps even all—political honors to Washington.[43]

If these claims are cogent, then the collective integrity has no obvious disadvantages in comparison to the individualist approaches when it comes to the withdrawal of political honors. But this finding actually understates the point, since the collectivist understanding of withdrawal decisions has two fundamental *advantages* over the individualist alternatives, and especially over the individual desert account. First, the collectivist outlook avoids the mistake of attributing to past honorees *any* moral claim to have "their" honors preserved. Second, the collective outlook can capture differences in the moral reasons that pertain to different political communities who may be considering, even at the same time, the withdrawal of honors accorded to the same individuals.

The case of honors to Mahatma Gandhi can illustrate these advantages. While Gandhi celebrated non-violent protest as a "feminine" principle, critics also accuse him of "monstrously sexist views," including the belief that "Indian women who were raped lost their value as human beings," and that "fathers could be justified in killing daughters who had been sexually assaulted for the sake of family and community honour."[44] In his own writings, Gandhi described how he had personally cut the hair of women followers who were harassed by men.[45] Now, suppose that in light of these disturbing facts, feminist activists in India, protesting pervasive sexual violence against women,[46] sought to remove certain monuments to Gandhi, "the father of the nation," as a symbolic indication of the extent to which India ought to re-examine its core values with regard to women's rights. According to the desert-based approach, this feminist demand would have to be assessed with an eye toward what Gandhi the individual deserves. This means, first, that if Gandhi's leadership of India's anti-colonial struggle were deemed to "outweigh" his legacy with regard to the status of women, so as to make him deserving of honors "overall," then feminists would be (at least presumptively)

[43] Would these reasons be dispositive? The answer, it seems to me, would not hinge solely on the newly revealed information about Washington. It would also depend on the extent to which that information comes to taint the public perception of Washington, in the manner akin to how the public perception of Calhoun has been irrevocably tainted by his views regarding slavery. Whether that tainting does in fact occur is in turn something that seems best left for free public discourse and civil society to settle. It may very well be the moral responsibility of government to seek to correct various prevalent falsehoods distorting the public perception of politically prominent figures. But, at least within a certain range, government should probably leave civil society to continuously negotiate, in pluralistic fashion, which of all of the relevant facts about a given political figure exert the most impact on how that figure is perceived.

[44] See Michael Connellan, "Women Suffer from Gandhi's Legacy," *The Guardian*, January 27, 2010. Connellan obviously admits that Gandhi "isn't singularly to blame for India's deeply problematic attitudes to sex and female sexuality." Yet although Gandhi's views became more moderate in his later years, "the damage was done, and the legacy lingers."

[45] See the quotes from Gandhi and the description of the case in Rajmohan Gandhi, *Mohandas* (New Delhi: Penguin Books, 2006), 161–2.

[46] See, e.g., Belinda Goldsmith and Meka Beresford, "Poll Ranks India the World's Most Dangerous Country for Women," *The Guardian*, June 28, 2018.

wronging Gandhi by removing the relevant monuments commemorating him. Second, the desert-based solution would be unable to explain why *other* nations with their own monuments to Gandhi would face completely different moral questions with regard to these monuments, even at the very same point in time. If a political honor is supposed to conform to desert as an "objective measure," as Walzer puts it—if the evaluation of desert is supposed to be an "absolute judgement"—then exactly the same desert "verdict"[47] should apply whether the relevant honor is a monument to Gandhi in New Delhi or (say) in London. This perspective would identify no qualitative difference between the moral reasoning in which English society must engage when considering its honors to Gandhi, and the moral reasoning in which Indian society must engage.

The collectivist approach avoids both of these shortcomings. First, on this approach, to reiterate what I said earlier in this chapter, no individual, no matter how widely admired, has *any* moral claim to any special forms of symbolic recognition by political entities. And so it is simply not true that a feminist call to remove any honors to Gandhi would wrong him even presumptively.[48] Second, on the collectivist outlook, what matters is the collective context surrounding a certain individual honor. And because the collective context faced by foreign societies who have chosen to honor Gandhi is fundamentally different from the collective context of Indian society, there are no grounds at all to expect any parity in the moral reasoning that these societies should employ when deciding about the fate of these honors. Whether the English should retain Gandhi's statue in London's Parliament Square, for example, is a question that concerns, first and foremost, England's collective commitment to distance itself from its colonialist past.[49] This question can and should be entirely separate from Gandhi's treatment of women. But when considering the status of monuments to Gandhi *within* India, there are going to be at least some cases where such separation will be much harder to sustain. The collectivist approach, unlike the individual desert approach, can capture this fundamental difference between the two contexts.

Given the complexity of this case, it might be helpful to offer a few more thoughts about how the collectivist approach might adjudicate moral questions concerning honors centered on Gandhi, at least within India. Even if—as I just said—Gandhi himself would not be wronged by the removal of various honors

---

[47] All of these terms come from Walzer, *Spheres of Justice*, 259.

[48] Notice, moreover, a broader dilemma here for the desert-based view, extending far beyond Gandhi's specific case. The desert theorist can rely on a conception of desert that somehow fades over time, at the cost of counter-intuitive results in cases such as the aforementioned Medal of Honor awarded after decades of discrimination. Or such a theorist can insist that honorees have an enduring claim to special symbolic recognition that is oblivious to the passage of time. But this stance runs afoul of the powerful intuition that as political circumstances change, posing new moral questions for the political community to tackle, even honors that were morally appropriate at a certain point can (and sometimes ought to) give way to others. The collectivist alternative faces no such dilemma.

[49] See James Dunn, "Gandhi Statue Unveiled in Parliament Square—Next to His Old Enemy Churchill," *The Independent*, March 14, 2015.

focused on him, it does *not* automatically follow that any (let alone many or all) existing such honors ought, all-things-considered, to be removed. Whether that is true depends on other morally relevant factors. For example, the clearer it is that a given government decision to honor Gandhi is based (partly) on a direct dismissal of the significance of gender equality, the stronger is the moral case for withdrawing the relevant honor. If, for instance, Indian public officials created an "all citizens are equal" campaign, but named new public buildings devoted to the campaign after Gandhi, there would be a clear moral case for removing this honor, insofar as it would imply that women do not really belong in the category of "all citizens" whose equality is supposed to be advanced. Similarly, imagine that a given Indian government set up a huge new Gandhi monument with the hope that it would be a significant tourist attraction,[50] and then actively suppressed new disquieting revelations about Gandhi's treatment of women, so as to maintain touristic "buzz" and thus "protect the investment." If this silencing effort was eventually exposed, then any future government aware of the effort would have to view it as morally tainting the monument. It would therefore be morally appropriate for any government in that position to replace the relevant monument with some alternative tourist attraction, even if such replacement would leave government revenue unchanged.

What, finally, of public monuments that are clearly meant to commemorate India's liberation from colonial rule? Should such monuments featuring Gandhi be removed as well? Insofar as there is no *automatic* reason to view these specific monuments as conveying a collective acceptance of Gandhi's views regarding women, there is also no automatic reason to think that there is a moral duty to remove these monuments in the name of gender equality.[51]

That said, there is a clear moral duty that lies in the vicinity—namely, to erect many more prominent public monuments (and other forms of state honors) featuring female protagonists. This moral duty, once more, is based not on individual desert claims, but rather on the weighty and stringent moral need to distance Indian society as a collective from any acceptance of gender hierarchy—whether propagated by Gandhi or by anyone else.

---

[50] In late 2018, Indian Prime Minister Narendra Modi used tourism as a justification for erecting the world's tallest statute, of another Indian freedom fighter, Sardar Vallabhbhai Patel, at the astonishing cost of nearly half a billion dollars. Critics have portrayed this initiative as a transparent Modi ploy at self-aggrandizement. See, e.g., Sonia Faleiro, "Let Them Eat Statues," *Foreign Policy*, November 30, 2018.

[51] It is important not to confuse this claim with the "compartmentalized desert" approach I criticized earlier. Unlike that approach, the argument I am presenting here does not seek to isolate a certain area of activity regarding which an individual "deserves" to be honored. To reiterate: the relevant distinction has to do with the different *collective context* surrounding different honors, not with what honorees might deserve.

5.5 In Lieu of a Conclusion

I have spent this chapter arguing in favor of a collective integrity approach to the morality of political honors. In defending this approach, I have once again sought to show that the integrity framework not only avoids implausibly saintly political conclusions, but also avoids the kind of internal indeterminacy that would threaten its value as a practical political guide. What was true for our discussion of media demagogues and their collaborators in Chapter 4 thus also turns out to be true for this chapter's discussion of political honors: even when individual and collective integrity point in conflicting practical directions, an internally coherent, systematic solution to such conflicts can be found. Rather than rehearse the specific claims I have made here in defense of this conclusion, however, I want to close with a brief observation on normative political theory's neglect of political honors, which provided a key part of the motivation for this chapter's discussion.

This neglect, I believe, is likely due to the thought that the symbolic recognition reflected in political honors often seems secondary to substantive political action. Indeed, reflecting on the entire arc of this book, one could certainly understand a skeptical reader who believes that whereas questions about integrity's implications for practical political decisions matter greatly, questions about integrity's implications for symbolic politics do not. It may matter greatly, on this view, whether dissidents such as Václav Havel—with whom this book started—truly had independent reasons of moral integrity to contest the dictatorships under which they lived. But it does *not* matter greatly how Czech society balances Havel's controversial policies as president[52] with his dissident legacy, when deciding whether and how to honor him.

This skeptical view is sensible, but only up to a point. It is true that we should be careful not to overestimate the significance of political symbols. But we should also not underestimate them.[53] Thus, for example, it is certainly true that an average Czech concerned about growing corruption in his country's political class[54] is unlikely to take much comfort in any enduring monument to Havel, however prominent. But this does not mean that it is a matter of moral indifference whether any such monument is removed, or replaced with a groveling monument to the Chinese president. Similarly, the removal, throughout the former Soviet bloc, of statues honoring figures responsible for the most egregious aspects of Soviet rule will not by itself mend families still scarred by the history of Gulag torture and other violations of basic rights. But this does not mean that it is

---

[52] Including, for example, the controversial general amnesty that Havel issued upon assuming office. See, e.g., "New Czech Leader Orders Amnesty for Up to 30,000," *Reuters*, January 2, 1990, at http://articles.latimes.com/1990-01-02/news/mn-175_1_amnesty-announcement.

[53] As emphasized, for example, in Schulz, "Must Rhodes Fall?," passim, e.g. at 167.

[54] See for instance Freedom House's 2018 Czech Republic report, at https://freedomhouse.org/report/freedom-world/2018/czech-republic.

a matter of moral indifference whether these statues are to be re-installed.[55] And what is true for these monuments is true, more generally, for the numerous political honors that are present in social life—from school and street names to national rituals. Such political symbols form much of the (often transparent) background of our everyday activities. And while it would be seriously misguided to think that "fixing" this symbolic background can by itself fix political realities, it would also be misguided to continue to neglect this background. This fact alone suffices to makes it worthwhile to close a book on personal and political integrity with the morality of political honors.

---

[55] See, e.g., Sarah Rainsford, "Russian Communists Look to Reinstate 'Iron Felix' Statue," *BBC News*, July 19, 2015, at http://www.bbc.com/news/av/world-europe-33549850/russian-communists-look-to-reinstate-iron-felix-statue.

Conclusion

A Chilean Struggle

December 2006 saw the passing of General Augusto Pinochet, who ruled Chile through a military dictatorship that lasted almost seventeen years. Pinochet's regime, which had its roots in a 1973 military coup against Salvador Allende's democratically elected government, murdered thousands and tortured tens of thousands. Upon Pinochet's passing, the Chilean government allowed the military to hold official ceremonies mourning him, but refused to honor the military dictator with a head-of-state funeral.[1]

Particularly telling, however, was the reaction of Chile's President at that point, Michelle Bachelet. Bachelet refused to attend Pinochet's funeral, publicly explaining that to do so would be a "violation of my conscience."[2] This public statement was widely understood to reflect not just President Bachelet's general moral condemnation of Pinochet's regime, but also her specific personal history, as a direct victim of this regime. Bachelet was personally subjected to torture by Pinochet's henchmen, as was her father, a high-ranking military officer who died in Pinochet's prison for his fidelity to democracy.[3] When Bachelet cited her "conscience," then, she was not only invoking her integrity as a moral reason. She was also invoking a personal history that made this integrity reason especially salient.

Whereas on this particular occasion, Bachelet's focus was quite squarely on her personal integrity, other key events during her time at the center of the political stage showed complex links between this individual integrity and the collective integrity of Chilean society. In October 2007, for example, reporters asked Bachelet to comment on the arrest of several of Pinochet's family members on corruption charges. The President's brief response—"in this country no one is

---

[1] Chile's Minister of the Interior at the time, Belisario Velasco, observed that on the day of the coup against Allende's government, Pinochet had ordered the bombing of the presidential palace, known as La Moneda: "I didn't see the flag [put] at half mast at La Moneda by General Pinochet, the flag was shot down, not put at half mast... That's why the government has decided that General Pinochet does not have the necessary requirements to give him a funeral as a head of state." Quoted in Jonathan Franklin, "Chilean Government Rejects State Funeral for Pinochet as Thousands Queue to Pay Respects," *The Guardian*, December 12, 2006.

[2] Quoted in "Pinochet Grips Chile Beyond the Grave," *CNN*, December 11, 2006, at http://edition.cnn.com/2006/WORLD/americas/12/11/pinochet.legacy/index.html.

[3] See, e.g., "Former Chilean Military Officers Jailed for 1974 Death of President Bachelet's Father," *The Guardian*, November 21, 2014.

Integrity, Personal, and Political. Shmuel Nili, Oxford University Press (2020). © Shmuel Nili.
DOI: 10.1093/oso/9780198859635.001.0001

above the law"[4]—had a complex integrity subtext. True to her promise not to be an "avenging angel,"[5] Bachelet did not express any personal glee at the Pinochet family's predicament. Instead, Bachelet's emphasis on the rule of law implicitly invoked a collective commitment to break away from certain aspects of Chile's past—including not only the period of Pinochet's actual dictatorship, but also the long period following the dictatorship during which Pinochet was formally protected from legal prosecution for his crimes.[6]

This collective integrity theme, of Chilean society reshaping its identity-grounding institutions as a negation of its Pinochet-laden past, was more explicit during Bachelet's second term as President (2014–18). Thus, for instance, in her victory speech following her second electoral success, Bachelet proclaimed that "Chile has looked at itself, has looked at its path, its recent history, its wounds, its feats, its unfinished business and this Chile has decided it is the time to start deep transformations."[7] And while many politicians could be expected to use such collective integrity-style talk, there was little doubt that in Bachelet's case, this talk was intimately linked with a personal commitment that gave collective reforms a different kind of urgency. This link was evident, for example, in Bachelet's consistent refusal, despite recurring political failures, to endorse more gradual reforms of the Pinochet-era constitution that still governs Chile, insisting until the very end of her presidency that this constitution is "illegitimate in its origins" and must be "designed from scratch."[8]

---

[4] Quoted in Monte Reel, "Widow, Children of Pinochet Arrested in Hiding of Millions," *Washington Post*, October 5, 2007, at www.washingtonpost.com/wp-dyn/content/article/2007/10/04/AR2007100401574.html. Later on, during her second term in office, when Bachelet's son and daughter-in-law were implicated in a corruption scandal, Bachelet—to her credit—insisted on the same equality before the law (see, e.g., Pascale Bonnefoy, "Daughter-in-Law of Chile's President Faces Corruption Charge," *New York Times*, January 29, 2016). A sympathetic survey of this period observed: "When confronted with a wave of destabilizing conflict of interest scandals implicating actors on all sides of the political spectrum, including her own son, she tackled the problem with a systematic, sober and (critically) bipartisan presidential commission...to propose ethics and campaign finance reforms. To date, 63 percent of the commission's slate of 236 recommendations has been enacted. Bachelet could have responded to the scandals with a political dogfight. Instead, she pursued a consensus response. In doing so, Bachelet arguably ended up taking most of the public blame for corruption—but was also able to guarantee meaningful progress against structural corruption. According to a poll in 2016, 60 percent of Chileans believe that these measures could restore trust in politics." See Beryl Seiler and Ben Raderstrof, "Michelle Bachelet's Underappreciated Legacy in Chile," *Americas Quarterly*, March 9, 2018, at http://www.americasquarterly.org/content/michelle-bachelets-underappreciated-legacy-chile.
[5] Quoted in Phil Davison, "Single Mother Poised to Be Chilean President," *Belfast Telegraph*, December 12, 2005, at https://archive.is/20130628092707/http:/www.accessmylibrary.com/coms2/summary_0286-12015452_ITM; see also Larry Rohter, "A Leader Making Peace with Chile's Past," *New York Times*, January 15, 2006.
[6] Primarily because of Pinochet's status as a "senator for life," which in turn resulted from the constitution enacted in 1980 by his own dictatorship.
[7] Dan Collyns and Jonathan Watts, "Bachelet Pledges Radical Constitutional Reforms After Winning Chilean Election," *The Guardian*, December 13, 2013.
[8] See, e.g., "Chile's Bachelet Proposes New Constitution in Last Days in Office," *Reuters*, March 6, 2018, at https://www.reuters.com/article/us-chile-politics/chiles-bachelet-proposes-new-constitution-in-last-days-in-office-idUSKBN1GI07I; see also Rachel Kennedy, "Replacing the Chilean Constitution," *Constellations* 24 (2017): 456–69.

The link between Bachelet's personal commitments and personal history on the one hand, and Chile's collective transformation on the other, was even more evident when her role as head of state directly fused with her personal story. This was the case, for example, in a 2016 ceremony, in which Bachelet formally responded to a ruling against the Chilean state, issued by the Inter-American Court of Human Rights. The Court had found that, following the military coup against Allende, Pinochet's dictatorship denied justice to twelve air force officers who were tried in a "war council" and who—like Bachelet's father, another air force officer—were steadfast in their loyalty to the over-thrown democratic government. Bachelet formally recognized the Court's verdict on behalf of the state, an acknowledgment described by the *Associated Press* as follows:

> Chilean President Michelle Bachelet recalled with deep emotion the torture of her father and...recognized the role of the state in human rights violations during the country's 1973–1990 military dictatorship. Referring to last year's human rights court ruling, Bachelet said in a speech broadcast on CNN: "Thanks to this finding, other victims of the war councils will be able to ask for revision of their cases and restore their dignity and military honor." She added, in a voice cracking with emotion, "Today the state of Chile solemnly recognizes that you, the victims, suffered grave human rights violations." Bachelet then openly cried, in a rare display of public emotion.[9]

The case of Bachelet, Chile, and Pinochet's shadow represents a fitting coda to the inquiries of this book. One obvious reason has to do with the multiple ways in which different aspects of this case relate to the book's core ideas. The independent moral significance of certain appeals to one's conscience; the way in which the presence of a particular history amplifies the moral force of such appeals; the parallels between the polity's moral history and the history of an individual person; the moral significance of the polity's effort to define itself against its "past self"; the moral significance and complexity of symbolic political recognition in general, and symbolic recognition of the politically prominent in particular—all of these key themes of the book receive concrete expression in the Chilean episodes I just described.

The less obvious reason to end the book with this case has to do with some of the questions to which the book's arguments point. While many such questions could be mentioned, the following three seem particularly worth highlighting.

[9] "Chilean President Bachelet Shows Deep Emotion at Human Rights Event," *AP*, October 8, 2016, at https://www.reuters.com/article/us-chile-politics/chilean-president-bachelet-shows-deep-emotion-at-human-rights-event-idUSKCN127217.

First, how can a moralized conception of collective integrity, such as the one I have defended throughout this book, inform our thinking about entrenched political disagreement? More specifically, how can moralized collective integrity inform our thinking about disagreement that results from the continued salience of morally untenable views? This has been a live question in the case of Chile, where a non-trivial portion of the population, especially among the middle class, continues to regard Pinochet as a hero whose "excesses" were heavily outweighed by his "saving" of the country's politics and economy from "destruction by communists."[10] Such views, I assume, go beyond the bounds of reasonable disagreement in a liberal democracy, not least because they ultimately call into question liberal democracy's very foundations. As I stressed in Chapter 2, a society can have collective integrity even when its members disagree—intensely—on a wide range of policy questions. But the relevant disagreements are supposed to be premised on a basic acceptance of democratic procedures for the resolution of political disputes, as well as on respect for basic rights and liberties. It is therefore a philosophically complex question precisely how the appeal to collective integrity can help us deal with those who call these basic liberal-democratic premises into question. It is also a practically important question, whether one is thinking about the many Chileans who publicly mourned Pinochet upon his death,[11] or about the many sympathizers of contemporary authoritarians around the world, or even about the sizeable populations supporting elected media demagogues of the kind that this book discussed in detail.[12]

A second set of questions has to do with the integrity of collective agents regulated by the state. The Chilean military is a case in point. In 1973, the military coup that eventually placed Pinochet in power was partly encouraged by right-wing politicians who simply decided to ignore the electoral results that brought Allende's leftist government to power. And one would clearly want politicians—in Chile and elsewhere—to uphold the integrity of liberal democracy by unconditionally committing to keeping the military out of politics. But can we use the language of collective integrity to say anything about the military's own ethical responsibilities as a collective agent? How do the responsibilities of such a powerful collective actor relate to the integrity of the political community? And what should we make of this relationship when it concerns other powerful actors who are at least nominally subject to regulation by state authorities, such as major corporations?

---

[10] See, e.g., Heraldo Munoz, *The Dictator's Shadow* (New York: Basic Books, 2008).

[11] See, e.g., "Pinochet's Funeral Shows Chile's Divide," AP, December 12, 2006, at http://www.nbcnews.com/id/16172516/ns/world_news-americas/t/pinochet-funeral-shows-chiles-divide.

[12] For an interesting discussion of how to engage "unreasonable" supporters of media demagogues, see Gabriele Badano and Alasia Nuti, "Under Pressure: Political Liberalism, the Rise of Unreasonableness, and the Complexity of Containment," *Journal of Political Philosophy* 26 (2018): 145–68.

Finally, I have intentionally left open, throughout the book, a deep philosophical question concerning individuals' moral integrity in general, and their moral integrity concerning political repression in particular. From the very beginning of the book, starting with Havel's famous grocer, I have devoted considerable space to the multiple links between individual moral integrity and opposition to political repression. But "opposition to repression" can take two very different forms. On the one hand, such opposition can take the form of refusal to be complicit in repression and other political evils—perhaps even, at the limit, going into exile, as many Chileans had done after Pinochet consolidated his hold on power.[13] On the other hand, "opposition to repression" can also take a more active form, of the kind exemplified in Chapter 3's discussion of Dietrich Bonhoeffer, who eventually chose to return from a short-lived exile in the United States, and to entangle himself in the Nazi war machine, in order to increase his chances of helping to destroy this machine from the inside.[14]

My discussion, in Chapters 3 and 4, of the complex relationship between integrity and clean hands obviously bears on this difficult choice. But active opposition to political repression need not always take the form of dirty hands. Therefore, the idea of integrity might have more implications for the choice between different modes of opposition to political repression—and to grave political wrongs more generally—than I have acknowledged.[15] If I did not expand on the moral questions surrounding this choice, this is not because I think these questions insignificant, but because I have not yet been able to identify satisfactory answers. Perhaps readers convinced of integrity's value can help.

---

[13] Though some of the exiles, like Bachelet and her mother, were effectively forced into exile by the regime.

[14] Confronted with the full scale of Nazi crimes through his service in German military intelligence, Bonhoeffer wrote: "the ultimate question for a responsible man to ask is not how he is to extricate himself heroically from the affair, but how the coming generation shall continue to live." Dietrich Bonhoeffer, *Letters and Papers from Prison* (New York: Touchstone, 1997), 7.

[15] For a remarkable literary exploration of how different dimensions of integrity bear on this choice, see Kurt Vonnegut's tale of an American spy who spends the Second World War spreading Nazi propaganda from Berlin, in *Mother Night* (New York: Random House, 2009 [1961]). Numerous elements of this novel dovetail with the themes of this book, but especially pertinent is Vonnegut's choice to close the novel with the protagonist's self-indictment for "crimes against himself"—an unusual and yet eminently appropriate turn of phrase.

Index of Names

For the benefit of digital users, indexed terms that span two pages (e.g., 52–53) may, on occasion, appear on only one of those pages.

Index

For the benefit of digital users, indexed terms that span two pages (e.g., 52–53) may, on occasion, appear on only one of those pages.